An introduction to applied biogeography

Biogeography is about the geographical distribution, both past and present, of plants, animals and other organisms. Ian Spellerberg and John Sawyer bring a modern and new approach to an old subject, writing in a lively and sometimes provocative manner. Throughout, the applications of biogeography in conservation management, economic production, environmental assessment, sustainable use of resources, landscape planning and public health are emphasised. Applications of island biogeography in conservation are critically appraised, analysis of biogeographical data is explained, the concept of wildlife corridors is questioned and the role of humans and their cultures in biogeography is explored. The authors pay warm tributes to important events and people in biogeography and conclude by discussing the future roles for biogeography.

IAN F. SPELLERBERG is the Director and Head of the Environmental Management and Design Division at Lincoln University, Canterbury, New Zealand. He was previously the Director of the Centre for Environmental Sciences at the University of Southampton, UK, where he played a major role in the establishment and teaching of a range of environmental courses. He has undertaken research for a number of agencies, including the Nature Conservancy Council, the Forestry Commission, English Nature and the Department of Conservation (NZ), and has been an expert adviser for the European Directorate for Sciences, Research and Development. He has written eight textbooks, has published extensively in a range of journals and is on the editorial board of three scientific journals. His current research is on the ecological effects of new roads on natural areas.

JOHN W. D. SAWYER is a Senior Conservation Officer at the Department of Conservation, New Zealand, where his responsibilities include biological surveys, threatened plant species recovery, plant pest control programmes, habitat management and ecological restoration. He also has experience of conservation and environmental issues in Central and Southern America, Canada, Europe and Australia.

An introduction to applied biogeography

Ian F. Spellerberg and John W. D. Sawyer

CAMBRIDGE
UNIVERSITY PRESS

PUBLISHED BY THE PRESS SYNDICATE OF THE UNIVERSITY OF CAMBRIDGE
The Pitt Building, Trumpington Street, Cambridge CB2 1RP, United Kingdom

CAMBRIDGE UNIVERSITY PRESS
The Edinburgh Building, Cambridge CB2 2RU, UK   http://www.cup.cam.ac.uk
40 West 20th Street, New York, NY 10011–4211, USA   http://www/cup.org
10 Stamford Road, Oakleigh, Melbourne 3166, Australia

First published 1999

Printed in the United Kingdom at the University Press, Cambridge

Typeset in Garamond 11/13 pt [VN]

A catalogue record for this book is available from the British Library

Library of Congress Cataloguing in Publication data

Spellerberg, Ian F.
 An introduction to applied biogeography/Ian F. Spellerberg and John W.D. Sawyer
  p.   cm.
 Includes bibliographical references.
 ISBN 0 521 45102 7 (hb). – ISBN 0 521 45712 2 (pb)
 1. Biogeography.   I. Sawyer, John W. D. (John William David),
 1965–   . II. Title.
QH84.S7   1999
578.09 – dc21   98–21967 CIP

ISBN 0 521 45102 7 hardback
ISBN 0 521 45712 2 paperback

Contents

Foreword

There is an island in Indonesia with a particularly beautiful parrot that lives nowhere else. Local people trap large numbers of the birds for export to bird fanciers around the world and are more than happy to do so because they feel it is a pest. However, there was growing concern that the population was dropping to alarming levels. Conservationists working there conducted surveys of the population size, trapping pressures, breeding biology, and crop damage, thereby determining a way in which the wild population could be harvested at a sustainable rate and crop damage limited. During discussions with officials who would have to monitor and control the rate of harvesting there was only half-hearted preparedness to cooperate. Then they were told that this bird was found nowhere else, and attitudes changed completely. The officials had thought that the parrot was found everywhere, but that they somehow had a monopoly on the supply to those strange people who wanted a pest as a pet. Once those in charge were given a grasp of biogeography their support was won.

Of course, knowledge of biogeography is not in itself going to save the world's biodiversity, but it does at least put into perspective the increasing global concern for the massive decline of populations and loss of species in all ecosystems. It forms the basis of the many and varied exercises to assess conservation priorities around the world, even though the complexities mean that the answers are never precisely the same. This prioritization is essential, since, although there are far more financial resources available now than ever before for global conservation, there are not nearly enough to right every wrong and cure every ill, and decision makers need to allocate funds in as rational a way as possible.

It is over twenty years since Ian Spellerberg taught me biogeography, ecology and behaviour at Southampton University and captured my interest in these fields to the extent that I went off and became wholly engrossed and enmeshed in them. I am thrilled that he, this time together with John Sawyer, has produced another clear and important book which I hope will be used and read widely, and perhaps translated into other languages to touch as many people as possible.

Tony Whitten
Biodiversity Specialist
The World Bank
Washington, DC

Preface

Biogeography is the study of the distribution and patterns of distribution of plants, animals and other organisms across the globe, on land, in the sea and in the air. Information from biogeography provides the basis for environmental protection and resource management. It has a very important role to play in managing the world's biological diversity and can be applied in many areas. It can be used to show where species and groups of species are distributed, to provide information which can be used in environmental impact assessments and to provide information to ensure sustainable use and conservation of those biological resources. Biogeography is an interesting and developing subject and is particularly important in providing a basis for understanding the critical relationships between humans and the environment.

In almost any area of natural sciences there are general components, underlying themes and specialist aspects. Biology, for example, is the general name for the study of life but there are many aspects of biology, such as molecular biology, population biology and human biology. Under the general heading of biological sciences we could include genetics, ecology, immunology and biogeography. Similarly, biogeography has a general theme as well as underlying themes and specialist aspects. Underlying themes include historical biogeography, analytical biogeography, ecological biogeography and applied biogeography.

This book is an introduction to applied biogeography. It is an introduction to a subject that underpins human understanding of ecology and it also describes some of the many applications of biogeography in resource management and environmental protection. The text provides structured and analytical ways of looking at the distribution patterns of plants and animals and also the complex patterns of interactions between humans and the environment. We describe patterns of distribution at scales ranging from global to agricultural fields. We also describe research that seeks explanations for those patterns and the processes which maintain them. The patterns may be found on land, sea and in the air and at many spatial scales. The patterns may also change over periods of time (thousands of years, centuries, months or days). One of the challenges of writing this book was to choose the spatial limits for the examples in the text. For example, whereas species patterns of grasses in a whole country would certainly be considered as biogeography, would a study of the distribution pattern of beetles in a woodland also be considered as biogeography? For us the answer was yes.

Chapter 1 includes an introduction to the nature of biogeography and also explains the rationale for the structure of the rest of the book. Biogeography may have had a poor image in the past but we believe that biogeography from an ecological perspective is a challenging science and one which has many applications in a changing world. The most valuable application is provision of the necessary information for sustainable use of some species and conservation of other species.

We commenced researching and writing this book in England and finished it in New Zealand. By chance, both of us had independently moved across the world from a relatively new continental island to an ancient island. That move has helped to enrich our understanding of biogeography. We have used our own experiences of research in ecology and biogeography but have also included a synthesis of some of the most modern aspects of the latter. As well as relying heavily on the results of many recent research programmes, we also pay tribute to many of the historical developments in the discipline and in so doing we put those developments into perspective. We feel that it is important not to interpret historical developments in a modern setting. The work of the earlier biogeographers and actual populations are best understood if we are able to have a glimpse of their time, their culture and their way of life. Although what was thought and known during their time may have been modified and corrected, the same process applies to us today; what we have written will be corrected and modified in the future.

Biogeography has developed largely from descriptive studies, mapping plant and animal distributions, and may therefore appear uninteresting. The biogeographical studies of the 18th century were bold and innovative for their time and, for some of the early biogeographers, it required much courage to make public their discoveries and beliefs. We must ensure that applied biogeography is both rigorous and objective – as a tribute to the early biogeographers. We believe that applied biogeography will continue to play an important role in environmental management and that it will continue to underpin ecological research and conservation well into the 21st century.

Ian Spellerberg and John Sawyer

Acknowledgements

This project has spanned two hemispheres in a period of a few years. In that time many people have kindly contributed to the project and consequently made large improvements. We are particularly grateful to all those people and organisations who have kindly allowed us to use material from printed sources. We have endeavoured to contact all persons and organisations for all the copyright material used in this text, and we apologise if we have overlooked any person or any organisation.

Many people have kindly provided information and have found time to read parts of the text. To all those who assisted in this way, we are truly grateful. In particular we would like to acknowledge the help of the following: Ian Abbott, Keith Barber, Andy Barker, Jack Chernin, Jonathan Cowie, Paul Curran, Peter de Lange, Gina Douglas, Richard Duncan, Rowan Emberson, Neil Enright, Dianne Gleeson, Collin Hindmarch, Peter Hopkins, Sandi Irvine, Michael Johnston, John Marsden, John Mitchell, Keith Morrison, Hugh Possingham, Amanda Reid, Alan Saunders, Gillian Sawyer, J. Michael Scott, Phillip Simpson, Kathryn Spellerberg, Bianca Sullivan, Ian Thornton, Geoff Tunnicliffe, Nigel Webb and Tony Whitten.

Finally we owe much to the staff of Cambridge University Press and our ever-patient editors.

1

Biogeography: the nature of the subject, its history and its applications

1.1 Introduction

In 1994, an article in the journal *New Scientist* proclaimed that 'Since biogeography holds the key to the survival of life, it deserves more attention' (Bowman, 1994). That statement is a very fitting opening to this first chapter.

Biogeography is about the geography of plants, animals and other organisms, that is, the study of the geographical distribution of plants, animals and other organisms. Biogeographical research helps us to understand the patterns and processes of distribution and the factors that cause and maintain those patterns and processes. The patterns of distribution that we find today amongst living organisms have been determined by many things, including the following:

Evolution
Physiological and behavioural adaptations
Dispersal mechanisms and levels of dispersal abilities
Competition between species
Ecological succession
Climate change
Sea level changes
Moving continents through a process called plate tectonics
Direct and indirect impact of humans

The distribution and abundance of plants (phytogeography) and animals (zoogeography) have been the two main divisions of biogeography. Both those divisions embrace elements of several disciplines including biology, geography, taxonomy, geology, climatology and ecology. Many biologists, taxonomists, geologists, climatologists and ecologists have interests in various aspects of biogeography and indeed some have particular views as to the precise nature of biogeography. Those differences in views are based partly on differences of scale, be it in time or spatially. For example, a geologist's view might be particularly biased by an interest in evolutionary processes over very long periods of time (millions of years) perhaps in relation to plate tectonics. Geographers might take a special interest in researching the distribution of plants and animals over the last few thousand years, perhaps in relation to the post-glacial periods. An ecologist's view of biogeography might be dominated by those factors which determine and maintain the distribution of plants and animals within certain localities and over much shorter periods of time (perhaps in relation to the reduction and fragmentation of habitats in the last few decades). These different views contribute to the rich and varied nature of biogeographical research and its many important, practical applications. The common theme in all approaches to the study of biogeography is the study of the geographical distribution of groups of plants, animals and other organisms from a spatial or space perspective (that is, over land, in the soil, in water and in the air) and a temporal or time perspective (that is changes in distribution that occur over time). Biogeography provides a valuable link between traditional single disciplines (such as ecology, taxonomy and conservation biology) and a focus for interdisciplinary studies. That is important because many if not all environmental problems facing us today require an interdisciplinary approach (that is an integration of several disciplines, including ecology, geology, economics, policy and sociocultural factors).

Biogeography is more than about mapping the geographical distribution of organisms (present and past) at different spatial scales or merely dividing the land and sea into regions which are based on groups of characteristic organisms. Once a predominantly descriptive discipline, biogeography is now a quantitative science. It has applications in conservation, helping to establish a strategy for the location, extent and management of protected areas. It has applications in trying to achieve sustainable use of living resources and in environmental assessment by helping to ensure the least impact on the natural environment. It has applications in helping to tackle many aspects of environmental change, whether it be modelling the effects of changing weather patterns on agriculture or those of introduced and invasive species on native (indigenous) commercial fish species.

Before we can look in more detail at biogeography we need to know what we are dealing with and thus a brief introduction to the classification of organisms is helpful. We then go on to introduce the subject of biogeography and the history of biogeography. The relation between ecology and biogeography is then discussed and finally we look at some applications of biogeography.

1.2 An introduction to plants, animals and other organisms

There are approximately 1.7 million named species of living oganisms. The total number of living species is of course not known and we can only estimate what the figure might be. Estimates range from about 11 to 30 million or more. What is certain is that human impacts are causing species to become extinct faster than they can be named. Also of concern is our lack of knowledge about the named species. Scientists have intensively investigated only 10 per cent of plant species and a far smaller proportion of animal species (information from the World Commission in Environment and Development 1987 publication *Our Common Future*, Oxford University Press).

There are many terms used to refer to different groups of animals, plants and other kinds of living organism such as fungi, bacteria and viruses. The classification of biota (living organisms) has been reviewed and changed many times as a result of new information. In 1969, R. H. Whittaker of Cornell University suggested five groups of living organisms (Box 1.1). More recently, new taxonomic levels and regrouping of major taxa have been proposed as a result of studies in molecular biology.

Commonly used terms for living organisms include 'wildlife' and more recently the widely misunderstood term 'biological diversity' (often abbreviated to biodiversity). Wildlife is often used only with reference to mammals and birds. In this book it refers to any kind of wild organism (plants, animals, fungi and other groups) and therefore not to domesticated animals or plants.

The term biological diversity is often used in connection with conservation, not because it is fashionable to do so but because of the important concept embodied in its use. Conservation of wildlife conjures up lists of species which are endangered. There is nothing wrong with that but biological diversity draws attention to the need to conserve variety at different levels of biological organisation (from the genetic level to ecosystem levels). Biological diversity is an all-embracing term that means the variety of life at all levels of biological organisation, including 'diversity within species, between species and of ecosystems' (from the 1992 Convention on Biological Diversity). There is biological diversity at different levels of ecological organisation, genetic organisation and taxonomic organisation.

Box 1.1. The diversity of life. Classifications and definitions of biological diversity (see also Table 5.1)

In this five-kingdom system (developed primarily by R. H. Whittaker of Cornell University) living organisms are arranged on the basis of level of biological complexity and mode of nutrition. This is merely a summary of what is a much more detailed classification and it omits many groups within the major taxonomic levels of phylum, class, order, family, genus and species.

The numbers in brackets are the approximate number of named species (numbers are in thousands and are given only where there is good agreement about the number).

Kingdom Monera: Bacteria and blue-green algae.
Kingdom Protista: Primitive fungi, slime moulds, green algae, etc.
Kingdom Fungi: (mode of nutrition by absorption) three main groups of fungi (40).
Kingdom Plantae: (mode of nutrition photosynthesis):
Division Bryophyta: Mosses and liverworts.
Division Tracheophyta: This division includes the most complex and advanced plants such as the three classes – ferns, conifers and flowering plants.
Class Filicineae: Ferns (10).
Class Gymnospermae: Conifers (0.6).
Class Angiospermae: Flowering plants (286).
Subclass: Monocotyledonae: Grasses, lilies, palms, orchids, etc.
Subclass: Dicotyledonae: e.g. Rose Family, . . . Genera in other families such as *Fagus* (northern beech) and *Nothofagus* (Southern beech).

Kingdom Animalia: (mode of nutrition ingestion):
Phylum Porifera: Sponges (10).
Phylum Coelenterata: Sea anemones, corals, jellyfish, etc. (10).
Phylum Platyhelminthes: Flatworms, tapeworms, flukes, etc. (125).
Phylum Nematoda: Roundworms (30).
Phylum Mollusca: Shellfish or molluscs, squid, snails, etc. (110).
Phylum Annelida: Earthworms, leeches, etc. (15).
Phylum Onychophora: Velvet worms, e.g. the genus *Peripatus*.
Phylum Arthropoda: Insects (800), spiders (130), crustacens (30), etc.
Phylum Echinodermata: Starfish, sea urchins, sea lilies, etc. (6).
Phylum Hemichordata: Acorn worms.
Phylum Chordata: The vertebrates including fish (20), amphibians (2.5), reptiles (6.3), birds (8.5) and mammals (4).

This table indicates the variety of known life in terms of taxonomic diversity. However, this is only one aspect of biological diversity.

Box 1.1 (*cont.*)

The 1992 Convention on Biological Diversity defines Biological diversity 'the variability among living organisms from all sources including, amongst other things, terrestrial, marine and other aquatic ecosystems and the ecological complexes of which they are part; this includes diversity within species, between species and of ecosystems'.

Biological Diversity occurs at different levels of organisation (after Angermeier & Karr, 1994):

Taxonomic	Genetic	Ecological
Species	Gene	Population
Genus	Chromosome	Community
Family etc.	Genome	Ecosystems

Plants, animals and other organisms are collectively known as biota or organisms. Aggregations of the same kind of organisms are known as populations, for example trout populations, or oak tree populations. A population of organisms such as trout lives in a habitat; a habitat is usually linked to a population and is the locality or area occupied by the populations. Habitats can be characterised by the physical features, soil conditions, and by the other kinds of organism found in the area. Biological communities are made up of different kinds of populations of organisms; for example a coral reef community consists of coral populations, fish populations, crustaceans, algae and other marine life. Different kinds of community have sometimes been classified on the basis of recognisable mixes or assemblages. Different kinds of woodland or grassland can be recognised by the different composition of the species; for example, we could refer to the mixed-species deciduous woodlands of the temperate climate region.

At a higher level of ecological organisation there are ecosystems. An ecosystem has no boundaries and is characterised by cycles and flows of water, energy, minerals and other elements through both the living components and physical components of the ecosystem. Ecosystems comprise three categories: individual organisms, species etc.; processes such as energy flow or ecological succession; and properties such as fragility and condition.

Biota, living and extinct, have long been classified into different groups; the science of classifying organisms and the study of relationships between those groups is systematics. The science of taxonomy is the oldest of all biological sciences and is about the study and description of the diversity of organisms and how that diversity arose. Living organisms include more than just plants and animals (Box 1.1).

Taxonomic classifications have a hierarchical structure, in which the basic unit is the species (see also Table 5.1). A species is a group of organisms that are recognised as being distinct (in form and reproductively) from other groups. When a species is identified or named, it is typically given a binomial (Latin) name which includes a generic and a specific component. The designation of a binomial name follows an agreed convention and is the same when used within any language. An example of a binomial name is that used for beech trees, of which there are many kinds or species. In northern temperate climate regions, species belong to the genus *Fagus* whereas in southern temperate climate regions there is a different genus, *Nothofagus*. Note the convention of putting the scientific names in italics. There are different species within each of the genera; for example, in the genus *Nothofagus* there are the species *Nothofagus fusca*, *Nothofagus menziesii* and *Nothofagus solandri*.

In much of this book we consider the biogeography of species – the distribution patterns and the reasons for those patterns. This does not mean that biogeography is concerned only with one level of taxonomic organisation, the species. It deals with other levels such as genera and families.

1.3 A history of biogeography

The presence and distribution of plants and animals has been recorded by humans for many thousands of years. Cave drawings of animals could be said to be the beginning of biogeography. The earliest written records and books mention the occurrence, abundance and absence of various plants and animals. Similarly, maps depicting plants, animals, dragons and other creatures have been made for centuries. Until early this century, many of these maps depicted actual organisms rather than indicating their distribution. However, as early as 1697, animals were drawn on an economic map of Hungary and later, in 1845, Heinrich Berghaus's *Physikalischer Atlas* has animal distribution maps (George, 1969). Throughout the 20th century there has been an ever-growing interest in how best to map, survey, record and distribute information about the distribution of plants, animals and natural biological communities. The books listed in Table 1.1 are testament to the varied nature of that mapping, etc. In recent years, the interest in mapping has been greatly facilitated and enhanced by developments in computer and satellite technologies (see Chapter 6).

Biogeography, in the sense of identifying geographical faunal and floral characteristics, probably emerged from early attempts to classify organisms

Table 1.1. *One hundred years of biogeography books*

Charles Darwin's *The Origin of Species* was the first great landmark in books that greatly influenced subsequent writing on biogeography. This table is a list of books or chapters in books (in English or translated into English) published during the 100 years following 1859 and which have been relevant to the advancement of biogeography. This list excludes those publications which specialise on island biogeography (see Section 3.2).

These books represent a history of literature on biogeography which has brought the subject to a wider audience. Underlying these books is a wealth of material from expeditions and research, most of which is published in scientific journals.

1859. *On The Origin of Species by means of Natural Selection, or the Preservation of Favoured Races in the Struggle for Life*, by C. Darwin. London, John Murray.

1869. *The Malay Archipelago*, by A. R. Wallace. London, Macmillan. (Wallace dedicated this book to Charles Darwin with whom he had shared thoughts about the theories of natural selection.

1876. *The Geographical Distribution of Animals*, by A. R. Wallace. London, Macmillan.

1887. *The Geographical and Geological Distribution of Animals*, by A. Heilprin. London, Kegan Paul, Trench & Co.

1911. *Atlas of Zoogeography*, by J. G. Bartholomew, W. E. Clarke & P. H. Grimshaw. Edinburgh, J. Bartholomew and the Edinburgh Geographical Institute.

1913. *The Wanderings of Animals*, by H. Gadow. London, Cambridge University Press.

1934. *The Life Forms of Plants and Statistical Plant Geography*, by C. Raunkiaer. Oxford, Clarendon Press.

1935. *Zoogeography of the Sea*, by S. Ekman. German edition first published in 1935 and translated into English in 1953. London, Sidgwick and Jackson.

1936. *Plant and Animal Geography*, by M. I. Newbigin. London, Methuen.

1937. *Ecological Animal Geography*, by R. Hesse, W. C. Allee & K. P. Schmidt, New York and London, John Wiley.

1944. *Foundations of Plant Geography*, by S. A. Cain. New York and London, Harper & Bros.

Table 1.1. *(cont.)*

1951. *Zoogeography of the Land and Inland Waters*, by L. de Beaufort. London, Sidgwick & Jackson.

1953. *Zoogeography of the Sea*, by S. Ekman. London, Sidgwick & Jackson (originally published in Germany in 1935).

1953. *Evolution and Geography*, by G. G. Simpson. Eugene, Oregon State System Higher Education.

1954. *The Distribution and Abundance of Animals*, by H. H. Andrewartha & L. C. Birch. Chicago, University of Chicago Press.

1957. *Zoogeography: The Geographical Distribution of Animals*, by P. J. Darlington. New York and London.

1957. *Biogeography: An Ecological Perspective*, by P. M. Dansereau. New York, Ronald Press.

1958. *Panbiogeography or An Introduction Synthesis of Zoogeography, Phytogeography, and Geology; with notes on Evolution, Systematics, Ecology, Anthropology* etc. by L. Croizat. Caracas, published by the Author.

---

and in the origins of taxonomy and systematics. Georges Louis Leclerc, Comte de Buffon (1707–1788), a wealthy French nobleman had, as early as 1761, observed that the Old World (Europe, Asia and Africa) and the New World (North and South America) had no mammalian species in common. Buffon's work was monumental: 44 large volumes published over a period of 50 years.

The early explorers, the natural history excursions of the 19th century and scientific expeditions of the 20th century, have moulded the study of the geographical distribution of life on land and in the sea. Amongst the notable biogeographers (Fig. 1.1), one stands out as having made a notable contribution and that was the Prussian naturalist and explorer of South America, Alexander, Baron von Humboldt (1769–1859). He was interested in the manner by which plants contributed to the landscape and is sometimes referred to as the father of plant geography.

Early studies (Table 1.1) of plant and animal distributions played a key role in the development of the theory of evolution; for example the observations made by both Charles Darwin (1809–1882) during his passage on the ship *HMS Beagle* (1831–1836) and Alfred Russel Wallace (1823–1913) during his expedition to the Malay archipelago, returning to England in 1862 with a

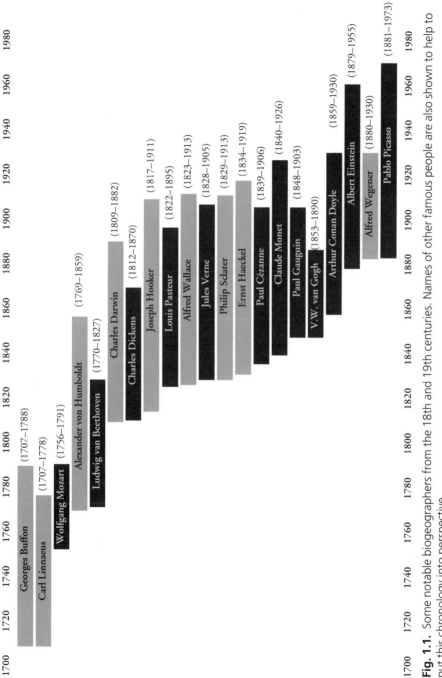

Fig. 1.1. Some notable biogeographers from the 18th and 19th centuries. Names of other famous people are also shown to help to put this chronology into perspective.

Table 1.2. *Texts on biogeography mentioned by Hans Gadow*

The 18th and 19th centuries were rich in biogeographical studies of animals. (References taken from Hans Gadow, 1913, *The Wanderings of Animals*, London, Cambridge University Press).

1707–1788. *Historie Naturelle*, by G. Buffon. 44 volumes published over 50 years during the life of Buffon. (Contains the first general ideas about geographical distribution.)

1777. *Specimen Zoologiae Geographicae Quadrupedum*, by E. A. W. Zimmerman. (The first special treatise on the subject and, according to Gadow, deals in a statistical way with mammals.)

1778. *Philosophia Entomologica*, by J. C. Fabricius. (The first to divide the world into eight regions.)

1803. *Biologie*, by G. R. Treviranus. (This included a chapter on the distribution of the whole animal kingdom.)

1810. *Anatomie und Naturgeschichte der Voegel*, by F. Tiedemann. (Deals with the influence of environment, distribution and migration of birds.)

Text by Latrielle (Date not mentioned). (Proposed that temperature is the main factor in the distribution of animals.)

1822. Text (unknown) by Desmoulins. (Suggested analogous centres of creation – meaning that similar groups of creatures may have arisen independently in different parts of the world.)

1835. Text (not stated) by W. Swainson. (The first book dealing with the geography and classification of the whole animal kingdom.)

1830–1833. *Principles of Geology*, by Charles Lyell. London. Looks at the history of the distribution of animals over time.)

1852. *Physikalischer Atlas: Thiergeographie*, by H. Berghaus. Gotha. (Has the earliest maps dealing with animal distributions.)

1853. Text (not stated) by L. K. Schmarda. (The distribution of the whole animal kingdom. He discusses the possible physical causes and modes of dispersal from original centres of creation and divides the land into 25 'realms'.)

1857. 'On the geographical distribution of the members of the Class Aves'. *Journal of the Proceedings of the Linnean Society, Zoology*, **11**, 130–145, by P. L. Sclater. (He suggests six 'regions' which have been the basis for a classification of biogeographical regions until this day.)

1859. *The Origin of Species*, by Charles Darwin. (A benchmark in biogeographical studies; especially mapping and characterising regions.)

1866. *Geographical Distribution of Mammals*, by A. Murray. (101 coloured distribution maps.)

Table 1.2. (*cont.*)

1868. Text (not stated) by Huxley. (Gives reasons for dividing the world into an Arctogaea or North World and Notogaea or South World.)

1872. Text (not stated) by Alexander Agassiz. (A morphological systematic revision of sea urchins, leading to the suggestion of four realms of the oceans, justified by climatic and other physical conditions.)

1876. *The Geographical Distribution of Animals*, by A. R. Wallace. (The second great landmark.)

1887. *The Geographical and Geological Distribution of Animals*, by A. Heilprin. London, Kegan Paul, Trench & Co. (Caused much discussion when he combined the Nearctic and the Palearctic into a Holarctic region.)

1890. Text (not stated) by W. T. Blanford. (Recognised three main divisions: Australia, South America, and the rest.)

---

huge number (125 660) of specimens of natural history. Another great contribution to early biogeography came from botanist Joseph Dalton Hooker (1817–1911), who took part in many collecting expeditions and published a classic work entitled *Flora of the British Isles*. He was a friend and confidant of Charles Darwin.

The early part of the 20th century saw the publication of many and varied books on the distribution of plants and animals (Table 1.1). One of these was the delightful publication by Hans Gadow on *The Wanderings of Animals* published by Cambridge University Press in 1913 (Table 1.2). The need for an interdisciplinary approach to biogeography is suggested in his Foreword:

> These outlines of the distribution of animals deal with a rather young branch of science. An attempt has therefore been made to sketch its rapid growth from small beginnings until it has become boundless, because the interpretation of at first seemingly simple facts in the domain of the zoologist, had soon to enlist the help of well-nigh all the other branches of Natural Science.

Many, but not all of these early works were totally descriptive; for example, Hans Gadow mentions Zimmermann's volume (Table 1.2), *Specimen Zoologiae Geographicae Quadrupedum*, which deals in a way with mammals and statistics of mammals. Such works were to be the forerunners of a growing interest in an analytical approach to biogeography.

Biogeography has evolved from geographical studies to specialist studies of regions and of various taxonomic groups. Many countries throughout the world now have their own biogeographical texts. Biogeographical studies have ranged in scale from the biogeography of 'mega-zoos' in the USA (studies for conservation of nature reserves) to biogeography of urban areas. There are specialist marine biogeographical texts and there are specialist taxonomic texts (see references at the end of each chapter).

Patterns and processes over different time scales from geological, through the Pleistocene and Holocene epochs (see Fig. 4.3), to historical times have provided incentives for biogeographers to define different, specialist kinds of biogeography (sometimes causing acrimonious debates about the existence and relevance of such areas of specialist study). One kind is historical biogeography (Box 1.2) and this has been associated largely with attempts to relate geological processes to sequences of the origins, dispersal and extinctions of taxonomic groups. Historical biogeography can be further divided into dispersal and vicariance biogeography. The former is concerned mainly with patterns of dispersal and the latter focuses mainly on the splitting of biota in a region (vicariated) as a result of barriers which inhibit dispersal of the organisms. Vicariance biogeographers are concerned with the general question 'What is the historical relationship among biotas or what is the relationship among areas?' (see for more detail, Andersson, 1996). For example, southern beech (*Nothofagus*) and the invertebrate 'velvet worm' (*Peripatus*) (see Section 4.2) are found in South America, New Zealand and Australia. How could the beech, with its heavy seeds, spread between continents and how could a small terrestrial invertebrate such as *Peripatus* (many of which are inhabitants of rotting logs or forest litter) disperse across continents? Vicariance explanations suggest that these organisms were previously more widespread and that more recently their distribution has become fragmented as a result of barriers, including the break-up of Gondwanaland (see Section 4.4).

Two modern philosophical and methodological approaches to vicariance biogeography have emerged; one is called panbiogeography and the other cladistic biogeography. Panbiogeography was a term first used by the botanist and biogeographer L. Croizat (1958) to refer to a global view of biotic interrelationships (Croizat had spurned Charles Darwin's ideas in favour of a quite novel approach to evolution based on the distribution of organisms). In panbiogeography, phylogenetic relationships between taxa are less important than are spatial and temporal patterns (for an example see Chapter 13 by Craw in Myers & Giller (1988)). Cladistic biogeography contrasts with panbiogeography by being closely associated with phylogeny and taxonomy

Box 1.2. Biogeography and specialist areas of study

Biogeography has many 'schools' or areas of specialist study and it is not a unified science. Consequently there are many 'kinds' of biogeography. The following is a synoptic account of the main kinds of biogeography.

Biogeography:
> Phytogeography: Deals with biogeography of plants.
> Zoogeography: Deals with biogeography of animals.
> Ecological biogeography: Deals mainly with patterns and processes over short time scales and within small spatial scales.
> Historical biogeography: Deals with patterns and processes over evolutionary and geological periods of time.
> Dispersal biogeography: Deals with patterns and processes of dispersal.
> Vicariance biogeography: Deals with splitting biota in a region, based on the barriers which inhibit dispersal.
> > Panbiogeography: Uses both endemic and non-endemic taxa. Based not so much on phylogenetic relationships but on spatial and temporal analysis of distribution patterns.
> > Cladistic biogeography: Cladistics deals with classification of biota based on common ancestry rather than using similarities in form. Thus cladistic biogeography uses phylogeny and relationships between areas (with endemic species) are based on shared, derived taxa.
> Analytical biogeography: Has an integrated approach to patterns and processes of organisms.
> Regional Biogeography. Examples include; *Biogeography and Ecology of the Rain Forests of Eastern Africa* (ed. J. C. Lovett & S. K. Wasser, Cambridge University Press); L. R. Heaney, 1986, 'Biogeography of mammals in Southeast Asia: estimates of rates of colonization, extinction and speciation', *Biological Journal of the Linnean Society*, **29**, 127–165.
> Taxonomic biogeography: The biogeography of various taxa.
> Applied biogeography: The application of biogeography for management and conservation of biota, communities and ecosystems.

(for more detail see Chapter 12 by Humphries *et al.* in Myers & Giller (1988)).

In this small book we have had to be selective with reference to the areas of biogeography discussed. We have chosen not to include any further information in this introductory text on cladistic and vicariance biogeography, despite the current popularity of these subdisciplines.

1.4 Ecology and biogeography

In 1870, the German biologist Ernst Haeckel (1834–1919) first coined the term 'ecology' and defined it as 'the total relations of the animal both to its inorganic and organic environment'. In some ways that encapsulated what ecology is today; the study of the interactions between organisms and their environment; but also including (1) the study of the abundance of organisms in space and time and (2) the processes in biological communities. Early in the 20th century, ecology emerged from natural history and wildlife management as a science. Developments in early ecology occurred simultaneously in both North America and Europe. Landmarks in early animal ecology textbooks included Arthur Pearse's *Animal Ecology* (published by McGraw-Hill in 1926) and the work of Charles Elton (*Animal Ecology*, published by Sidgwick & Jackson in 1927). Much of the stimulus for the emergence of plant community studies came from the work of Tansley (1935) and Watt (1947) in Britain and from F. E. Clements in North America (*Dynamics of Vegetation*, published by Hafner Press in 1949). The establishment of the British Ecological Society in 1913 and the Ecological Society of America, founded in 1916, provided a professional basis for ecology. Ecology has become a well-known word but sadly the discipline of ecology is not well understood and is even equated with environmentalism and being 'green'. That is another topic which cannot be discussed here.

As the science of ecology (objective, quantifiable, experimental) began to emerge early this century it was, not surprisingly, going to have close links with biogeography – not surprising because both ecologists and geographers were interested in the patterns of distribution of organisms in space and in time and the processes which determined those patterns. As early as 1924, Richard Hesse in his *Tiergeographie auf Oekologischer Grundlage* wrote about 'ecological animal geography' as a young science. When this work was later translated and published in 1937 it made a marked impact on ecological and biogeographical studies in both Europe and North America. Later academics such as the Americans Robert McArthur and Edward Wilson (see Box 3.2) wrote as if there were no real difference between biogeography and ecology. The term 'ecological biogeography' has since been widely used.

Although the distribution of organisms and the factors and processes causing those distributions is central to the study of biogeography, ecology is concerned mainly with interactions between organisms and their environment, patterns and processes in ecosystems, as well as with the distribution and abundance. But the study of distribution could also be considered to be a part of the study of abundance; factors affecting distribution will also affect abundance. Studies of distribution and abundance can be undertaken at different levels of organisation, including populations, species and biological communities. Previously, community-based ecological studies were prominent in Europe and North America in the early part of the 20th century. Then in the 1950s came the publication of a particularly important contribution to the scientific study of distribution and abundance. This was a book called *The Distribution and Abundance of Animals* by two Australian biologists, H. G. Andrewartha and L. C. Birch (1954). Rather than studying biological communities, these authors had established a strong statistical and analytical approach to population ecology involving three aspects: (1) physiology and behaviour of animals; (2) physiography, climate, soil and vegetation; (3) numbers of individuals in populations.

Andrewartha & Birch stressed the spatial relations between 'local populations'. Also, in the previous work of early ecologists such as Watt (1947), there was reference to shifting mosaics of populations; that is, species found on naturally occurring patchy and transient habitats. These references to population processes have more recently found their way into the literature dealing with the theory of metapopulations (see Section 7.2.1).

Later, we give examples of how biogeographical information can be analysed (see, for example, Box 7.2). In addition to examples of analysis we also describe some theories and models that have been used in biogeographical studies. But why theories and what is a model? In biogeography, theories (that is, sets of ideas to try to explain or test something) are used to try to understand processes (for example, the processes which determine the number of species on an island). Models are theories that can be tested to some extent and therefore may be used to predict the effects of certain impacts on the natural world (for example, climate change on the distribution of biological communities).

1.5 Applications of biogeography

Biogeography has had a very important role to play in the development of our understanding of biology. For example it was biogeography that was the key to developing the theory of the evolution of life. Today, not only does biogeographical research have important applications in a world of rapidly increasing human population densities and diminishing resources, it has crucial applications for conservation and sustainable use of many levels of biological diversity. If we are to make the best uses of limited resources for conservation we must know much more about the geography and ecology of the many kinds of biological diversity.

Some questions in biogeography may seem rather academic. For example, why are certain species and certain groups of organisms found in certain localities and nowhere else? What has caused these patterns on a world scale? Why is it that for many groups of organisms there are fewer and fewer species in the north and in the south compared to the tropical regions? Why is it that in some regions there are few species but the abundance of some individual species is very high? Answers to these questions help us to understand the processes and interactions that have resulted in present distribution patterns and the mechanism by which they are currently maintained. In turn, that information can be used to help to reduce human impact on the environment and can help us to use the environment in a sustainable manner.

We cannot make good decisions about the conservation of nature if we do not know what is there and where it is. Therefore many questions in biogeography are crucial for conservation. For example, what is the location and distribution of species throughout the world – on land, in the water and in the sea? Where are the highest levels of species richness? Where are the different levels of biological diversity to be found? Where do you find the highest levels of biological diversity? Biogeography has important applications, particularly because of the huge gaps in our knowledge and because of the increasing rate at which so many levels of biological diversity are being damaged and lost (see examples of mapping and gap analysis in Section 2.5).

Conservation of wildlife and habitats is achieved in part by the establishment of various kinds of protected area such as nature reserves on land, in rivers and lakes and in the sea. Where should nature reserves be located and why? How large should they be? How should they be managed? Should protected areas be buffered from perturbations arising from land use activities around the protected areas? Biogeography has played a major role in answering these questions (see Section 7.6).

Biogeography also has a part to play in assessing possible impacts on the environment that might be caused by new developments in land use. Determining the likely effects of major projects on the natural environment (land, water or sea) by way of the formalised procedure of an Environmental Impact Assessment has become a statutory requirement in many countries throughout the world. The probable effects of construction of dams and tidal barrages, for example, have been at the centre of many large investigations. Some years ago there was a proposal to construct a tidal barrage (for electricity generation) in the estuary of the River Severn, between Wales and England in the UK. The distribution of estuarine invertebrates is determined largely by salinity levels. A tidal barrage would change the salinity distribution, which would affect the distribution of estuarine invertebrates. This in turn would affect the distribution of estuarine birds that feed on the invertebrates. The biogeographical and ecological studies of the distributions of organisms and factors determining their distribution in an estuary is an example of the ecological aspect of biogeography and its value in determining impacts arising from habitat modification.

Biogeography is important in developing strategies for biological control of pests. In 1962 a book with the evocative title *Silent Spring* was published. Written by Rachael Carson, this book was a clear statement of her concern about the extensive use of chemicals in agriculture and the possibility that intensive use of herbicides and insecticides could affect organisms other than pest species. Since that time the study of pest control has become more and more integrated endeavouring to combine minimum use of chemicals with maximum use of biological control. Encouraging the presence of predators of insect pests in horticulture and in agriculture is not new. However, manipulating agricultural landscapes to facilitate movements of predators of agricultural pests has become an exciting and important aspect of integrated pest control. This could not have come about without an understanding of the patterns of movements and distribution of the predators (see Section 8.5).

Development of computers, computing and information technology has enabled new applications to occur in biogeography. One of these applications has been in connection with researching the role of tropical forests, deforestation and regenerating forests in the carbon cycle. Every year, about 8.5 gigatonnes of carbon move between the land, the air and the oceans. There has been much recent concern about increases in the levels of atmospheric carbon brought about by the release of carbon when forests are burnt. Increased levels of carbon dioxide have implications for climate change and consequently there has been much research on carbon 'sinks' or the processes which take up atmospheric carbon. Mature tropical forests absorb carbon (photosynthesis) and release it (respiration), resulting in a carbon balance. However, regenerating forests are major sinks of carbon dioxide (CO_2). Knowing where these sinks are, their area and their stage or condition in ecological terms is of great importance in helping to mitigate human impact on the carbon cycle. A highly advanced tool with which to estimate areas of forest at regional and global scales which may be acting as carbon sinks is remote sensing from satellites. One example of this kind of detection has been undertaken by a group of researchers based in the UK but working on tropical forests in Ghana (Foody & Curran, 1994). Data gathered by satellite have been used to characterise tropical forest regeneration and in turn to help to analyse the nature and role of forest regeneration in the carbon cycle.

We live at a time when there are many environmental issues and concerns. One well-known environmental issue is climate change and the implications of any change on agriculture, horticulture and the distribution and abundance of living organisms. Determining the rate of climate change and extent of change depends on the time scale being used. Although there appears to have been an increase in the frequency of extreme weather conditions during the last ten years, some would say that this is variety in nature. Depending on the time scale being used, it could be said that the world climate could be becoming more variable, warmer or cooler. Environmental change occurs not only over different time scales but at different spatial scales. We could consider global changes or regional environmental changes. For example, in New Zealand, river temperatures have been getting slightly lower; at least that is the conclusion after just six years of monitoring river temperatures.

Environmental change has come to dominate much research and even public concern. The implications of climate change on biota are being modelled and researched at many centres by biogeographers and there seems to be no doubt that in the future some aspects of climate change could have severe implications for the way of life of people throughout the world. Climate change could have major impacts on agriculture practices, forestry and fisheries, as well as on the availability of water. These changes could also affect the distributions of wild plants and animals and have implications for the role of protected areas such as nature reserves.

Biogeography provides essential information for the conservation of species (and other taxonomic groups) and for restoration of biological communities. Human actions have 'shaken' and 'stirred' the world's biota (as well as having caused many taxa to become extinct). Consequently there are many parts of the world where the group of taxa does not constitute a natural biological community. In many parks and gardens there are plant species that would not normally occur in those biogeographical areas. The implications of moving species around the world are many. Some introduced species may supplant native species, they may become invasive and they may act as hosts for pests. Human-assembled collections of exotic plants (not native to that area) such as trees and shrubs in a city park or in an urban garden may be attractive visually and may be a living museum of flora. Such collections, however, fail to recognise the rich dynamics and variety of interactions that occur in natural biological communities or plant assemblages. A single exotic (non-native) specimen tree in a park or botanic garden (for example, Fig. 1.2)

Fig. 1.2. A single, isolated 'specimen' tree in a botanic garden.

will interact with other organisms that occur in that area, but in the sense of natural biological communities such a specimen tree is like a single member of an orchestra playing only their part in a Beethoven symphony without the existence of other players and an audience. That single specimen tree is of little significance in terms of biogeography, biological diversity and biological communities. Such a tree may as well be made of plastic for its visual appearance is its only importance.

Biogeography is helping ecological restoration projects throughout the world at many different scales. There are large-scale, country-wide forest restoration projects and there are local initiatives. There seems to be a growing interest in trying to turn around our practice of mixing species around the world. But restoring native species is just the first simple step. Restoring the biological communities with both the species and the interactions between species is a challenge being helped by biogeography and ecology.

Of all the environmental issues facing us today, what is the most serious in terms of the costs and damage incurred? Climate change, pollution, loss of indigenous forests, or fragmentation of habitats? There is a widely held view amongst many ecologists that the most important and most threatening aspect of environmental change is that caused by introduced and invasive organisms. The most damaging of all pests are introduced organisms. The problems of invasive species are likely to become even more severe in the future, with increasing global trade and reduction in trade barriers. There are many, many examples of introduced species which have had dramatic consequences on both ecology and economics. Examples include the klamath weed or St John's wort (*Hypericum perforatum*) from Eurasia and North Africa in the USA, the North American grey squirrel (*Sciurus carolinensis*) in Britain, the Australian brush-tailed possum (*Trichosurus vulpecula*) in New Zealand (see also Section 4.8.3), and the South American cactus *Opuntia* in Australia. Humans have certainly mixed, stirred and changed the distribution of many plant and animals species throughout the world, either deliberately via introductions or by acting as vectors for the transport of organisms. Many species have been introduced to new biogeographical areas and many of those species have become pests. The damage caused by these pests has had very serious economic implications. The costs of control may be extremely high each year. For example, the distribution of the zebra mussel (*Dreissena polymorpha*) from Europe has been extended after being carried in ballasts of ships. The spread of this species in the Great Lakes of North America and cost of subsequent damage now runs into several billion dollars.

Ecologists and biogeographers will have an increasingly important role in identifying possible future invasive species and in mitigation of the effects of current invasive species.

1.6 Last frontiers for human exploration

We find it ironic that so much effort and so many resources are put into the exploration of outer space, at a time when humans are progressively using resources to depletion and when so little is known about the biological diversity of the earth. Why is there all this publicity about ancient life discovered on the planet Mars when there are regions of the Earth where life has yet to be explored? Life at the extremes of environmental conditions are to be found on the Earth. For example, studies of life at great depths in the oceans has hardly begun. Recently, an entire new kingdom of deep sea organisms, the Archaea, has been recognised; although discovered some decades ago, genetic analysis has shown them to be quite unlike any other kind of life (Earle, 1996).

We have been concerned to read of proposals for using deep oceans for disposal of global waste – waste that is inert or rich in metals or even in organic compounds (but not industrial organic compounds). Quite rightly, some proponents of these methods of global waste management have recommended the need for appropriately scaled experiments and further research on the processes that maintain the diversity of benthic assemblages (Angel & Rice, 1996).

The oceans are truly one of the last frontiers for exploration and the challenges of undertaking such exploration are huge. The mechanics of sampling are difficult, little is known about the taxonomy of the biota at great depths, and the low density of some organisms and the cryptic nature of the many creatures make them difficult to locate. Once located and if captured (which is not easy), there are more difficulties because there are no well-developed techniques for ensuring that the material is not damaged during retrieval. The biogeography of the sea, particularly the biogeography of the ocean depths is worthy of much greater attention and can justify much greater support for research than questionable work on the possible existence of life on another planet.

1.7 Structure of the book

While recognising recent and valuable new developments in biogeography, such as cladistic biogeography, this book is concerned mostly with the ecological approach to biogeography. In so doing we look at biogeography at different spatial scales, from global patterns to patterns within biological communities and even individual species distributions and future opportunities to model and predict in the light of environmental change.

The sequence of chapters is based on the following structure: (a) the patterns of distribution, (b) causes of the patterns, (c) data collection and analysis (d) biogeography in practice. Chapters 2 and 3 consider biogeography at different scales, commencing with global patterns and ending with island patterns. Island biogeography deserves a special mention, partly because of the many historical studies of island organisms but also because there are some very real and modern issues to do with the conservation of island fauna and flora.

What has caused the patterns we observe today? There are geological, environmental, evolutionary, biological and human aspects (see Chapter 4). Evolution through long periods of geological history and dispersal of organisms has shaped present distributions of biota but in recent history, human social and cultural aspects have been important. The patterns and types of species distribution pattern (in space and in time) are introduced in Chapter 5.

Throughout this book the emphasis is on the applied aspects of biogeography. It seems logical therefore to consider how biogeographical information is obtained (Chapter 6). What are the field techniques and what role does computer technology have in biogeography?

The process of loss of habitat and subsequent breaking up of habitats into smaller and smaller fragments is a major concern amongst conservation biologists. Chapter 7 looks at the role of biogeography in understanding the ecological aspects of habitat fragmentation and restoration of habitats. A very popular concept has been wildlife corridors; 'What are they?' Do they work?' are two main questions discussed in Chapter 8.

Finally, what of the future? In Chapter 9 we look into the crystal ball of biogeography suggesting ideas for the future. The appendices comprise a glossary of technical terms used in the text and a list of addresses of organizations with biogeographical interests.

1.8 References

At the end of each chapter a small number of references is included either to allow further details to be obtained or as a source of authority for main points.

References

Andersson, L. (1996). An ontological dilemma: epistomology and methodology of historical biogeography. *Journal of Biogeography*, **23**, 269–77.

Andrewartha, H. G. & Birch, L. C. (1954). *The Distribution and Abundance of Animals*. Chicago & London, University of Chicago Press.

Angel, M. V. & Rice, T. L. (1996). The ecology of the deep ocean and its relevance to global waste management. *Journal of Applied Ecology*, **33**, 915–926.

Angermeier, P. L. & Karr, J. R. (1994). Biological integrity versus biological diversity as policy directives. *BioScience*, **44**, 690–697.

Bowman, D. (1994). Cry shame on all humanity. *New Scientist*, **144**, 59.

Carson, R. (1962). *Silent Spring.* Boston, MA, Houghton Mifflin.

Croizat, L. (1958). *Panbiogeography or an Introductory Synthesis of Zoogeography, Phytogeography, and Geology.* Caracas, published by the author.

Earle, S. A. (1996). Oceans, the well of life. *Time,* 44, 52–53.

Foody, G. M. & Curran, P. J. (1994). Estimation of tropical forest extent and regenerative stage using remotely sensed data. *Journal of Biogeography,* 21, 223–244.

Gadow, H. (1913). *The Wanderings of Animals.* London, Cambridge University Press.

George, W. (1969). *Animals and Maps.* London, Secker and Warburg.

Myers, A. A. & Giller, P. S. (1988). *Analytical Biogeography.* London, Chapman & Hall.

Tansley, A. G. (1935). The use and abuse of vegetational concepts and terms. *Ecology,* 16, 284–307.

Watt, A. S. (1947). Pattern and process in the plant community. *Journal of Ecology,* 35, 1–22.

2

Patterns of distribution and biogeographical classifications

2.1 Introduction

The distribution of plants, animals and other organisms can merely be portrayed as maps. Indeed for thousands of years there have been attempts to map the distribution of various groups of plants and animals. In the 19th and early 20th centuries, biogeographical studies were much influenced by 'centres of creation' or centres of origin; that is, there were attempts to identify the localities where it was thought that plant and animals groups originally arose. Then, from about the time of the theories of Charles Darwin and Alfred Wallace in the mid 19th century, more attention was paid not only to mapping various taxa but also to the geological, historical and ecological reasons for the patterns observed.

Common to all these early studies were attempts to classify various regions from biological and environmental perspectives. Biogeographical realms and biomes, and many other types of region, subregion and zone have been suggested. Some classifications were based on the types and groups of fauna and flora characteristic of the area. An alternative approach was to focus on a combination of environmental and biotic variables.

Today, with the use of modern mapping techniques, computer technology and satellites there continues to be much effort devoted to dividing the world up into different kinds of biogeographical region. Why this emphasis on 'mapping' and what relevance does this have today? The reason is simple. Before we can either utilise or conserve biota (and establish management strategies) we must know what is there, what it consists of, what state it is in, how abundant it is, where it occurs and when it occurs. That information can then be used for many purposes; for example, it could be used for establishing conservation priorities and conservation gaps (see Section 2.5).

In this chapter we first look at the foundations of biogeographical mapping and classification before examining modern methods and their applications and limitations.

2.2 A history of classification systems

As is the case now, biogeographical studies in the 18th and 19th centuries came in many forms. Evidence for this can be seen amongst some of the literature recorded in Hans Gadow's book *The Wanderings of Animals* published in 1913. In it he gives a delightful, brief insight into these early publications, the main volumes of which are listed in Table 1.2.

At about the time when Charles Darwin and other naturalists were reporting their observations on the distribution patterns of plants and animals throughout the world, others were intent on identifying centres of creation. Those early studies prompted much lively discussion and it is difficult for us today to have insight into the cultural, social and scientific atmosphere at the time. However, there is one notable and historic place, which can be visited today, where anyone can begin to enter the world of the early naturalists and biogeographers. This is the home of the Linnean Society, a scholarly society in the centre of London, founded in 1788 and named in honour of that most significant early naturalist Carl Linnaeus (1707–1778). In the stately building of Burlington House, a short distance from Piccadilly in the centre of London, there are the rooms of the Linnean Society (Fig. 2.1), including offices, meeting rooms and a library of around 100 000 books, periodicals and manuscripts as well the library and collection of Linnaeus. Walking into a meeting room or the library of the Society is like walking into history – a rich tapestry of natural history, biogeography, biology and taxonomy.

The agenda for a meeting in June of 1857 of the Linnean Society is relevant to our discussion here. We will never know what the atmosphere of the meeting was like but it took place at a time when there was much controversy and indeed bitter arguments within the natural sciences; theories of natural selection were emerging amidst strongly held views about the creation. The agenda for the meeting (Box 2.1) is included in the published proceedings of the Society and can be read at the Linnean Society. There were contributions from Lord Wallace and from Philip Lutley Sclater, Esq. (1829–1913) a notable English zoologist who travelled widely throughout Europe, the Mediterranean region and North America. He was not alone at the time in his

Fig. 2.1. Photographs of the Linnean Society Meeting Room and Library. (Courtesy of the Linnean Society of London and M. B. Spellerberg.)

Box 2.1. Agenda for the Meeting of the Linnean Society of 16 June 1857. (Reproduced with kind permission of the Linnean Society of London)

June 16th, 1857.

Thomas Bell, Esq., President, in the Chair.

Read, first, a "Catalogue of the *Hymenoptera* collected at Sarawak, in the Island of Borneo, Malacca, and Singapore, by Mr. A. R. Wallace;" by Frederick Smith, Esq.; communicated by W. W. Saunders, Esq., F.L.S. (See "Zoological Proceedings," vol. ii. p. 42.)

Read, secondly, a "Note on the Occurrence of *Rotatoria* in *Vaucheria*;" by Daniel Oliver, Jun., Esq., F.L.S.

Read, thirdly, a Memoir "On the growth and composition of the Ovarium of *Siphonodon,* Griff.;" by Joseph Dalton Hooker, Esq., M.D., F.R.S., F.L.S. (See "Transactions," vol. xxii. p. 133.)

Read, fourthly, a Note "On a Monstrous Development in *Habenaria chlorantha*;" by the Rev. John Stevens Henslow, M.A., F.L.S. (See "Botanical Proceedings," vol. ii.)

Read, fifthly, a Note "On a Monstrous Development of the Spike of a species of Banana;" by Sir Robert H. Schomburgk; communicated by George Bentham, Esq., F.L.S. (See "Botanical Proceedings," vol. ii.)

Read, sixthly, a Memoir "On the Geographical Distribution of the Members of the Class *Aves*;" by Philip Lutley Sclater, Esq., F.L.S. (See "Zoological Proceedings," vol. ii.)

efforts to try to demonstrate 'centres of creation'. If he could show the existence of separate centres of creation in different parts of the world, he considered it would be possible to avoid

> the awkward necessity of supposing the introduction of the red man into America by Bering's Straits, and of colonizing Polynesia by stray pairs of Malays floating over water-like cocoa nuts *Proceedings of the Linnean Society*, 16 June 1857.

On the evening of 16 June 1857, at a meeting of the Linnean Society, Sclater presented a proposal for six regions based on the distribution of birds. In his talk he bemoaned the fact that previous maps showing the world's fauna and flora paid scant attention to the fact that two or more geographical regions may have closer relations to each other than to a third. He commenced by saying (the language by today's standards is delightful):

> An important problem in natural History, and one that has hitherto been too little agitated, is that of ascertaining the most natural primary divisions of the earth's surface, taking the amount of similarity or dissimilarity of organized life solely as our guide *Proceedings of the Linnean Society*, 16 June 1857.

He set about demonstrating his views by examining the geographical distribution within the vertebrate class, Aves, noting first that birds 'being of all the animated creation the class most particularly adapted for wide and rapid locomotion would at first sight, seem to be by no means a favourable part of nature's subjects for the solution of such a problem.' But some groups of birds do have extremely local distributions and it was possible for Sclater to recognise regional differences in the avifauna. A distribution scheme for birds by Sclater is shown in Fig. 2.2.

The six regions shown in Sclater's scheme do not (as expected) have names which reflect political or cultural boundaries. Those six regions provided a basis on which Alfred Wallace devised his zoogeographical regions, an example of which is shown in Fig. 2.3. The term 'realm' is more appropriate than 'region' at this scale because a realm is the largest of the biogeographical units embracing a large climatic area and physiographical units. Within a realm there are regions and within regions there are zones.

Not everyone at that time agreed with the geographical boundaries and the number of realms. For example, one person well known to Wallace was Angelo Heilprin (working from the Academy of Natural Sciences at Philadelphia); he adopted a suggestion that the two large realms of the Nearctic and the Palearctic should be combined into an even larger realm, the

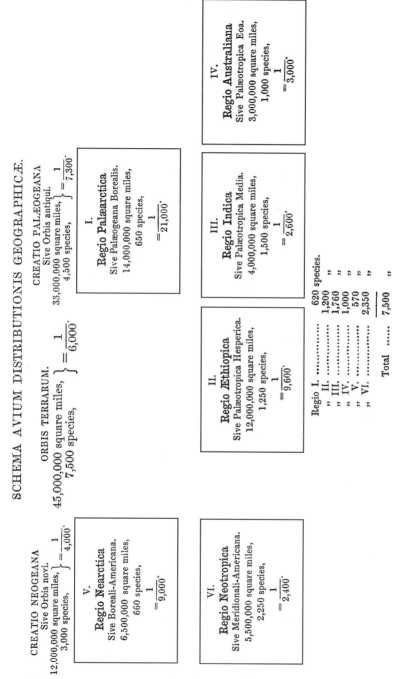

Fig. 2.2. Philip Sclater's (1857) scheme for classifying the geographical distribution of birds. (Reproduced with kind permission of the Linnean Society of London.)

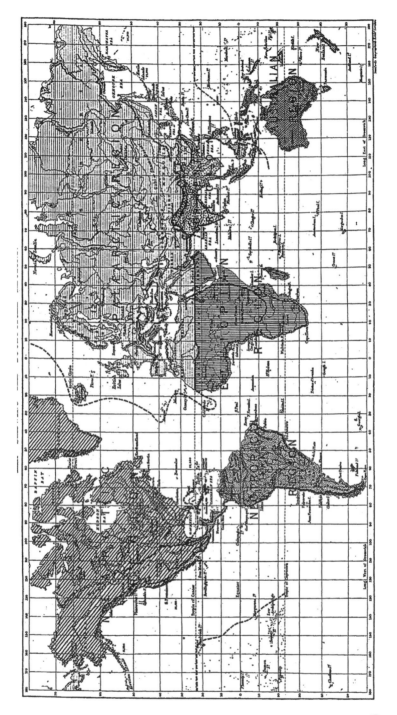

(a)

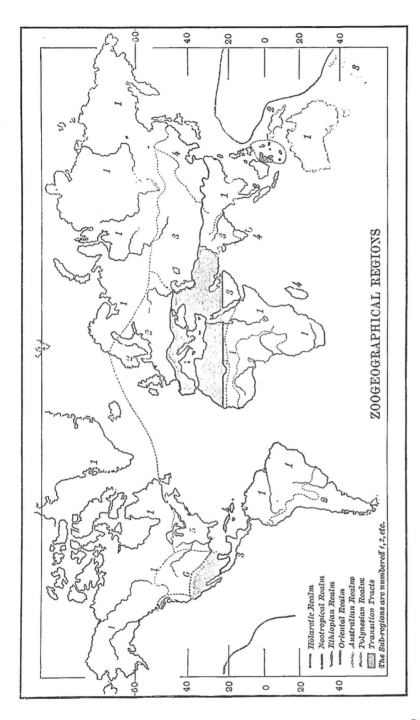

Fig. 2.3. Zoogeographical realms (regions) according to (**a**) Alfred Wallace (from his book *Island Life* published in 1880 by MacMillan and Co.) and (**b**) Angelo Heilprin (from his book *The Geographical and Geological Distribution of Animals* published in 1887 by Kegan Paul, Trench & Co.). Note that Heilprin has combined the Nearctic and the Palearctic into one huge region, the Holarctic.

(*b*)

ZOOGEOGRAPHICAL REGIONS

Holarctic Realm
Neotropical Realm
Ethiopian Realm
Oriental Realm
Australian Realm
Polynesian Realm
Transition Tracts
The Sub-regions are numbered 1, 2, etc.

Holarctic (Fig. 2.3). That suggestion has not been well supported. Wallace's basic classification of the zoogeographical regions of the world remains as one of the major landmarks in biogeography and is still used today. In some parts of the world, these regions are subdivided into subregions. For example, one scheme for subregions in Australia has three areas (Fig. 2.4).

New zoogeographical regions, some for particular taxa, continued to be recognised after Wallace's work. For example in 1926, Theodor Herzog published his *Geographie der Moose* and provided a basis for a single world-wide geographical classification for bryophtes (mosses, liverworts and hornworts). Although no map was given, there were sufficient data for a map to be created.

Regions that tended to be overlooked in the earlier classifications were the polar regions and particularly the southern oceans. The Antarctic continent and surrounding oceans is the focus of much biogeographical attention today because of concern about increasing human impacts on the marine ecosystems. As with other regions, there is a huge and growing amount of information about the biogeography and environmental science of Antarctica and the southern oceans. That information is deposited in widely scattered localities and until recently was not easily available. The growth in amount and complexity of biogeographical information has prompted the establishment of some independent centres for the purpose of gathering and handling environmental information. For example, the International Centre for Antarctic Information and Research (ICAIR, based at Christchurch, New Zealand) collects, analyses and distributes scientific, environmental and educational information relating to Antarctica.

Our knowledge of the biogeography of the polar seas has advanced considerably in recent years and, whereas some marine groups previously appeared not to be abundant, that picture has now changed. For example, prior to the 1960s it was recorded that bivalve molluscs in Antarctic waters were not very abundant and numbered fewer than 90 species. Recent surveys of gastropods and bivalves in Antarctica and sub-Antarctic waters have revealed that the southern ocean mollusc fauna is quite diverse, comprising more than 750 species. The species richness of these groups in warmer waters is greater by only a hundred or so species. There is much yet to be learnt about the biogeography of the southern oceans.

The vertical divisions of the oceans include the Epipelagic (sunlit) Zone down to about 200 metres, the Mesopelagic (twilight) Zone down to 1000 metres, the Bathypelagic (sunless) Zone down to 6000 metres and the Hadopelagic (trench) Zone which is below 6000 metres. In the early part of the 20th century it appeared that there was no good biological reason for dividing the deep sea into geographical regions but in the 1950s a simple

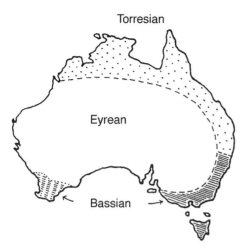

Fig. 2.4. One scheme adopted for the zoogeographical subregions of Australia. Other schemes include more than three subregions.

division into four regions was recognised by some biogeographers: the Atlantic, Indo-Pacific, Arctic and Antarctic. Later, and owing to the work of Russian scientists, a more substantial zoogeography of the deep sea came to be recognised. For example, studies of the fauna of the Abyssal Zone (the great depths below about 4000 metres) and Hadal Zone (the trenches and canyons at depths below 6000 metres) have provided a basis for clear divisions of those zones (Vinogradova, 1979).

Zoogeographical regions are based on the observation that certain taxonomic groups of organisms occur together, providing a basis for a classification of regions or zones. But taxonomic groups are only one way of looking at the world's biota. Another is to look at the structure of the biota, such as the form and shape of the vegetation, for example grasses, deciduous forests and coniferous forests.

In the 1800s, European botanists were studying groups of taxa based on the structure of the plants or on the adaptations of the plants to environmental variables. This led in 1903 to the Danish botanist Christen Raunkiaer writing about his observations of different major plant forms which seemed to have become well adapted to the climate and therefore dominated different climatic regions. He suggested the concept of plant life forms, a link between plants and their environment (Fig. 2.5): in some regions, plants were generally shrub like and low growing, whereas in other regions the dominant form might be trees. He based his system of plant life forms on a single characteristic, the position of the resting (or perennating) buds of the plant in relation to the soil

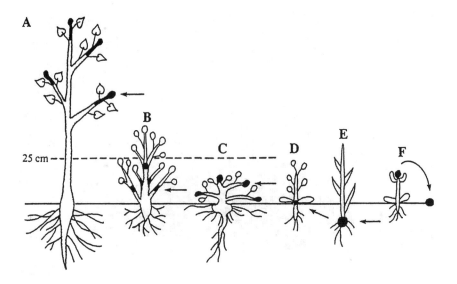

Fig. 2.5. Some of the plant life forms based on Raunkiaer's (1934) classification. The chief plant life forms include (A) phanerophytes (tall woody plants, trees or shrubs with their resting buds greater than 25 centimetres above the ground); (B and C) chamaeophytes (semi-shrubs with buds less than 25 centimetres above the ground); (D) hemicryptophytes (perennial herbs with buds at the ground surface); (E) geophyte, perennial herb with perennating organ below ground surface; (F) therophyte, annual plant that survives unfavourable periods as a seed. (From Raunkiaer, C. (1934), The life forms of plants and statistical plant geography, Clarendon Press, Oxford. By permission of Oxford University Press.)

surface. An account of plant life forms can be found in most plant ecology textbooks. It was this recognition of geographical differences in plant life forms that provided a basis for the concept of biomes; that is, geographical regions characterised by distinctive life forms.

But it is not only plants which have become well adapted to different climatic regions; animals have done the same. Two authors, F. E. Clements and J. E. Shelford in 1939 published their book *Bio-ecology* and this was part of a movement which drew together the 'ecological studies' of botanists and zoologists. It was obvious that no plant community existed without animals and vice versa (except at the ocean depths). The 'bioecologists' defined the term 'biome' as an ecological unit.

Terrestrial biomes are characterised by the dominant plant life form (based on the concept put forward by Raunkiaer) and especially those in a climax community (the 'final' stage or life form in an ecological succession). One classification of the terrestrial biomes of the world (Fig. 2.6) includes the

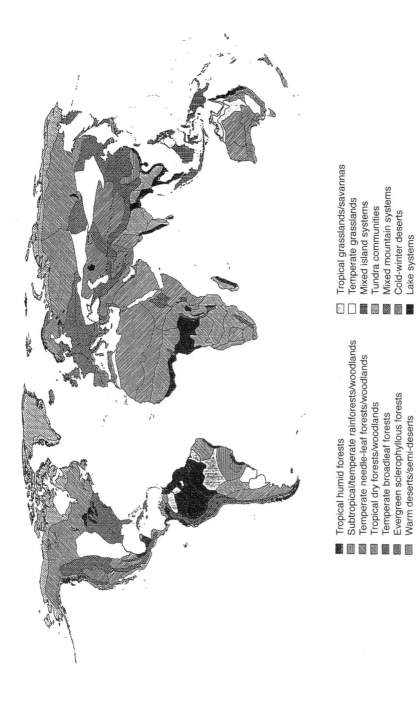

Fig. 2.6. A classification of biomes by Udvardy (1975). (Redrawn from *Global Biodiversity, Status of the earth's Living Resources* published by Chapman & Hall (1992) and compiled by the World Conservation Monitoring Centre. With permission of the World Conservation Monitoring Centre.)

Tropical humid forests
Subtropical/temperate rainforests/woodlands
Temperate needle-leaf forests/woodlands
Tropical dry forests/woodlands
Temperate broadleaf forests
Evergreen sclerophyllous forests
Warm deserts/semi-deserts

Tropical grasslands/savannas
Temperate grasslands
Mixed island systems
Tundra communities
Mixed mountain systems
Cold-winter deserts
Lake systems

tundra, the northern coniferous forest, temperate broad-leaved forest, tropical dry forest, temperate grasslands and cold winter deserts. This type of classification combines characteristics of the life forms of mainly dominant climax vegetation with climate (see also Fig. 5.6).

There are also marine biomes: the three main marine biomes are the oceanic biome (including the planktonic sub-biome, the nektonic sub-biome and the benthic sub-biome), the rocky shore biome and the sandy or mud shore biome.

As biomes are easily recognised large units and because they demonstrate that the distribution of various groups of organisms (not necessarily taxonomic groups) is determined by their adaptations and interactions with the environment including climatic factors and edaphic factors (pertaining to the soil), they serve a very useful purpose as units of biogeographical study. However, the present boundaries of biomes are unlikely to remain fixed. If changes in the world's climate do occur then it is almost certain that the geographical positions will change (see Fig. 9.1).

Over millions of years, plants have evolved and have adapted to edaphic factors, regional climate and other environmental variables. But just what precise variables and to what extent environmental variables determine the biogeography of vegetation has been at the centre of much challenging research. Climatic variables such as precipitation, wind, temperature, insolation (exposure to solar radiation) and combinations of these affect the geographical distribution of plant life forms, so much so that vegetation types can be classified in relation to climatic variables. For example, in 1947 L. R. Holdridge at the Botany Department, University of Michigan, proposed a classification where each biome had a unique combination of climatic variables. The Holdridge 'Life Zone System' is based largely on three long-term climatic variables: mean annual total precipitation, mean annual 'biotemperature', and potential evapotranspiration. This is a broad-based system which has a number of shortcomings with respect to some vegetation patterns. For example, seasonality is largely omitted. The concept of 'biotemperatures', while innovative, is perhaps not easily justified.

2.3 Biogeographical classification at different spatial scales

Many classification systems have been developed for different levels of biological diversity (such as communities and ecosystems), for application at various spatial scales (such as global, national and regional) and for a variety of

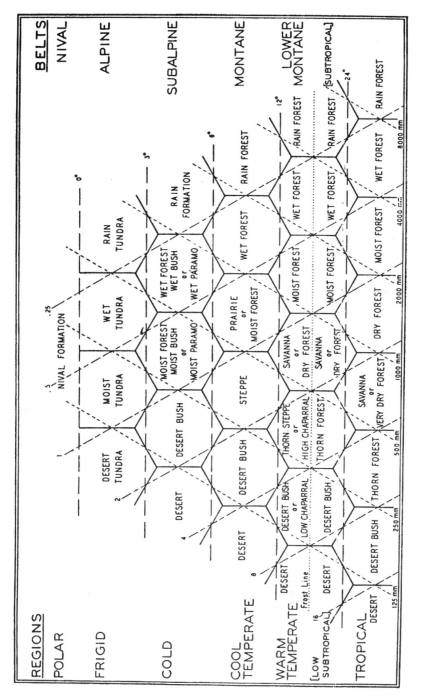

Fig. 2.7. The classification system used by Holdridge for vegetation types and climatic variables. (Reprinted with permission from Holdridge, L. R. 1947, *Science*, **105**, 367. Copyright 1947 American Association for the Advancement of Science.)

different purposes; some of these are shown in Box 2.2. A variety of classification systems have been developed because some of them work better in some parts of the world than others and because of the different uses to which those systems will be put.

A classification system can be relied upon only at the scale for which that system was developed. That is because at a global scale the vegetation of, say, Central Africa may be classified as 'tropical rain forest', but that is not to deny that a far more heterogeneous mix of vegetation types exists. Local variations in topography or microclimate can strongly influence the biological nature of vegetation, creating greater diversity that can only be recognised if the vegetation types are classified at a higher level of resolution. Therefore, classification systems used to describe global patterns cannot be relied upon for local details and systems to describe local patterns cannot be extrapolated to generate global information. The use of one classification system at one spatial scale does not preclude the use of other systems (more or less detailed) at another scale or level of resolution.

An example of a vegetation classification system is that published by UNESCO in 1973 for the primary purpose of mapping. It was an attempt to classify the world's terrestrial vegetation and is a good example of a global approach. It is based primarily on structural and physiognomic characters of the terrestrial vegetation, which means that the physical state of the vegetation is described rather than the species within the vegetation. 'Closed forest', for example, is defined as being 'formed by trees at least 5 metres tall with their crowns interlocking'.

At a national level there are many examples of classification systems (see Box 2.2). For example, in the USA one classification is based on 52 ecoregions (USDA, 1995). Ecoregions are defined as ecosystems of regional extent and are differentiated according to a hierarchical scheme that uses climate and vegetation as indicators of their spatial extent. The vegetation and fauna of an ecoregion are described using indicator species that are either unique to that region or abundant in it. The hierarchy of classification within each ecoregion recognises three levels: domains, divisions and provinces. Domains and divisions are based on broad ecological climate zones and a province is classified based on the macro-features of the vegetation.

Another example from the USA is the ecosystem classification system developed for use by the United States Fish and Wildlife Service (USFWS, 1995). That system delineates hydrological units (such as the Lower Mississippi River and the Columbia River Basin) and treats each unit as an ecosystem for the purpose of management. Such a classification system is

---

Box 2.2. Classification systems for physical or biologically equivalent units of land, water and vegetation have been developed and applied at a variety of different spatial scales including global, national and regional

Global

1. The UNESCO system for classification of the world's terrestrial vegetation was published in 1973 and is based on structural and physiognomic characters of the vegetation (UNESCO, 1973).
2. The ecoregions of the world have been classified using three hierarchical levels: domains and divisions are based on broad ecological climate zones; divisions are further subdivided into provinces on the basis of macro-features in the vegetation (Bailey, 1989).

National

1. In the USA a national classification has been completed of the ecoregions of that country using climate and vegetation as indicators of the extent of each region (USDA, 1995).
2. In the UK the National Vegetation Classification (NVC) is a comprehensive classification of British vegetation types including vegetation from all natural, semi-natural and major artificial habitats of Great Britain (Rodwell *et al.*, 1991).
3. In New Zealand ecological regions and districts have been identified and are differentiated on the basis of differences in geology, landform, climate, soil and flora and the extent of the remaining indigenous vegetation (Simpson, 1982). See also Harding & Winterbourn (1997).

Regional

1. In Canada the Biogeoclimatic Ecosystem Classification System (BEC) has been developed for use at regional and local levels and attempts to identify biologically equivalent sites based on characters of the ecosystem (Mackinnon *et al.*, 1992).

---

appropriate for aquatic organisms or those species whose distribution is determined primarily by the geographical extent of a watershed. However, for some plants and animals, a watershed boundary may not affect their geographical distribution and so such a classification system can have limitations.

In the UK one national system in use is the National Vegetation Classification (NVC) (Rodwell *et al.*, 1991). The NVC is a systematic classification of over 250 plant communities covering all natural, semi-natural and major artificial habitats of Great Britain. A summary of the vascular plants, bryophytes and lichens of each community is provided in the classification.

That system also recognises ecological assemblages and many different kinds of vegetation types (such as oak woodlands) that are classified on the basis of the mix of plant species characterised by that vegetation.

In addition to national classifications there are regional and local attempts to identify levels of biological diversity (Box 2.2). One example is the Biogeoclimatic Ecosystem Classification System (BEC) which is used in Canada at local and regional levels (Mackinnon *et al.*, 1992). The BEC seeks to define biologically equivalent site units based on characters of the ecosystem. The classification of sites is based on shared environmental characteristics (such as equivalent physical properties, including the soil moisture and nutrient régime) that will produce similar plant communities at climax (that is, at their point of stability). The system is hierarchical so that, at the local level, vegetation and site classifications differentiate vegetation and site units. At the regional level a climatic classification is used to differentiate between homogeneous bioclimatic units that are areas of the landscape characterised by a uniform macroclimate.

2.4 Applied aspects

Biogeographical classifications have many applications in ecology, in conservation and in management of biological diversity, in ecological monitoring and also in resource management (Box 2.3). One example is an atlas showing the distribution of the plant communities of Australia (Specht *et al.*, 1996). To produce the atlas, each plant community was classified on the basis of its structure and floristics (which means the structural attributes of the vegetation and the species within the community). After mapping the distribution of the plant community types it was found, not surprisingly, that some were far more common than others. Of the 344 major plant communities identified, those that are less common and those that are not currently found in conservation reserves are to become the focus for conservation efforts.

For use with continents a classification of the ecoregions has been proposed by Bailey (1989). The purpose of the classification system and the subsequent map has been to facilitate a regional rather than site-by-site approach to planning land use. That classification system and map provided the geographical framework to identify areas that are similar in a biological or physical sense and from which similar responses may be expected and to which similar management policies may be applied.

Biogeographical classification systems have been used in ecology for analysis of distribution patterns of populations or communities of species. The

---

Box 2.3. Biogeographical classifications have various applications including environmental protection, monitoring and in resource management

1. Conservation management and environmental protection

A classification system was used to produce a conservation atlas showing the geographical distribution of the plant communities of Australia (Specht *et al.*, 1996).

Gap analysis (performed using classification systems) is used to identify gaps in the protective network for the conservation of biological diversity in any particular region (Scott *et al.*, 1993).

2. Ecology

Classification systems, such as the Biogeoclimatic Ecosystem Classification System in Canada are used in ecology as a framework in studies to explain why certain species of plant or animal are distributed as they are (Mackinnon *et al.*, 1992).

3. Ecological restoration

Classification systems are used in ecological restoration initiatives. A classification system of soils and climate was used to determine the potential role of islands in the restoration of the complete variety of New Zealand's terrestrial environments (Meurk & Blaschke, 1990).

4. Environmental monitoring

Classification systems are used to provide a framework for storing baseline information about the distribution of various levels of biological diversity for comparative analysis of future changes in their distribution.

5. Resource management

Classification systems are used in sustainable resource management. The Biogeoclimatic Ecosystem Classification System is used to improve management of production forestry and to manage the sustained development of forest resources in west Canada (Mackinnon *et al.*, 1992).

---

systems can be used to identify reasons for the performance of some plant or animal species (or communities of species) under certain environmental conditions or a particular management régime. In Canada, the BEC has been used as a basis for identifying units for wildlife management. The homogeneous bioclimatic units (defined by similar macroclimates) are stratified into habitats (for example, estuaries and old-growth forests) of importance to wildlife. Wildlife associated with each of those habitats is identified and a summary of information is generated about wildlife in each unit (in the system). When some species of wildlife are observed to occur regularly at sites that are biologically or physically equivalent, it may be possible to identify what determines the distribution of those species and limits their potential distribution. Classification systems therefore provide a basis for ecological biogeography, providing ecological explanations for observed distribution patterns.

Classification systems have applications in evaluation of land for ecological restoration or species recovery. For example, in New Zealand, which is made up of two main islands and many offshore islands, Meurk & Blaschke (1990) have characterised the range and extent of climate and soil types. They then determined the extent to which each of the islands of New Zealand is representative of New Zealand environments as a whole. That classification and analysis showed the limited potential of island environments for ecological restoration of the complete range of New Zealand temperate communities.

Classification systems can be used to evaluate areas of economic potential; that is, for production of natural resources. One example is in Canada where the BEC has been used in the development and management of the timber production industry. The BEC is now an integral part of silviculture in British Columbia. The treatment of particular sites for production forestry takes into account the understanding of the unit, based on experiences in dealing with equivalent units elsewhere. A body of management experiences has been compiled by staff about each biologically equivalent site unit in the system. The predicted responses of those units to particular management régimes are used by staff when they decide on the most suitable crop tree species for reafforestation at a particular site. The BEC is therefore used to manage the sustained development of forest resources in west Canada.

For monitoring environmental change, a classification system can be used to provide baseline information for comparative analysis of future changes in the geographical distribution of each of the elements of the system. If it is assumed that similar responses can be expected from biologically or physically similar units in a classification system then their use can reduce the need for environmental monitoring and analysis on a site-by-site basis.

When applying biogeographical classifications, it is necessary to recognise their limitations. This is not to be critical of such classifications but it does acknowledge the limitations to ensure best use of the methods. In some classification systems the units may be defined vaguely or may be subjective. For example, in the UNESCO world vegetation classification system (UNESCO, 1973) terms such as 'often' and 'generally' are used. Use of those vague terms may create uncertainty or ambiguity, may not provide an objective means for classification and can make an observer's field diagnosis of vegetation types inconsistent.

Classification in the field can sometimes be subjective and can lead to inaccuracies in the consistency of the vegetation classification. For example, the system distinguishes between two types of tropical rain forest – alluvial forest and submontane forest – by observing that alluvial forest is richer in palms and in undergrowth life forms. Making that distinction in the field without use of more quantitative criteria could lead to inaccurate classification of some types of rain forest.

Incompatibility may be a difficulty. That is to say classification systems that have been developed in different parts of the world and for use at different spatial scales may be incompatible. For example, one vegetation classification system may define forest as vegetation with a minimum height of 7.5 metres (see UNESCO, 1982), whereas forest may be defined elsewhere as vegetation of 10 metres in height (see White, 1983). Inconsistency in definitions between classification systems may prevent the compilation of information from different systems from different parts of the world.

It is not always clear what are the true geographical limits to units of a classification system. A classification system generally separates two regions by means of a single line. However, boundaries between regions may not take the form of abrupt discontinuities as represented by a line on a map. Instead there may be a gradation from conditions in one region to conditions in another. Geographical boundaries identified in a classification system therefore may be far more sharply defined than they really are in nature. Furthermore the boundaries between regions may change such that a classification system may become inaccurate over time.

The extent to which a classification is comprehensive has often been debated; that is, some classification systems for vegetation may exclude certain vegetation types such as human-modified vegetation. These may be disturbed areas and areas cultivated by humans such as forest plantations. Some systems such as the National Vegetation Classification include all major artificial habitats; however, other classifications such as the UNESCO system ignore human-modified vegetation such as wheat fields, vineyards and plantations, despite the fact that these areas of land use occupy a considerable portion of the earth's surface.

The ever-changing nature of biological communities presents a challenge for any classification. Systems of classification, for vegetation in particular, can be limited because of the dynamic nature of vegetation. Vegetation at one site may be classified but can then change in time so that the original classification becomes out of date. Not all categories in a vegetation classification system (such as that of UNESCO) represent climax vegetation conditions, so for these vegetation types the areas may need to be inspected regularly to observe changes that may have occurred. Previous site classification could quickly become out of date as one vegetation type succeeds another and the vegetation structure changes.

2.5 Gap analysis

Identifying gaps is one further aspect of applying biogeographical classifications. Gap analysis is a technique for identifying vegetation types and species that are not adequately represented in an existing protective network of biologial diversity. Gap analysis projects can help to locate priority areas for conservation action and research. The technique can therefore be used as a means to prioritise human effort in habitat protection and management to achieve the conservation of a region's biological diversity (see Scott *et al.*, 1996).

The principal application of gap analysis is to describe spatially, in any particular region, where are the priority areas for habitat protection to conserve species and plant and animal communities that are not already protected. In short, gap analysis is a rapid method for evaluating conservation requirements for protection of biological diversity.

In North America, for example, gap analysis has been used to identify shortfalls in conservation programmes to protect biological diversity. To perform that analysis a vegetation classification system was first used to determine biologically equivalent units of vegetation so that their geographical distribution could then be determined.

Some tasks required to implement a gap analysis project are shown in Table 2.1. To undertake gap analysis the geographical distributions of vegetation types and individual plant and animal taxa are used. The vegetation must therefore have already been classified so that the geographical distribution of the various types can be mapped. Gap analysis is not a classification system but relies on existing systems for its application. In fact classification systems for vegetation are fundamental to the success of gap analysis projects. To date, gap analysis has been performed commonly for terrestrial conservation but the method can also be used in marine conservation.

Once biologically equivalent vegetation units have been classified the geographical distribution of those units can be determined. These are two important stages in the implementation of a gap analysis project (see Table 2.1). The geographical distributions of species of plants and animals are then mapped where those distributions are known (stage 3). In particular the distributions are mapped of uncommon species or species whose existence in the wild is threatened (stage 4). The distribution of areas set aside for the

Table 2.1. *Some tasks required to implement a gap analysis project. (Note how classification of the vegetation is the first stage)*

Stage 1: Classify the vegetation types
Stage 2: Map the geographical distribution of vegetation types
Stage 3: Map the geographical distribution of species of plant and animal (where known)
Stage 4: Map the location of populations of uncommon species or species whose existence in the world is threatened
Stage 5: Map the distribution of areas set aside for the protection of biological diversity
Stage 6: Map the distribution of habitats of greatest importance to wildlife such as streams and wetlands
Stage 7: Overlay the above maps (drawn to the same scale) to identify gaps (for example, species that are not already represented in the protected area network)
Stage 8: Prioritise conservation efforts towards those geographical areas that will protect the greatest number of the new species, new habitats, and new plant and animal communities not already represented in existing reserves

protection of biological diversity is then mapped (stage 5). Habitats of greatest importance to certain plants, animals and other organisms such as streams and wetlands are then mapped (stage 6). All the above maps drafted at the same spatial scale are then overlaid (stage 7). At this point gaps are identified – the location of species or vegetation types not already represented in the network of protected areas is shown. Stage 8 is then the filling of those gaps through prioritisation and implementation of conservation efforts to protect the greatest number of species, habitats, and plant and animal communities that do not already occur in existing reserves.

Gap analysis projects have several applications, including the following: they can be used to determine the representation of species and natural plant and animal communities within areas being managed for biodiversity conservation, they provide data to model wildlife habitat distributions, and they provide a baseline of information about the distributions of plant and animal species and communities that can be used for comparative analysis of future changes in those distributions (that is, monitoring environmental change).

Although gap analysis generates information, it is not a substitute for biological inventory. That is because field inspections are still necessary for acquiring biological information about each area and about the species

GAP ANALYSIS:

PROTECTING BIODIVERSITY USING GEOGRAPHIC INFORMATION SYSTEMS

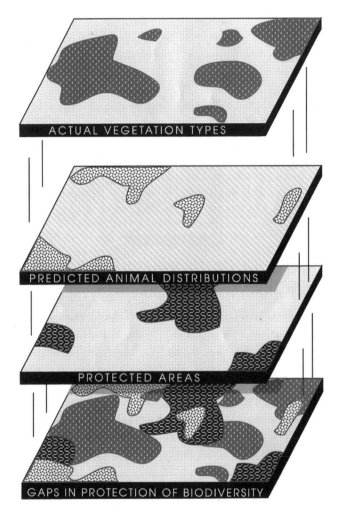

Fig. 2.8. Data layers may be overlain to show gaps in the protective network for biological diversity. (From Scott *et al.*, 1993. Gap analysis: a geographic approach to protection of biological diversity. *Wildlife Monographs*, **123**. Supplement to the *Journal of Wildlife Management*, **57**(1) Published with kind permission of the Wildlife Society who hold the copyright.)

occupying those areas. Different species tend to have different spatial require-ments and it cannot be assumed that filling gaps for one group of species will satisfy the conservation needs of another. Many birds, for example, are highly mobile and the conservation of vegetation across an entire landscape may not be necessary for their protection whereas other groups may require continu-ous tracts of preserved habitat. The identification of areas on the ground where species occur, or where there are vegetation types not represented in existing biological reserves, does not imply that setting aside those areas will result in conservation in perpetuity of those resources. A larger area may have to be set aside for the conservation of a wide-ranging species. Gap analysis provides only a first assessment of the immediate protection needs for the conservation of biological diversity in a region.

One effective way to perform gap analysis is through the use of a com-puterised Geographic Information System (GIS) and representing the spatial data as layers within a GIS (see Sections 6.7 and 9.9). However, gap analysis can be performed without such a system (see Fig. 2.8).

Gap analysis may also be used as a basis for ecological biogeography and ecological modelling. Information gathered for gap projects can focus field survey efforts on particular species or communities of species. Changes in the geographical distribution of plants and animals and their respective commu-nities may also be predicted using information from gap projects (see also Section 9.9).

References

Bailey, R. G. (1989). Explanatory supplement to ecoregions map of the continents. *Environmental Conservation*, **16**, 307–309. [With separate map at 1: 30,000,000.]

Clements, F. E. & Shelford, V. E. (1939). *Bio-ecology*. New York, Wiley.

Harding, J. S. & Winterbourn, M. J. (1997). An ecoregion classification of the South Island, New Zealand. *Journal of Environmental Management*, **51**, 275–287.

Holdridge, L. R. (1947). Determination of world plant formations from simple climatic data. *Science*, **105**, 367–368.

Mackinnon, A., Meidinger, D. & Klinka, K. (1992). Use of biogeoclimatic ecosys-tem classification system in British Columbia. *Forestry Chronicle*, **68**, 100–120.

Meurk, C. & Blaschke, P. (1990). How representative can restored islands really be? An analysis of climo-edaphic environments in New Zealand. In Towns, D. R., Daugherty, C. H., & Atkinson, I. A. E. (eds.), *Ecological Restoration of New Zealand Islands*, 52–72. Conservation Sciences publication no. 2. Wellington, Department of Conservation.

Rodwell, J. S. (ed.), Pigott, C. D., Ratcliffe, D. A., Malloch, A. J. C., Birks, H. J. B., Proctor, M. C. F., Shimwell, D. W., Huntley, J. P., Radford, E., Wigginton, M. J. & Wilkins, P. (1991). *British Plant Communities*, vol. 1 *Woodlands and Scrub*. Cambridge University Press, Cambridge.

Scott, J. M., Davis, F., Csuti, B. *et al.* (1993). *Gap Analysis: A Geographic Approach to Protection of Wildlife Diversity.* Wildlife Monographs **123**. Supplement to *Journal of Wildlife Management,* **57** (1).

Scott, J. M., Tear, T. H. & Davis, F. W. (1996). *Gap Analysis: a landscape approach to Biodiversity Planning,* MD, American Society for Photogrammetry and Remote Sensing, Maryland, USA.

Simpson, P. (1982). *Ecological Regions and districts of New Zealand: A Natural Subdivision.* Wellington, Biological Resources Centre Publication.

Specht, R. L., Specht, A., Whelan, M. B. & Hegarty, E. E. (1996). *Conservation Atlas of Plant Communities in Australia.* Lismore, Australia, Centre for Coastal Management in Association with Southern Cross University Press.

Udvardy, M. D. F. (1975). A classification of the biogeographical provinces of the world. *IUCN Occasional Paper,* no. 18. Gland, IUCN.

UNESCO (1973). *International Mapping and Classification of Vegetation.* UNESCO Ecology and Conservation Series no. 6.

UNESCO (1982). *Vegetation Map of South America.* Paris, UNESCO.

USDA (United States Department of Agriculture) (1995). *Description of the Ecoregions of the United States.* Forest Service. Miscellaneous publication no. 1391.

USFWS (United States Fish and Wildlife Service) (1995). *An Ecosystem Approach to fish and Wildlife Conservation.* Washington, DC, Department of the Interior.

Vinogradova, M. E. (1979). The geographical distribution of the abyssal and hadal (ultra-abyssal) fauna in relation to the vertical zonation of the ocean. *Sarsia,* **64**, 41–50.

White, FD. (1983). *UNESCO Vegetation Map of Africa.* Paris, UNESCO.

3

Islands

3.1 Introduction

How often have you seen those wonderful advertisements inviting you to have a holiday on a tropical island (Fig. 3.1)? What is it about islands, whether in the tropics or polar regions, that suggests romance, excitement and adventure? Is it because of a sense of escape from the pressures and stress of a bustling way of life, or the opportunity to savour sun-soaked beaches, or the adventure of rocky unexplored shores, or perhaps the chance of seeing unique island wildlife? It is for all these reasons that there is a growing tourist industry for many islands around the world.

The wildlife of islands, especially oceanic islands, has long been of special significance in biology, ecology, conservation and biogeography. Studies of island species have also been of historical significance for evolutionary biology. Many of the world's islands have high levels of endemic flora and fauna; that is, taxa found only on a particular island and no other place (see Table 3.2; also Figs. 5.9–5.11 and Box 5.1 with regard to centres of diversity and endemism). Island biota has often been devastated by the effects of introduced species, whether that be by accident or by deliberate means. In the last few hundred years human beings have been the main carriers of introduced species to islands, sometimes with drastic consequences for the indigenous biota. For example, information assembled by the World Conservation Monitoring Centre shows that most vertebrate extinctions have been on islands and a high proportion of endangered vertebrates occur on islands. A growing tourism industry could, without careful planning, contribute further to the continuing and growing loss of wildlife on islands.

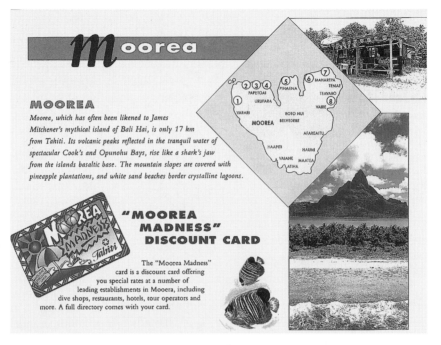

Fig. 3.1. Advertising holidays on islands. (Information reproduced with kind permission of Passport Holidays.)

We commence this chapter by describing what an island is and then give a brief introduction to the historically important island biogeographical studies. Then we mention some intriguing aspects of island biology and finally introduce the topic of island conservation and restoration.

3.2 Islands and island biogeography

It seems curious to ask 'What is an island?' The answer is straightforward but there are different kinds of island. An island is an area of land permanently surrounded by water. Islands occur in rivers, within lakes, in estuaries and some are oceanic. On the basis of geological history, at least three types of oceanic island have been recognised (resulting from movements of the Earth's tectonic plates). There are oceanic ridge islands, so called 'hot spot' islands and those of island arcs. The first two result from volcanic activity but form as the volcano emerges from the ocean floor. Islands of island arcs are also volcanic but are formed where geological plates collide; the descending plate gives rise to series of volcanic activity and the visible results are islands distributed along an arc.

But the question 'What is an island?' is important because island biogeography can include studies of more than just pieces of land surrounded by water. At the very least, in biogeography, it is important to state how the term 'island' is used. For some people, island biogeography includes islands as defined above and also 'mainland islands' or 'island habitats', for example the upper levels on mountains or remnants of woodland surrounded by agricultural land.

The theories of island biogeography (Section 3.6) have often been discussed along with theories about the effects of fragmentation of habitats and biological communities, hence sometimes mixing the ecology of islands and the ecology of isolated habitats (sometimes called habitat fragments or 'island habitats'). Islands are small areas of land surrounded by water whereas isolated habitats include remnants of what were once larger expanses of biological communities. Other examples include lakes and ponds where populations of a species are isolated from each other. There are also examples of isolated alpine plant and animal communities.

Mixing the biogeography of islands with the spatial ecology of mainland habitats has commonly and regrettably occurred with respect to ideas about the design of nature reserves and other kinds of designated conservation area. For reasons which we hope will become clear, our appraisal of the application of island biogeography to nature reserve design has been given over to Chapter 7. In this chapter we use the term island to refer only to a piece of land surrounded by water.

3.3 Historically important studies

Islands have attracted the interest of explorers, natural historians and biologists for hundreds of years and indeed the study of island life has made significant contributions to the advancement of evolutionary biology, ecology and biogeography. Charles Darwin's study of the Galapagos Islands was pivotal to his theory of evolution and David Lack's later study of Darwin's finches (Lack, 1947) on the Galapagos Islands made a significant contribution to the development of ecology. R. H. MacArthur and C. O. Wilson's work on islands was the precursor to island biogeography. There are many publications which are testaments to this long and rich interest in islands, and their human history, geology, fauna and flora. A few of the important books on island biogeography are listed in Table 3.1.

Table 3.1. *One hundred and twenty-seven years of books, or chapters in books, and monographs (in English or translated into English) which have been relevant to the study of island biogeography*

Note the several references to the Galapagos Islands and to Madagascar. This is not an exhaustive list but serves to show the varied interest in those ancient islands and also to indicate that literature which is more easily available to a wider readership.

The important milestones in the literature on island biogeography are to be found amongst the scientific journals. Those reports of original research and reviews of the subject (of which there are many) provide the detailed and illuminating accounts of the development of island biogeography. Some of those papers are in the references at the end of this chapter.

1869 *The Malay Archipelago. The Land of the Orang-utan and the Bird of Paradise. A Narrative of Travel with Studies of Man and Nature*, by A. R. Wallace. London, Macmillan and Co.

1880. *Island Life or the Phenomena and Causes of Insular Faunas and Floras, Including a Revision and Attempted Solution of the Problem of Geological Climates*, by A. R. Wallace. London, Macmillan and Co.

1881. *Island Life*, by A. R. Wallace. New York, Harper and Brothers.

1924. *Galapagos: World's End*, by W. Beebee. New York, G. P. Putnam's and Sons.

1947. *Darwin's Finches*, by D. Lack. Cambridge, Cambridge University Press.

1957. *Island Patterns*, Chapter 8 'Zoogeography: the geographical distribution of animals', by P. J. Darlington, New York and London, John Wiley.

1962. 'New Zealand biogeography. A paleontologist's approach. *Tuatara*, **10**, 53–108, by C. A. Fleming, Victoria University, New Zealand.

1963. *Man's Place in the Island Ecosystem*, by F. R. Fosberg, Tenth Pacific Science Congress, Honolulu, Bishop Museum.

1965. *Island Life*, by S. Carlquist. New York, Natural History Press.

1967. *The Theory of Island Biogeography*, by R. H. MacArthur and E. O. Wilson. Princeton, NJ, Princeton University Press.

1968. *Galapagos. Island of Birds*, by B. Nelson, Longmans.

1971. *Darwin's Islands. A Natural History of the Galapagos*, by I. Thornton. New York, The Natural History Press.

1971. *Flora of the Galapagos Islands*, ed. I. L. Wiggins & D. M. Porter. Stanford, CA, Stanford University Press.

1972. *Island Patterns*, Chapter 5, 'Geographical ecology. Patterns in the distribution of species, by R. H. MacArthur. Princeton, NJ, Princeton University Press.

1972. *Biogeography and Ecology in Madagascar*, ed. R. Battistini & G. Richard-Vindard. The Hague, Junk.

1974. *Island Biology*, by S. Carlquist. New York, Columbia University Press.

1974. *A field guide to the birds of the Galapagos*, by M. Harris. London, Collins.

1975. *Biogeography and Ecology in New Zealand*, ed. G. Kischel. The Hague, Junk.

1976. *Island Biology, Illustrated by the Land Birds of Jamaica*, by D. Lack. Berkeley, CA, University of California Press.

1979. *Island Ecology*, by M. L. Gorman. London, Chapman & Hall.

1981. *Island Ecosystems. Biological Organization in Selected Hawaiian Communities*, ed. D. Mueller-Dombois, K. W. Bridges & H. L. Carson. Straoudsberg, PA, Hutchinson Ross.

1981. *Island Populations*, by M. Williamson. Oxford, Oxford University Press.

1982. *Biogeography and Ecology of New Guinea*, ed. J. L. Gressitt. The Hague, Junk.

1983. *Island Biogeography in the Sea of Cortex*, by T. J. Case & M. L. Cody. Berkeley, CA, University of California Press.

1983. *Patterns of Evolution in Galapagos Organisms*, R. I. Bowman, M. Berson & A. E. Leviton. San Francisco, CA, American Association for the Advancement of Science.

1984. *Biogeography and Ecology of the Seychelles*, by D. R. Stoddart. The Hague, Junk.

1984. *Key Environments: Madagascar*, by A. Jolly, P. Oberle, & R. Albignac. Oxford, Pergamon Press.

1986. *Ecology and Evolution of Darwin's Finches*, by P. R. Grant. Princeton, NJ, Princeton University Press.

1987. *The Ecology of Sumatra*, by A. J. Whitten, S. J. Damanik, J. Anwar & N. Hisyam. Gadjah Mada University Press.

1987. *The Ecology of Sulawesi*, by A. J. Whitten, M. Mustafa & G. S. Henderson. Gadjah University Press.

1987. *Biogeographical Evolution of the Malay Archipelago*, by T. C. Whitmore. Oxford, Clarendon Press.

1995. *Islands. Biological Diversity and Ecosystem Function*, ed. P. M. Vitousek, L. L. Loope & H. Anderson. Berlin, Springer- Verlag.

1995. *The Beak of the Finch. A Story of Evolution in Our Time*, by J. Weiner. New York, Alfred A. Knopf.

1996. *The Song of the Dodo. Island Biogeography in an Age of Extinctions*, by D. Quammen. London, Pimlico.

1996. *Krakatau. The Destruction and Reassembly of an Island Ecosystem*, by I. Thornton. Cambridge, MA, and London, Harvard University Press.

1996. *The Origin and Evolution of Pacific Island Biotas, New Guinea to Eastern Polynesia. Patterns and processes*, ed. A. Keats & S. E. Miller. The Netherlands, SPB Academic.

Our present-day knowledge of island fauna and flora has been much enhanced by several young men who went on various expeditions. Those men included Charles Darwin, Joseph Hooker and Alfred Wallace (see Chapter 1). Some of the most notable contributions to the study of island geology, biology and biogeography come from Charles Darwin's explorations. He visited and wrote about many islands but there was a visit to one group of islands in particular which later played a significant role in his writings. Charles Darwin visited the geologically ancient Galapagos Islands in September and October of 1835; this was a brief part of that now famous voyage of the ship *HMS Beagle*. The Enchanted Isles or Galapagos Islands (the Spanish had called them Las Islas Encantadas) consist of 123 islands (Snell *et al.*, 1996) lying on the equator, 900 kilometres off the coast of Ecuador (Fig. 3.2). At least that is the case today; as with all other islands there has been a long geological history and the number of islands and distance from the mainland will have changed. It was on the Galapagos Islands that the young and excited Darwin (26 years old at that time) found examples of many species which were endemic to single islands. He also found remarkable variation amongst the tortoises and the finches; variations in the latter were to provide convincing evidence of speciation and adaptive radiation (Lack, 1947). That evolution of the finches, as with evolution in general, does not stand still and has been observed to continue to this day. Jonathan Weiner in his book *The Beak of the Finch* (see Table 3.1) described observations of continuing evolution amongst the finches of the Galapagos.

On these islands there are also examples of very unusual animals and animal behaviour; these include a nocturnal gull, a flightless cormorant, a penguin (at the equator!), and a lizard that feeds on seaweed at the bottom of the sea. Darwin wrote of these islands and their biology in his journals and

Fig. 3.2. The Galapagos Islands and some of their fauna: (a) the geographical location in the east-central Pacific with the main ocean currents and submarine ridges shown; (b) the islands of the archipelago; (c) The flightless cormorant and marine iguanas. (Reproduced with kind permission from Thornton, I., 1971. *Darwin's Islands, A Natural History of the Galapagos*, New York. The Natural History Press, New York. Copyright (©) 1971 by Ian Thornton. Reproduced with permission of the Author and Doubleday, a Division of Bantam Doubleday Dell Publishing Group Inc.)

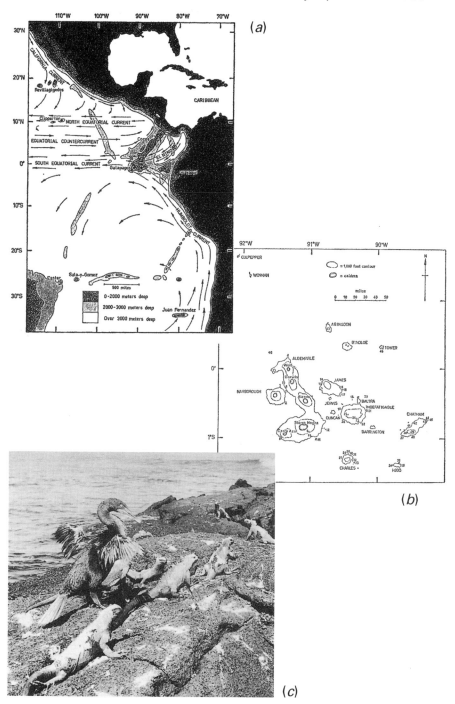

(a)

(b)

(c)

noted the following:

> September 15th, 1835.
> The *Beagle* arrived at the southernmost of the Galapagos Islands. This
> archipelago consists of ten principal islands, of which five much exceed
> the others in size. They are situated under the equatorial line, and
> between five and six hundred miles to the westward of the coast of
> America.

> September 17th.
> The natural history of this archipelago is very remarkable; it seems to be
> a little world within itself; the greater number of the inhabitants, both
> vegetable and animal, being found nowhere else.

> September 29th.
> These lizards were occasionally seen some hundred yards from the shore
> swimming about.
>
> In the thirteen species of ground-finches, a nearly perfect gradation
> may be traced, from a beak extraordinarily thick to one so fine, that it
> may compared to that of a warbler. I very much suspect, that certain
> members of the series are confined to different islands.

Extracts from the Journals of Charles Darwin.

Back in England, the material collected from the Galapagos Islands and the
many observations made by Darwin were to provide much valuable material
for studying not only island biology but also for developing his theories on
natural selection. Many other biologists of that time took part in studying the
island material. For example, Joseph Hooker helped Darwin to study and
analyse the plant specimens and published the results in one of the journals of
the Linnean Society in 1847.

Joseph Hooker was an avid plant collector and at the age of 22 he had been
assistant surgeon and 'botanist' on an expedition to the southern and Antarctic regions, captained by James Clark Ross (during the years 1839–1843). In
1866 he gave lectures about the characteristics of island floras and noted
amongst other things the taxonomic peculiarities of these floras; there were
often fewer species on an oceanic island than on a similar sized area of the
mainland. Since then there has been much quantitative research on the
phenomenon known as 'island impoverishment'. The number of species
(species richness) on different islands was also of interest to Hooker because,
as early as 1847, he wrote about the number of plant species (collected by
Darwin) on the different islands of the Galapagos.

Another one of the early landmarks in the exploration of islands, their geography, biology and peoples was that of Alfred Russel Wallace. During the time when, independently of Charles Darwin, he proposed the theory of natural selection, he was a professional zoological collector spending much time among the islands of Indonesia. In 1876 he published his classic book *The Geographical Distribution of Animals* (Table 1.2) and in 1880 his book *Island Life* (Table 3.1). When Wallace was thinking about designation of zoogeographical regions, he had some difficulty himself in deciding how islands should be classified. Like many others at that time he had come to appreciate the often unusual adaptations of island life and high levels of endemism on islands. For him and others, islands did not fall easily into any of the previously proposed methods of classification of zoogeographical regions. In his book on island life he wrote:

> If we visit the great islands of the globe, we find that they present similar anomalies in their animal productions, for while some exactly resemble the nearest continents others are widely different ... These examples will illustrate the kind of question it is the object of the present work to deal with. Every continent, every country and every island on the globe, offers similar problems of greater or less complexity and interest, and the time has now arrived when their solution can be attempted with some prospect of success. Many years' study of this class of subjects has convinced me that there is no short and easy method of dealing with them ...

Eventually Wallace classified islands with reference to their distribution (and methods of formation) and suggested two types of island (1) oceanic islands, for example islands of volcanic or coral formation (usually found far from continents); (2) continental islands of which there are two marked groups, ancient and recent continental islands. Examples of oceanic islands studied by Wallace were the Azores, Bermuda, the Galapagos Islands, St Helena and the Hawaiian Islands. Examples of recent continental islands discussed by Wallace were Great Britain, Borneo, Java, and Japan. An example of ancient continental islands was the Madagascar group. Curiously, Wallace also considered what he called anomalous, ancient continental islands, for example Sulawesi (previously the Celebes) and New Zealand.

In 1857, Philip Sclater had helped to set the scene for identifying and mapping zoogeographical regions (see Section 2.2). This kind of work fascinated Wallace and, in his early thirties, he carried out meticulous studies of the Malay Archipelago over a period of eight years (1854–1862). A tribute to Wallace's work in that region is what is now called Wallace's line (Fig. 3.3).

Fig. 3.3. A map of Southeast Asia showing the position of the biogeographical line, Wallace's line.

In earlier studies of biogeographical regions there had been some preoccupation with defining the limits. Where one biogeographical region ends or commences has attracted many biogeographers intent on ensuring that these regions are well defined. Traditionally, boundaries between major biogeographical regions have been called biogeographic lines. There are several examples of these lines and sometimes more than one has been suggested for just one region. For example, between Southeast Asia and Australia, several lines including Wallace's line have been proposed (Fig. 3.3) as a result of many studies dating back to the 1840s. These lines have been attempts to define the boundaries between the biota of the Oriental and Australian regions. Such has been the debate that some biogeographers proposed a separate region, 'Wallacea' between the Oriental and Australian regions.

There has been much interest in, and much written about, the relationships between the biota of the Oriental region and the Australian region. That interest has been promoted by many biogeographical expeditions and surveys, notably that of Wallace. But detailed studies of the biogeography and ecology of many of the islands have been few and only in more recent times have there been extensive surveys. For example the biology of Sumatra and its many surrounding islands was poorly understood until the 1980s.

Tony Whitten (who kindly wrote the Foreword to our book) worked in Sumatra in the early 80s and together with several colleagues obtained data which were later to be published as *The Ecology of Sumatra* (Whitten *et al.*, 1984).

Within mainland Sumatra there are barriers for some organisms in the form of rivers and mountains and consequently at least 26 biogeographical units (Box 3.1). The diversity of many groups of organisms in Sumatra is therefore very striking, for example there are 4 species and 21 subspecies of leaf monkey (genus *Presbytis*).

3.4 Island biology

The biology of any island is the product of its history – the geology, the climate and sea level changes and ecological processes. Throughout geological history, single islands, groups of islands and island chains have come and gone. For example, there has been a long history of alternating presence and absence of islands between North and South America. Those islands have on occasions acted as barriers to dispersal and 'stepping stones' facilitating dispersal (stepping stones and other linear distribution features are discussed in Chapter 8). Perhaps not surprisingly the species composition of island chains between biogeographical regions has been influenced by those different regions.

The most important ecological processes contributing to the composition and abundance of island life are arrival, colonisation and extinction. Those organisms which are able to travel successfully over water are more likely to colonise islands. It is possible that the colonisers are likely to have less genetic diversity than the populations from which they have come. In the early days of population genetics (early 1940s), Ernst Mayr discussed this possibility and referred to the founder principle: only a small fraction of the genetic variation of a parent population of species is present in the small number of founder members of a new colony. The founder principle may have implications for the evolution and adaptive radiation of those organisms which manage to colonise islands.

That even remote islands, thousands of kilometres from the nearest sources of colonisation, have any life apart from those forms that fly or swim is indeed remarkable. How has it been possible for plants and animals to travel such distances in such hostile environments? There is a large element of luck involved and previously some scientists have likened the process to a sweepstake, making an analogy with betting on horse races. Many people put money on horses to win but few select the winner. Many organisms disperse from land

and inland waters (both unaided and aided) to the sea but few will make it to an island. From time to time, environmental conditions may be right to help an organism to succeed. For example, Clark & McInerney (1974) found that a species of freshwater fish, a chub called *Mylocheilus caurinus*, was able to move from the rivers of British Columbia to Vancouver Island in Canada because of long corridors of fresh water coming from the Fraser River, particularly during the spring when the snow thaw increases the volume of fresh water. Colonisation occurs rarely but is facilitated by special conditions.

It is because of these processes of dispersion and colonisation that some island biota are less complete compared to mainland biota. For example, some islands may be rich in bird life but have few or no mammalian species because of differences in dispersal ability. In the absence of mammals, the bird fauna may evolve many flightless species (as is the case in New Zealand).

Island biota has many interesting features. For example, the wildlife on islands is often relict, endemic and there are also unusual adaptations (see p. 55). There are two kinds of relict, taxonomic and biogeographical. The former are the sole survivors of what were once more diverse populations in terms of species. Biogeographical relicts are the survivors of a once far more geographically widespread group. For some species, both conditions often apply. For example, on some of the smaller islands of New Zealand, well known for many endemic plants and invertebrates, there still lives a relict of the dinosaur age, the curiously lizard-like reptiles called tuataras (*Sphenodon*). Now found on only 30 islands, the tuataras (Fig. 3.4) are both a taxonomic and a biogeographical relict. They have a long ancestral line and were once more widespread during the Triassic and Jurassic Periods, (see Fig. 4.3).

Box 3.1. Biogeographical units of mainland Sumatra and the biogeography of leaf monkeys. (From Whitten et al., *The Ecology of Sumatra*, Gadjah Mada University Press, 1984. Reproduced with kind permission of Tony Whitten and Gadjah Mada University Press)

Below opposite, from top left: Ptn, Presbytis thomasi nubilis; Pitt, P.t. thomasi; Pmm, P. melalophos margae; Pfpa, P. femoralis paenulata; Pfpe, P.f. percura; Pfn, P.f. natuna; Pfr, P.f. rhionis; Pm?, P. melalophos (subspecies not yet named); *Pfc, P. femoralis canus; Pm?, P. melalophos* (subspecies not yet named); *Pmfu^1, P.m. fuscomurina* (lowland form); *Pmfu^2, P.m. fuscomurina* (highland form); *Pmfl, P.m. fluviatilis; Pmme, P.m. melalophos; Pmm, P.m. nobilis; Ppp, P. potenziani; Pps, P.p. siberu; Pmf, P. melalophos ferruginea; Pmb, P.m. batuana; Pma, P.m. aurata; Pms, P.m. sumatrana.*

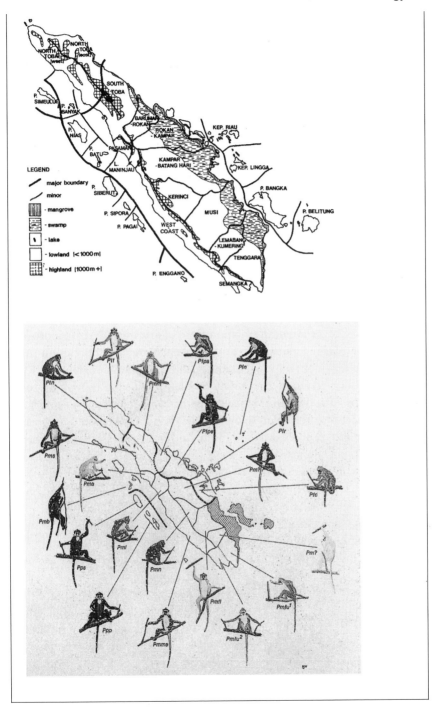

Fig. 3.4. The tuatara (*Sphenodon*) of New Zealand. Adults grow to about 62 centimetres in length. (From Spellerberg, I. F., 1982, *Biology of Reptiles*, Glasgow, Blackie.

Endemic forms (of which there may be different types) are those special to a particular area and are found nowhere else. The levels of endemism found on islands have come about in isolation from competitors and are a product of spectacular adaptive radiation. The number of endemic species on some islands can be very high; for some islands such as the islands of Hawaii, 90 per cent of the flora is endemic. Endemism on islands may also be high for some animal groups including amphibians, reptiles and mammals (Table 3.2). Endemism occurs at different taxonomic levels; subspecies, species, genera, etc. For example, Emberson (1995) in a study of beetles on the Chatham Islands off the east coast of New Zealand's South Island, found that the beetle fauna was closely related to that of New Zealand and also characterised by relatively high levels of endemicity at the species level (25 per cent) and lower at the generic level (less than 2 per cent).

Perhaps not surprisingly there is notable endemism on the Galapagos Islands (Fig. 3.2). For example, the study by Harris (1973) of the status of all birds recorded on the islands found that 57 species were known to have bred and, of those, about half (28) were considered to be endemic.

The species composition and species richness of islands have been analysed for many years and it has long been thought that dispersal ability and distance from the source of colonisation are important factors. Darlington (1957) was an earlier biogeographer who attempted to analyse the effects of distance on the composition and patterns of distribution of island faunas. Some fauna were seen as orderly or immigrant patterns and others were a relict pattern (Fig. 3.5). Robert MacArthur and Edward Wilson (see Box 3.2)

Table 3.2. *Numbers of endemic species in 18 'hot spots', including some islands*

Region	Higher plants	Mammals	Reptiles	Amphibians	Swallowtail butterflies
Cape Region (South Africa)	6000[2]	15	43	23	0
Upland western Amazonia	5000[1]	—	—	c. 70	—
Atlantic coastal Brazil	5000[1]	40	92	168	7
Madagascar	4900[1]	86	234	142	11
Philippines	3700[1]	98	120	41	23
Borneo (north)	3500[1]	42	69	47	4
Eastern Himalaya	3500[1]	—	20	25	—
SW Australia	2830[2]	10	25	22	0
Western Ecuador	2500	9	—	—	2
Colombian Chocó	2500[1]	8	137	111	0
Peninsular Malaysia	2400[1]	4	25	7	0
Californian floristic province	2140[2]	15	15	16	0
Western Ghats (India)	1600[2]	7	91	84	5
Central Chile	1450[2]	—	—	—	—
New Caledonia	1400[1]	2	21	0	2
Eastern Arc Mts (Tanzania)	535[2]	20	—	49	3
SW Sri Lanka	500[2]	4	—	—	2
SW Côte d'Ivoire	200[2]	3	—	2	0
Total	49655	363	892	c. 807	59

Sources for plants are from: (1) Myers, N., 1988, *The Environmentalist, 8*, 187–208; and (2) Myers, N., 1990, *The Environmentalist, 10*, 243–256. From Global Biodiversity, Status of the Earth's Living Resources, compiled by the World Conservation Monitoring Centre, published by Chapman & Hall, 1992. Reproduced with kind permission of the World Conservation Monitoring Centre.

A dash indicates no data yet available. All regions are classed floristically as tropical forest, with the exception of four regions which have Mediterranean-type floras, i.e. Cape Region South Africa, SW Australia, Californian floristic province and Central Chile.

in their theories also considered that distance from source would have an effect on species richness: the further from the source, the fewer would be the number of species (see Section 3.5). Since the 1950s there have been many more analyses of dispersion and island biota. For example, Adersen (1995)

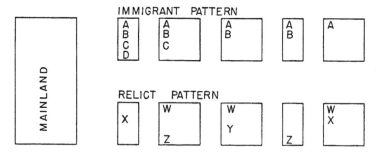

Fig. 3.5. A diagram from Philip Darlington's *Zoogeography: The Geographical Distribution of Animals* (1957, John Wiley and Sons Inc., New York) showing two patterns of dispersal, an immigrant pattern and a relict pattern. (Reprinted by permission of John Wiley & Sons, Inc.)

found that a clear pattern emerged (Fig. 3.6) when he looked at first the shortest distance to the continent and secondly the size of the diaspore (the part of an organism produced that is capable of giving rise to a new individual).

In addition to relict species and endemism, the biology of island biota often has special features. For example flightlessness is a common feature (Fig. 3.2). An ancient group of islands well known for the indigenous flightless birds is New Zealand (an archipelago since at least the Cretaceous Period). In the absence of native mammals (apart from bats and seals), many species of flightless birds evolved. These include many species now extinct such as the 11 species of moa (order Dinornithformes), an emu-like bird that ranged in height from about 0.9 to 3.6 metres. Many species of flightless bird are still to be found in New Zealand and its off-shore islands (for example, kiwis, penguins and wekas) but the predatory effects of introduced mammals and the damage done by grazing mammals has been devastating in terms of the threat to both species and their habitats.

Loss of flight has been found in other taxa, including beetles; for example on the Chatham Islands flightlessness has been found in 90 per cent of endemic beetle species (Emberson, 1995).

3.5 Island biogeography: patterns

One of the most commonly observed features of island biogeography has been the number of species on islands; for certain taxa or groups of biota, small islands had fewer species than larger islands. There was an apparent

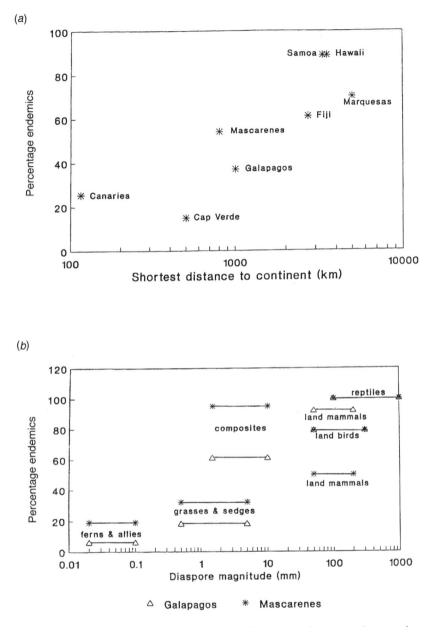

Fig. 3.6. Levels of endemism on islands and (a) distance to closest continent and (b) diaspore magnitude. (From Adsersen, H. 1995, *Research on Islands: Classic, Recent, and Prospective Approaches*, pp. 7–22. In Vitousek, P. M., Loope, L. L. & Adsersen, H. (eds.), Springer-Verlag, Berling. Material used with kind permission of the Author and Springer-Verlag, New York.)

Box 3.2.

(i) Robert H. MacArthur (a) and Edward O. Wilson (b). Authors of The milestone book *The Theory of Island Biogeography*, 1967, Princeton University Press. (Photographs kindly provided by Princeton University and Harvard University and reproduced with permission)

(ia)

(ii) Species–area curves for amphibians and reptiles of islands in the West Indies: (*a*) MacArthur & Wilson's species–area curve (Redrawn after MacArthur & Wilson, 1967); (*b*) for amphibians and reptiles on 63 different islands in the West Indies. The circles denote the seven islands in the graph from MacArthur & Wilson. (Reproduced with kind permission of the British Ecological Society from Spellerberg, I. F., Goldsmith, F. B. & Morris, M. G., 1991, *The Scientific Management of Temperate Communities for Conservation*, Blackwell Science)

(ib)

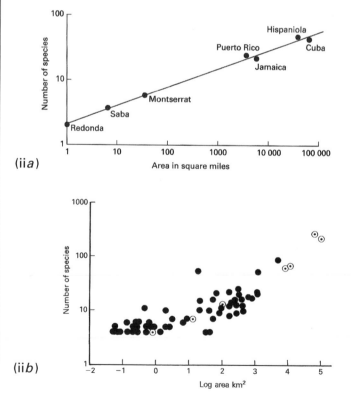

(ii*a*)

(ii*b*)

(iii) The equilibrium models from MacArthur & Wilson's 1963 paper in *Evolution*, 17, 373–387. (*a*) The equilibrium number of species for this single island is indicated by S. (*b*) The models for several islands of varying distance from the source of colonisation and of varying size. (Reproduced with kind permission of the *Journal of Evolution*)

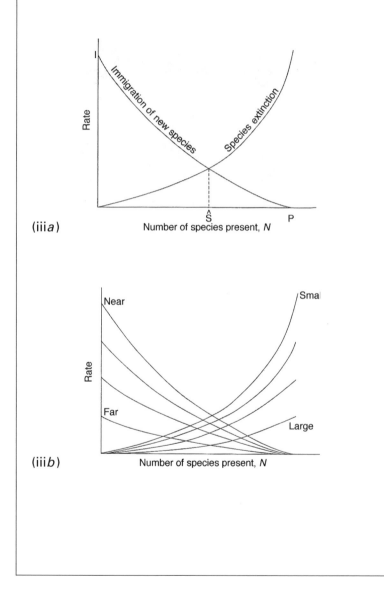

(iii*a*)

(iii*b*)

relationship between the number of species and the area of the island. For example, when Darlington (1957) tabulated published data on the genera and species of amphibians and reptiles found on different islands of the Greater Antilles (Cuba, Hispaniola, Jamaica, Puerto Rica and Trinidad) and the Lesser Antilles (Montserrat, Saba, Redonda, Sombrero), he found that, in general, larger islands had more species of amphibians and reptiles than did smaller islands.

Questions about species richness on islands are usually asked in relation to the number of species in certain taxonomic groups rather than how many species there are in total. One figure for species richness for many groups (plant, animal and other groups combined) is not very informative whereas numbers of specific taxa (grasses, reptiles, butterflies) or biological groups (saltmarsh plants, herbivorous insects, predatory spiders) start to tell us something about the structure of the island community and how it functions.

3.6 Island biogeography: the theories

Following the early studies based on the material from expeditions, some biogeographical studies led to theories not only about what determines the species composition but what maintains the species composition of island biota. However, not until the late 1950s and early 60s were there substantial attempts at quantitative studies of island biogeography. In the early 1960s, two scientists in particular made very important contributions to the development of island biogeographical theory. One was Robert MacArthur (1930–1972) and the other was Edward Wilson (Box 3.2). As well as contributing so much to island biogeography, MacArthur is remembered for his work as a mathematician, an ornithologist, and in community diversity and above all for his perceptive ecological research. It has been said that he once remarked that a good test for an ecologist was to walk through a field and see how many questions were asked. Edward Wilson, based at Harvard University, is very well known for his work on sociobiology, conservation biology and more recently biological diversity (with books such as *The Diversity of Life* published in 1992). MacArthur and Wilson looked at patterns of species abundance on islands and also the number of rare and common species which were found in biological communities (on islands and on mainlands). MacArthur and Wilson had seen a paper by Preston (published in 1962) in which there was a detailed analysis of the relationship between sampling area and the number of plant and animal species. That is, as the area of sampling, A, increases in area, the number of plant and animal species, s, increases in an approximately logarithmic manner:

$$s = cA^k$$
$$\log s = \log c + k \log A$$

where c is a constant (the number of species present when A has a value of 1) and k is a constant (the slope of the regression line).

Previously, Darlington (1957) had suggested a general rule that a ten-fold increase in area allowed a doubling of the number of species (a linear relationship between the log of the number of species and the log of the area). Six years later, MacArthur & Wilson (1963) published their classic paper in the *Journal of Evolution* entitled 'An equilibrium theory of insular geography' and drew attention to the observation that the 'species–area relationship' was true for islands as it was for biota on mainlands. Using data on the numbers of land and freshwater bird species (and other taxa such as ants) on various islands they took their analysis beyond the simple observation of the 'species–curve'. What was important was that they attempted to explain the variance in the data – variance caused not by observer bias, expertise or time of survey but by biological variables.

These and other ideas were later published in their book *The Theory of Island Biogeography* (1967), an unfortunate use of the definitive article because it implied that there is just one theory. As they had done so in their original paper, MacArthur and Wilson looked at variance in the data and indeed it is the variance which is particularly interesting and not the simple idea of drawing straight lines on a graph. One set of data in their book has been responsible for reinforcing the fascination of a simple species–area relationship and that was their use of previously tabulated data (in Darlington's book on zoogeography) on the numbers of amphibian and reptile species on islands (Box 3.2). That figure shows that, for those seven islands, more species are found on larger islands than on small islands.

There are, of course, more than seven islands in the West Indies and since the early 1960s there have been many more studies of the fauna (including amphibians and reptiles) of many of the islands. Today, therefore, there is an opportunity to see what pattern emerges when we examine the numbers of species of amphibians and reptiles of a larger number of islands (Box 3.2).

There is not a simple relationship between number of species and size of area and there is variation; that is, some moderately sized islands have far more species than might be predicted while other islands have fewer species than might be suggested by their size. The simple relationship with size of area seems to have dominated thinking about island biogeography. Surely more interesting questions are why does the slope (value of the constant k) seem to occur within certain limits (0.24 to 0.37)? What ecological factors keep the relationship within those limits? Why is there variation: why do some islands have relatively fewer or relatively more species compared to islands of a similar area? We discuss some of the answers in Section 3.7.

The island species–area relationship described by MacArthur and Wilson was nothing new at that time. It was other aspects of their work which were to become landmarks and hotly debated until this day. The many aspects of island biogeography considered by MacArthur & Wilson included what determined the number of species on an island and what factors maintained that number of species. Previous theories of island biogeography had not provided any quantitative analysis of island species richness and this is what MacArthur and Wilson were able to do. They suggested an innovative theory, a dynamic equilibrium model based on the idea that the number of taxa (species lumped together, such as birds or ants) was determined largely by the rates of immigration and rates of extinction. That is, with no change in environmental conditions, the number of species remains fairly constant although species composition may change as extinction and immigration take place. Interestingly, Preston in 1962 had also independently suggested that there might be a balance between immigration and extinction on islands.

In Box 3.2 we see that the two graphs (equilibrium models) show a hypothetical rate of immigration and extinction for taxa on an island. We start with a new island with no life. The rate of immigration is likely to be very high but that rate of immigration will decrease as the numbers of species become established. Similarly, we start with a very low rate of extinction but that rate increases as the number of species on the island grows. Where the two graphs cross, we could envisage (for a particular point in time) a balance between the rate of immigration and the rate of extinction. That point on the x-axis is what MacArthur and Wilson called the equilibrium number of species.

By using this approach, it was possible to explore the theoretical effects of island area and also the extent of isolation. For example in Box 3.2 we see that, theoretically, immigration rates for large and small islands are the same but extinction rates are larger for small islands (based on the idea that fewer species would be represented by fewer individuals and be more prone to extinction). Consequently the equilibrium number of species for small islands is less than that for large islands. When comparing near and far islands, extinction rates would be the same but immigration rates would be greater for islands closer to the source of immigration and therefore the equilibrium number of species would be higher for the less isolated islands.

Obviously it is not going to be as simple as that. Nevertheless, for the first time here was a model that provided opportunities for quantitative analysis. MacArthur and Wilson in their now classic book on island biogeography of 1967 took the central part of the theory and developed the mathematics much further. They also considered differences between taxa and the role of chains of islands or 'stepping stones' in colonisation, resulting in fringing archipelagos having a higher species richness than oceanic archipelagos.

The theories of island biogeography did not end with MacArthur and Wilson and there have been many more developments. Some of those deal with the effects of immigration on extinction ('rescue effect') and others deal with the 'supersaturation' of recently formed continental islands whose biota 'relaxes' or approaches equilibrium. In the 1970s, the Equilibrium Theory of MacArthur and Wilson prompted other ideas such as a theory of faunal collapse. This theory is derived from the Equilibrium Theory and it predicts certain levels of extinction, or losses, of fauna and flora on islands (or in fragmented biological communities) with increasing levels of isolation. Examples of faunal collapse have been given by Soule & Wilcox (1980).

3.7 Field studies of island biogeography

Although there are many studies showing that, for certain taxonomic groups, large islands tend to have more species than small islands, this does not necessarily mean that area per se determines the number of species. The apparent effects of area could be the result of many variables. For example, larger islands may, in general, have greater physical diversity or greater variety of habitats (habitat heterogeneity) and it is likely that physical diversity and habitat heterogeneity, rather than area per se, contribute somehow to island species richness. MacArthur and Wilson were interested in habitat heterogeneity but since that time relatively little research has been directed specifically at the implications of habitat heterogeneity. Why has there not been more research into this? Perhaps the reason is because habitat heterogeneity is not so easy to quantify and only in more recent times have there been efforts to do so for mainland habitats.

The fact that there could be a great deal of variance in the 'species–area' data did not escape MacArthur and Wilson; some studies show that this is particularly so amongst small islands (Whitehead & Jones, 1969). In other words there are certainly many variables which contribute to the numbers of species on an island.

Much work on island biogeography has been on birds and also flowering plants. One example for bird studies is that of Ian Abbott on 19 remote islands in the waters of the sub-Antarctic (Abbott, 1974). The main aim of the work was to assess the importance of island area as a predictor of the number of bird species and a secondary aim was to test for relationships among the number of plant species, insect species and land bird species inhabiting these islands. A total of 11 variables were considered: island area (A), island elevation (E), mean latitude (L), mean temperature of coldest month (T), distance from nearest mainland (D_1), distance from the nearest land (D_2), distance from the nearest land westward (D_3), number of native plant species (P), number of free-living insect species (I), number of breeding native species of passerines (B_1), and number of breeding species of land birds (B_2). In the analysis, Abbott considered both log–log and linear relationships.

He found that area was not of great importance: less than 5 per cent in explaining variation in the number of land bird species, passerine species, and insect species; and 33 per cent for plant species. He also found that a linear relationship explained variation better than log–log relationships for both the insects and the birds. A non-linear model explained 71 per cent of the variation in plant species. The plants in turn accounted for 73 per cent of the variation in insect species and 71 per cent of the total bird species. It seems therefore that, in this case at least, a log–log model linking S with A ($S = cAk$) is not a good descriptor.

The species area relationship is not confined to biota of islands (see examples in Section 3.6). However, the relationship has been a common feature of biogeographical studies, particularly those of islands. However, there still remain some intriguing aspects about the relationship. For example, Williams (1996) noted recently that some studies have erred by excluding islands for which $S = 0$ (see equation on p. 69). He looked at 13 published papers reporting data on island species number and found that islands with $S = 0$ were frequently excluded from the analysis. Excluding islands where $S = 0$ has the effect of biasing (upwards!) the estimate of S for islands of that size.

Many islands have been colonised by introduced species and consequently the ecology of interactions between native and introduced species on islands and the effects of introduced, invasive species on the native biota have been at the centre of much research. Most of that research has been directed towards attempts to remove the introduced species and restore the native species. Little or possibly even no research seems to have been undertaken on comparisons between the equilibrium numbers and turnover of introduced versus native species. Consequently very little is known about the differences between the two types of island biota with respect to their ecological processes.

There have been very few field studies in which the Equilibrium Theory has been investigated. This is mainly because of the great difficulty of accessing islands that are not being disturbed either by human beings or by natural events such as volcanic activity. Some researchers have taken an alternative experimental approach. Such experimental investigations have included studies of the fruit fly *Drosophila* on so-called laboratory islands, the removal of biota from a series of very small islands, and the colonisation of artificial marine sponges (see references cited in Spellerberg, 1991). None of these experimental investigations has provided convincing evidence for the Equilibrium Theory.

Looking for evidence to prove any island biogeographical theory is perhaps not as exciting and engaging as actually studying real island ecology and biogeography. Such studies require many years work and commitment from a range of people with expertise in many areas. There have been a few studies which have intensively investigated the patterns and processes on real islands over time. One notable study has been the work on the Krakatau archipelago between Sumatra and Java (Fig. 3.3). In 1883 on Krakatau there was a massive volcanic eruption which exploded with the force of thousands of hydrogen bombs. Since that time, biotic colonisation of the archipelago has attracted much attention from many biologists, the most recent being Ian Thornton and his team of colleagues and students, mainly from La Trobe University in Melbourne (Thornton, 1996). As well as providing much data about the community dynamics of several taxa, Thornton and his colleagues have established the most important baseline for long-term biogeographical studies on islands.

3.8 Conservation and restoration of island biota

The conservation and restoration of island biota has attracted much attention and has been the subject of some very intensive efforts. In a few of the islands around New Zealand, for example, introduced species have been successfully removed and there have been subsequent improvements in the status of some of the indigenous species. Often the decline of an island species is the result of loss of habitat and/or disturbance brought about by expanding agriculture and growth in tourism. Establishment of protected areas on islands and even the designation of whole islands as nature reserves have therefore played important roles in island conservation and restoration. However, any of these conservation and restoration projects can be expensive to implement and to maintain. It is therefore important that such measures can be justified on the basis of ecological and biogeographical research.

Conservation and restoration programmes can easily conflict with human beings and human activities on islands. There may be problems with re-sources and there may be conflicts of interests in new developments, particu-larly those that are tourism-related. Consequently many island conservation programmes have been rejected and even been subject to local hostility. Conservation and restoration cannot be achieved by biogeography and re-search alone; there has to be an integrated and shared approach involving as many of the interested parties as possible.

Despite existing efforts there is a case for international collaboration to help in the conservation of island biota. An international convention for conservation of island biota and biological communities is urgently needed, particularly with regard to the role of islands in preserving biological diversity and in terms of the need for their ecological restoration.

References

Abbott, I. (1974). Numbers of plant, insect and land bird species on 19 remote islands in the southern hemisphere. *Biological Journal of the Linnean Society*, **6**, 143–152.

Adsersen, H. (1995). Research on islands: classic, recent and prospective approaches. In Vitousek, P. M., Loope, L. L. & Adsersen, H., *Islands, Biological Diversity and Ecosystem Function*, pp. 7–33. Berlin, Springer.

Clark, D. W. & McInerney, J. E. (1974). Emigration of the peamouth chub *Mylocheilus caurinus*, across a dilute seawater bridge: an experimental zoogeo-graphic study. *Canadian Journal of Zoology*, **52**, 457–469.

Darlington, P. J. (1957). *Zoogeography. The Geographical Distribution of Animals.* New York and London, John Wiley & Sons, Inc.

Emberson, R. M. (1995). The Chatham Islands beetle fauna and the age of separ-ation of the Chatham Islands from New Zealand. *New Zealand Entomologist*, **18**, 1–7.

Harris, M. P. (1973). *The Galapagos Avifauna. Condor*, **75**, 265–278.

Hooker, J. D. (1947). On the vegetation of the Galapagos Archipelago, as compared with that of some other tropical islands and of the Continent of America. *Transactions of the Linnean Society, London*, **20**, 235–262.

Lack, D. (1947). *Darwin's Finches*. Cambridge, Cambridge University Press.

MacArthur, R. H. & Wilson, E. O. (1963). An equilibrium theory of insular zoogeography. *Evolution*, **17**, 373–387.

MacArthur, R. H. & Wilson, E. O. (1967). *The Theory of Island Biogeography.* Princeton, NJ, Princeton University Press.

Snell, H. M., Stone, P. A. & Snell, H. L. (1996). A summary of geographical characteristics of the Galapagos Islands. *Journal of Biogeography*, **23**, 619–624.

Soule, M. F. & Wilcox, F. (1980). *Conservation Biology: An Evolutionary-Ecological Perspective.* Massachusetts, Sinauer.

Spellerberg, I. F. (1991). Biogeographical basis of conservation. In Spellerberg, I. F., Goldsmith, F. B. & Morris, M. G., *The Scientific Management of Temperate Communities for Conservation*, pp. 293–322, Oxford, Blackwell Science.

Thornton, I. (1996). *Krakatau. The Destruction and Reassembly of an Island Ecosystem.* Cambridge, MA, and London, Harvard University Press.

Whitehead, D. R. & Jones, C. E. (1969). Small islands and the equilibrium theory of insular biogeography. *Evolution*, **23**, 171–179.

Whitten, A. J., Damanik, S. J., Anwar, J. & Hisyam, N. (1984). *The Ecology of Sumatra.* Indonesia, Gadjah Mada University Press.

Williams, M. R. (1996). Species–area curves: the need to include zeroes. *Global Ecology and Biogeography Letters*, **5**, 91–93.

4

Geological, evolutionary and human impacts on biogeography

4.1 Introduction

From the time when the Earth was first formed 4600 million years ago, it has gone through some huge and dramatic changes. Once upon a time the Earth was smaller and there was only one land mass and one ocean. As the earth expanded, like a slowly filling balloon, the single land mass fragmented in the same way as a layer of dry mud would fragment on the surface of an expanding balloon. Those fragments still move slowly and the oceans continue to grow as the earth steadily, but very slowly, expands.

The suggestion that the Earth has expanded is fanciful and is no more than a product of our imagination. We have used this brief introduction to emphasise the point that some scientific discoveries seem at first to be nothing but the product of someone's imagination. From time to time there are discoveries in science which seem totally implausible and which are consequently rejected by many. For example, when it was first suggested that continents had moved or drifted across the surface of the Earth, this was greeted as fantasy. It seemed highly unlikely that continents could move and so earlier this century the theory of continental drift received very little support. Today, it is well recognised that continental drift by a process called plate tectonics has had major implications for the distribution of biota over millions of years.

The patterns of distribution of groups of organisms have been determined by evolution, physiological and behavioural adaptations, dispersal mechanisms and levels of dispersal abilities, competition between species, ecological succession, climate change, sea level changes, moving continents and the direct and indirect impacts of human beings. This chapter is divided into two main sections. In the first we provide an introduction to evidence for changes in distribution patterns over millions of years, an introduction to the role of palaeoecology in helping to determine past distribution patterns, and an introduction to the effects of moving continents and sea level changes. The second section is devoted to an introduction to the impacts of human beings on biogeography and the impact of biogeography on human culture.

4.2 Clues to past events

What clues do we have today which tell us about past processes and events? The biogeography of some living groups of plants and animals is intriguing, either because of their very restricted and localised distribution or because of this they are geographically fragmented. This spread, or lack of it, holds clues to what has happened in the past and has helped to identify the major geological factors involved and their effects on the geographical distribution of groups of organisms throughout the world.

If one compares the present distribution of some living groups of organisms with that of related but extinct groups, it becomes clear that a relatively few species living today were once part of a more taxonomically diverse and geographically widespread group. Some present species have survived for millions of years with little change in their appearance and indeed their biology. For example there are some relict species (see Section 3.4) that could well be labelled 'living fossils'; that is, species that have survived for long periods of geological time with little or no change in their biology. Examples include that curious fish the coelacanth (*Latimeria chalumnae*) and also a reptile, the tuatara (Fig. 3.4). Trees that are considered to be living fossils include the *Gingko* and the *Metasequoia* (common specimen trees in parks and botanic gardens).

The story of the discovery of a living coelacanth (known as 'old four legs'), told by J. L. B. Smith (1956) in a book entitled *Old Fourlegs, The Story of the Coelacanth*, is as intriguing and fascinating as the fish itself. In 1938 a trawler off the coast of South Africa caught a very unusual fish (later to be identified as a coelacanth) about 1.5 metres in length, which was subsequently passed on to Miss Marjorie Courtenay-Latimer (curator of a local museum) before being brought to the attention of Professor Smith. At that time it was thought that the coelacanths had been extinct for at least 80 million years, but a chance discovery and subsequent events in 1938 brought this strange living fossil to the attention of science for the first time.

Although *Latimeria chalumnae* (Fig. 4.1) is not known in the fossil record, it does belong to a diverse group of ancient fish for which there are many fossil genera and species. Other fossil coelacanths are known from the Upper Devonian Period and the greatest diversity of this group occurred in the Lower Triassic Period (see Table 4.1) before becoming extinct in the Cretaceous. Many more specimens of *Latimeria* have since been found and we now know that this fish lives in the deep waters off western Madagascar and that it is indeed the one survivor of what was once a more diverse and widespread group of fish. During the Palaeozoic Era, some members of this group inhabited fresh waters and not surprisingly there has been a suggestion that they gave rise to the amphibians. Recent studies in molecular biology have suggested that lungfish and not members of the coelacanth group are likely to be the closest relatives of land vertebrates.

The coelacanth is one small key to our understanding of past geological and evolutionary events. It gives us some clues regarding the appearance and biology of fish from ancient geological times. The sole surviving species is one of the keys to our understanding of the great evolutionary, geological and climatic changes that have taken place over millions of years.

The maidenhair tree, *Ginkgo biloba* (an endemic of eastern China), is the only living representative of a much more diverse order, Ginkgoales, which first appeared in the Permian. Knowledge of the *Ginkgo* was brought to Europe in the early 18th century after the plant was collected and described from specimens in Japan (the correct spelling was ginkyo, meaning silver apricot, with reference to the fruit). These trees are unmistakable: they have fan-shaped leaves (Fig. 4.1) with radiating venation (thus maidenhair fern) and are often notched in the centre (thus *Ginkgo biloba*). The Ginkgoales, together with other gymnosperms such as cycads and conifers, and also ferns flourished in the Jurassic Period. The fossil material shows us that the *Ginkgo* of today has changed very little over many millions of years; it is indeed a 'living fossil' which has managed to survive in a climate similar to that which existed in the geological past.

The extinction of much of the flora of that time (later replaced by angiosperms) was accompanied by changes in climate. These changes accompanied by alterations in sea level and millions of years of geological change have not surprisingly had major impacts on the geographical distribution of biota, and thus biological evolution, resulting in some intriguing aspects of biogeography.

Another tree, native to China and once thought to be represented only by fossils, is *Metasequoia glyptostroboides*. This is the only living species of that genus and it was located as recently as 1944. Similar exciting discoveries

Fig. 4.1. Clues to biogeographical past from living fossils. *Above*: the coelacanth (*Latimeria chalumnae*). They reach up to about 1.8 metres in length. (From Parker, T. J. & Haswell, A., 1962, *A Textbook of Zoology*, London, Macmillan & Co., Ltd and redrawn from Millot's 1955 report in the journal *Nature*, **175**, 362. *Below*: The life form and the leaf (about half natural size) of the *Ginkgo biloba*, sometimes called the maidenhair tree.

continue to be made. For example, in Australia there was the remarkable discovery in 1994 of a new species of pine, the Wollemi pine, in the Blue Mountains of New South Wales. This living fossil has many features in common with Cretaceous and Early Tertiary fossil groups (Enright & Hill, 1995). Although new discoveries of living fossils are still made, the number of recently discovered living plant species is only a tiny fraction of the number of plant species which human beings are causing to become extinct.

Many groups of living organisms have geographically fragmented or disjunct distribution, some with close taxonomic links but yet found in different continents. For example the southern beech trees of the genus *Nothofagus* are found in climatically temperate regions of South America, New Zealand, Papua New Guinea and Australia.

Amongst the animal groups with an intriguing fragmented geographical distribution is a group of soft-bodied, caterpillar-like terrestrial animals restricted to habitats such as rotting logs and leaf litter in or near temperate forests (Box 4.1). This group is the phylum Onychophora, commonly known as *Peripatus* or 'velvet worms'. They are neither worm nor insect but in a phylum of their own. With a distribution that includes the temperate regions of Chile, southern Africa, New Zealand and the southeastern tip of Australia, these animals come from an era dating back more than 500 million years. How has the present distribution, with examples separated by vast oceans, come about? It is unlikely that *Peripatus* could have evolved in so many places because there are so many similarities between the living representatives. If there was only one centre of evolution then how did it disperse? The most likely explanation is that, at some stage in geological history, Australia, New Zealand, South Africa and South America were part of a larger land mass. We know now that there was indeed a large southern land mass, the supercontinent Gondwana, which included what is now Antarctica, South America, Australia, New Zealand and Africa.

Many biogeographers have studied freshwater fish to try to understand the nature and extent of historical events. There are some challenging aspects here, not least because of the difficulties of the systematics of some groups. One ecological classification proposed in the 20th century was based on tolerances of freshwater fish to sea water. Three groups are recognised: primary freshwater fish, intolerant of salinity; secondary freshwater fish, slightly tolerant sea water; a peripheral group, whose physiology enables them to live in sea or fresh water. The primary freshwater fish have been a particularly important focus of attention because of their presumed reliance on fresh water.

In the primary freshwater fish there are many endemic groups, most found in only one zoogeographical region. Other groups have widespread distributions. For example the catfish (suborder Siluroidei) are found on all continents and are particularly diverse in Asia and South America.

The lungfish are primary freshwater fish and belong to an ancient group that probably gave rise to the tetrapods. The Australian lungfish (*Neoceratodus*) is the sole surviving member of a family (Ceratodontidae) that was widespread in the Mesozoic (Fig. 4.2). It is noteworthy that the fossil record reveals much about the biogeography of organisms. For example, *Neoceratodus* is very restricted but fossil evidence suggests a wide-ranging distribution in geological history. Changes in climate, availability of fresh water, moving continents and competition from other similar and evolving species have helped to restrict the distribution of this freshwater fish.

4.3 Palaeoecology

Palaeoecology is the name given to the study of the ecology of fossil communities (combining ecology and palaeontology). In 1944 Stanley Cain described this area of study as 'the study of past biota on a basis of ecological concepts and methods insofar as they can be applied'. The fossil record, although very rich in fossil material is but a brief and fragmented glimpse of what life forms were like in the geological past and where they lived. Some fossils can help us piece together aspects of the ecology of those ancient communities. Palaeoecology has also had important commercial applications in the search for deposits of fossil fuels such as oil.

The location and abundance of certain fossils such as large quantities of shell deposits can shed light on the climate and sea levels of the time when the animals were alive. In New Zealand, for example, there are rich deposits of shells and other materials which provide us with evidence of land forms, climates and sea levels. Some of this material has been extensively researched by Sir Charles Fleming (1916–1987). It was he who did more for the advancement of biogeography in New Zealand than anyone else (see, for example, his article 'New Zealand biogeography. A paleontologist's approach', published in the journal *Tuatara* in 1962). Sediments with deposits of shell-bearing molluscs are common (Fig. 4.3) in New Zealand and incidence and locality of these have played a significant role in unravelling New Zealand's biogeography.

There are other sources which give us clues about past events. Those clues come from deposits of pollen from plants that were living thousands or even

Box 4.1. *Top*: The map shows the world distribution of the Onychophora (the solid black shading indicates the Peripatidae and grey indicates the Peripatopsidae. (Map reproduced with kind permission of Amanda Reid and the *Journal Invertebrate Taxonomy*, 1996, 10, 664)

Bottom: The Onychophora ('velvet worms' or *Peripatus*) is an ancient group (it has remained largely unchanged in appearance since its ancestors survived about 500 million years ago). Divergence amongst the group took place before the break-up of Gondwana. They are soft-bodied, terrestrial animals and avoid desiccation by inhabiting moist habitats. The world distribution and history of the group (together with their biology) is consistent with the widely accepted theories of continental drift and climate change. The photographs are of Australian species (those most commonly found in Australia are 2–4 cm in length). (Photographs by Jenny Norman, Macquarie University)

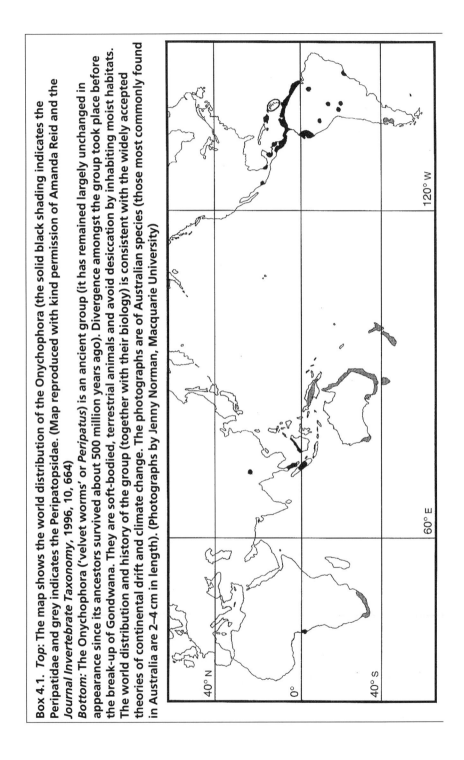

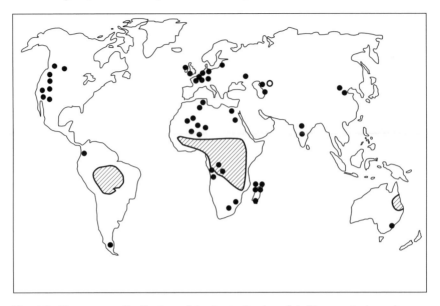

Fig. 4.2. The present distribution of the Australian lungfish (*Neoceratodus* sp.) (hatched) and distribution of fossil forms (family Ceratodontidae). (Redrawn from Sterba, G., 1966, *Freshwater Fishes of the World*, London, Studio Vista.)

millions of years ago. Analysis of pollen deposits and other material can help to reconstruct the features of past ecological communities, including the types of woodland (and other plant communities). It is also possible to determine previous levels of abundance of certain tree species. A combination of pollen analysis and carbon (and other dating) methods of sediments can be used to determine the nature of the climate and effects of past climate change on the geographical distribution of plant communities and species.

But it is not only past climate change that can be reconstructed. The effects of human impact and climate change on past biological communities can be determined from pollen studies. For example Barber *et al.* (1993), studying raised bogs in the border country of England and Scotland, have been able to construct a history of late Holocene environmental changes, both natural and cultural. The cultural record shows only small impacts during the Bronze and Iron Ages but large-scale deforestation during the time of the Roman invasions in southern England about AD 43. The degree of clearance is related to the distance from structures built by the Romans. By using data from pollen analysis we have been able to piece together information about changes in climate and land use, and thus the human and climatic impacts on the biological communities of that time.

CENOZOIC (TERTIARY)	RECENT 20,000 years	Lower river terraces and lower raised beaches	All of the species shown are now extinct, except *Notornis*
	PLEIOSTOCENE 2,000,000 years		1 Moa (*Dinornis*) 5 Goose (*Cnemiornis*) 2 Moa (*Pachyornis*) 6 *Notornis* 3 Eagle (*Harpagornis*) 7 Seal Jaw 4 N.Z. Swan
	PLIOCENE 13,000,000 years		1 Moa (*Dinornis*) 5 Foraminifer (*Bolivinita*) 2 Fan shell (*Pecten*) 6 Sand dollar 3 Oyster (*O. ingens*) 7 Leaf (*Knightia*) 4 Sea snail (*Struthiolaria*)
	MIOCENE 25,000,000 years		1 Bivalve (*Cucullaea*) 5 Foraminifer (*Orbulina*) 2 Sea snail (*Struthiolaria*) 6 Ostracod 3 Lamp shell (*Pachymagas*) 7 Shark's tooth 4 *Dentalium* 8 Coconut (*Cocos*) (*Carcharodon*)
	OLIGOCENE 36,000,000 years		1 Giant Penguin 5 Fan shell (*Janupecten*) 2 Whale tooth (*Kekenodon*) 6 Sea snail 3 Crab 7 Sea egg (*Bathytoma*) 4 Foraminifer (*Rotaliatina*) (*Hemipatagus*)
	EOCENE – PALEOCENE 63,000,000 years		1 *Monalaria* 5 Foraminifer (*Hantkenina*) 2 *Dicroloma* } Sea snails 6 Solitary coral 3 *Speightia* 4 Nautiloid (*Aturia*)
MESOZOIC	CRETACEOUS 135,000,000 years		1 Reptile (*Mauisaurus*) 5 *Inoceramus pacificus* 2 Belemnite (*Dimitobelus*) 5a Prismatic shell 3 Sea snail (*Conchothyra*) 6 Trigonia } Bivalves of 5 4 Ammonite (*Tainuia*) (*Iotrigonia*)
	JURASSIC 181,000,000 years		1 Ammonite (*Phylloceras*) 5 Brachiopod (*Kutchithyris*) 2 Belemnite (*Belemnopsis*) 6 *Cladophlebis* } Leaves of Extinct Plants 3 *Inoceramus* } 7 *Taeniopteris* 4 *Buchia* } Bivalves
	TRIASSIC 230,000,000 years		1 Reptile (*Mixosaurus*) 5 Brachiopod (*Spiriferina*) 2 *Monotis* 6 Leaf (*Linguifolium*) 3 *Halobia* } Bivalves 4 *Manticula*
PALEOZOIC	PERMIAN 280,000,000 years		1 *Atomodesma* 4 Productid 1a Prismatic shell of 1 5 *Neospirifer* 2 Sea Lily (Crinoid) 6 Solitary Coral 3 Pleurotomariid
	CARBONIFEROUS 345,000,000 years	Fossils not known in New Zealand	(Haast Schists of South Island probably partly Carboniferous).
	DEVONIAN 405,000,000 years		1 Crustacean (Trilobite) 4 Coral (*Cyathophyllum*) 2 *Hipparionyx* 5 Crustacean 3 Spiriferid } Brachiopods
	SILURIAN 425,000,000 years	Fossils not known in New Zealand	Silurian rocks probably present
	ORDOVICIAN 500,000,000 years		1 2 } Trilobites 3 Crustacean 4 — 7 Graptolites { Colonial animals, each point is an individual
	CAMBRIAN 600,000,000 years		1 *Dorypyge* } Trilobites 2 *Ptychagnostus* 3 Sponge spicules 6 Monoplacophoran 4 *Lingulella* } Brachiopods 7 *Hyolithes* 5 *Paterina* (Coniconchia)
	PRECAMBRIAN 2,000,000,000 years	Fossils not known in New Zealand	(Rocks in Nelson - Westland tentatively classed here).

Fig. 4.3. The 1962 geological time scale for New Zealand from Sir Charles Fleming's article 'New Zealand biogeography. A paleontologist's approach'. *Tuatara*, **10**, 53–108, 1962. Note the many references to shelled molluscs. (Reproduced with permission of Victoria University, New Zealand. Modified from an original drawing by Dr J. Marwick for National Broadcasting Service.)

Table 4.1. *The chief divisions of geological time with brief comments on climate and sea level changes (mainly with reference to Britain), continental drift and a few evolutionary stages. (See Figs. 4.3 and 4.4 for lengths of the divisions)*

Holocene and Pleistocene
Cool to glacial climate. Long-term, steady fall in sea levels. The mid-Atlantic ridge is spreading. Repeated transitions from Arctic steppe-tundra through boreal birch and conifer forest to temperate broad-leaved forest and back again. Rise and extinction of specialised Arctic tundra mammals

Pliocene
Warm to temperate climate. Long-term sea level falls with some fluctuations. Westward drift of the Americas as the Atlantic Ocean floor spreads from its central ridge. Large mammals abundant, many of which later became extinct.

Miocene
Temperate climate. Maximum sea level. European Alps formed as a result of northward movement of Italy. Grasslands increase in area at expense of forests. Large grazing mammals. Unspecialised apes abundant in Africa, Europe and Asia. Rise of the seals and walruses

Oligocene
Warm to temperate climate with sea level in the later part of the Period. Britain and much of northern Europe move northwards. Rise of many large ground-dwelling mammals but also widespread extinction of smaller arboreal ones

Eocene and Palaeocene
Climate warm and in parts of the south of Britain it was subtropical. A sea level rise preceded by slight fluctuations. Opening of North Atlantic and between Greenland and Europe (much volcanic activity). Whales, dolphins and seals evolve. First bats and representatives of nearly all main groups of birds appear. In the sea, modern gastropods and bivalves begin to proliferate

Cretaceous
Climate cooler than preceding period. Very high sea levels. Continents were moving outwards from Eurasia and Gondwanaland at different rates. South America separates from South Africa. Development and spread of the flowering plants (angiosperms). Many of the reptiles become extinct at the end of this period. Snakes appear; first birds with bills appear; many small insectivorous mammals. Intensive radiation of the insects

Jurassic

Climate warm and humid. A low then a high sea level. The first stages of the break-up of Africa and the Americas. Cycads, ferns and conifers well developed. Plankton becomes abundant. Large reptiles dominant on land. Toothed birds evolve. Insects increase in variety

Triassic

Hot climate with low then rising sea levels. Pangaea made up of Eurasia in the north and Gondwanaland in the south. Horsetails (Equisetites), ferns and the ginkgo (maidenhair tree), cycads and conifers present. Many marine invertebrates increase in variety. Mammal-like groups evolve. Beginning of the radiation of some insect groups such as beetles, the first flies and sawflies

Permian

Climate hot. Low sea levels. The final assembly of the supercontinent Pangaea has taken place. Gondwanaland (comprising South Amerrica, Africa, India, Australia, New Zealand) surrounded the southern polar region. Conifers abundant. Life in shallow seas greatly reduced in numbers and species, with some mass extinctions. Great spread of the reptiles. Insects diversify on land and in water

Carboniferous

Climate equatorial in Britain but glacial in Gondwanaland. Rise in sea levels follow a world low sea level. Africa converges northwards on combined land mass of America, Europe and Asia. Spread of the amphibians, bony fish and shark-like fish. Appearance of the first reptile

Devonian

Climate warm to moderate. Sea level rises then falls towards the end of the period. True seed plants evolved at the end of this period. Evolution of many plants. Amphibians evolve from air-breathing fishes. First spiders and primitive insects.

Silurian

Climate possibly warm. Marked rise in sea levels. First appearance of vascular land plants. Armoured jawless fish are abundant towards the end of the period.

Ordovician

Sea level rises. Climate probably mild or warm but glacial at the end of the period. Algae notable, many of which are reef-building types. Spread of the graptolites through the seas. Appearance of and increase in some corals. Spread of molluscs. Radiation of echinoderms

Cambrian

Low sea level after sea level rise. Climate uncertain. Lime-secreting algae present. Dominance of trilobites in shallow seas

4.4 Shifting continents

We can glean much about past biogeographical patterns and processes from the distribution of fossils and living organisms. Geological sciences, particularly palaeomagnetism, have also revealed much about what has happened in the past to determine biogeography. Many events throughout the millions of years of evolution of life (Table 4.1, Fig. 4.4) have affected the distribution of organisms as we find them today, but it has not been those events alone which have shaped the patterns. The sea, the inland waters and the land have been changed, or reshaped, often as the result of massive physical disturbances. Volcanic activity, earthquakes, floods and other phenomena have all affected the patterns of distribution of biota. Some islands have appeared from beneath the sea while others have sunk below it. Yet others have been destroyed by volcanic eruptions. The coastlines of the continents have changed but what about the shape and overall position of the continents on the Earth's surface?

As early as 1910, research suggested that there had indeed been movements of parts of the Earth's crust. The idea of continents moving across the face of the globe became refined through the concept of plate tectonics; this is now widely accepted. It was the German meteorologist Alfred Wegener (1880–1930) who early this century made the first and most significant claim that the continents had moved relative to each other. His observations were based on many disciplines including geology, geophysics and biogeography. Wegener's ideas were greeted with considerable scepticism until the 1950s, when some British scientists provided strong evidence from studies of palaeomagnetism (the magnetism preserved in rocks containing iron-bearing minerals) that Europe and North America had once been joined (Runcorn, 1962).

Thus for millions of years, continental drift was inextricably linked with changing biogeographical patterns. To appreciate what was happening over such epochs, we must look at one of the models of continental drift together with stages in evolution of plants and animals. The super continent Pangaea which existed about 200 million years ago towards the end of the Triassic Period comprised two slightly earlier land masses, Gondwana in the south and Laurasia to the north. It was in 1979 when two scientists from the Massachusetts Institute of Technology (MIT) in the USA published a report about a model for the evolution of the Indian Ocean and the break-up of the southern land mass, Gondwana (Norton & Sclater, 1979).

Some of the stages of the break-up of Gondwana are shown in reconstructions in Fig. 4.4. The most dramatic in terms of effects on distribution of terrestrial organisms occurred from the end of the Triassic Period through the Jurassic to the Cretaceous. During the Cretaceous (65 to 146 million years ago), the continents were moving outwards from Eurasia and Gondwana. It was a time when there was development and spread of the flowering plants (angiosperms), extinctions of many large reptiles and radiation of insectivorous mammals (Table 4.1).

Plate tectonics governs the relative positions of the land masses and affects their distribution. This must surely have had major and immense impacts on the distribution of ancient life forms. Evidence for such effects has indeed been found; for example, distribution of that curious group of invertebrates known as the Onychophora (Box 4.1) and the biogeography of freshwater fish (Section 4.2).

4.5 Land bridges and filters

Of all the non-human factors contributing to patterns in distribution (evolution, adaptations, dispersal, competition and succession, climate change, sea level changes and moving continents), it has been the changes in sea level together with changes in elevation of land masses which have prompted most speculation. Much of the theorising has been about so-called land bridges, which may have provided the links between land masses or islands. However, continental drift and plate tectonics have in many instances negated the need to postulate land bridges.

Even without continental drift, climate change involving warm, cool and cold (glacial) periods with fluctuating sea levels has important implications for patterns of geographical distribution. In areas such as the Bering Strait and Central America, climate and sea level changes did indeed at times facilitate or prevent changes in geographical distribution of some groups.

The term 'filter' is often used in connection with land bridges because different groups of organism may be prevented from dispersing, partly affected or even facilitated in their dispersal. Thus there is a filtering effect. The isthmus of Panama has been much studied as an area which over millions of years has acted as a filter for organisms moving south or north. The isthmus formed between four and six million years ago and since then there have been periods where certain groups, such as mammals, have moved south or north resulting in new mixes of species.

ERA	PERIOD	EPOCH
CENOZOIC	QUATERNARY	Holocene Pleistocene
	NEOGENE 22	Pliocene Miocene
	PALEOGENE 41.5	Oligocene Eocene Paleocene
MESOZOIC	CRETACEOUS 81	Late Cretaceous Early Cretaceous
	JURASSIC 59	Late Jurassic Middle Jurassic Early Jurassic
	TRIASSIC 46	Late Triassic Middle Triassic Early Triassic
PALAEOZOIC	PERMIAN 39	Late Permian (Zechstein) Early Permian (Rotliegendes)
	LATE (28) CARBONIFEROUS 63 EARLY (35)	Stephanian Westphalian Namurian Visean Tournaisian
	DEVONIAN 56	Late Devonian Middle Devonian Early Devonian
	SILURIAN 30	Pridoli Ludlow Wenlock Llandovery
	ORDOVICIAN 71	Ashgill Caradoc Llandilo-Llanvirn Arenig Tremadoc
	CAMBRIAN 40 Ma	Merioneth St. Davids Caerfai
PRECAMBRIAN TIME 4000 Ma	VENDIAN	Ediacara Varanger

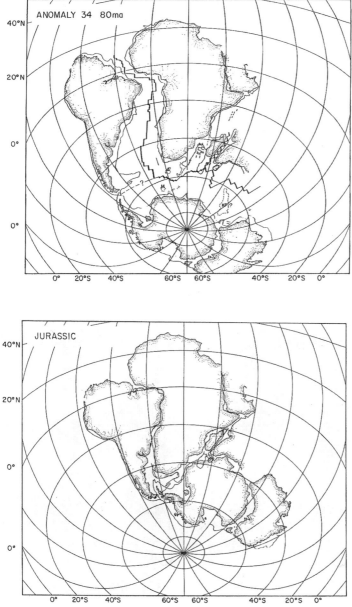

Fig. 4.4. Stages in the process of continental drift. Maps reproduced with kind permission of the American Geophysical Union from Norton, I. O. & Sclater, J. G., 1979, *Journal of Geophysical Research*, **84**, 6803–6830. Geological periods from the *Geological Column*, a Manchester Museum publication, Eager, R. C. M. and Dunning, F. W., 1992. Ma, millions of years ago.

4.6 Human impacts on biogeography

The interpretation or explanation of species distribution patterns may be incorrect if the effects of human beings are not taken into consideration. These effects on the biogeography of other species may be accidental; for example, some species of rat (*Rattus* sp.) were unintentionally transported aboard ships from Europe to the islands of the South Pacific. In other cases species distributions may have been deliberately modified by human beings. The indigenous people of the South Pacific intentionally moved the kumera (sweet potato) to islands in that region to provide the population with a new food crop.

More recently major changes have been made to the distribution of species by people living in the industrialised world. Species can now be easily transported rapidly around the world to environments in which they were not previously found. The increasing ease with which species can be moved globally has resulted in many countries now imposing restrictions on the export or import of certain organisms.

The translocation of species by humans (and latterly the imposition of restrictions on movement by way of national controls or world conventions such as CITES (the Convention on International Trade in Endangered Species)) has been primarily for economic reasons and for environmental protection. For example, humans introduced sitka spruce (*Picea sitchensis*) into Scotland and England from North America to use it as a timber crop. Similarly the Monterrey pine or radiata pine (*Pinus radiata*) was introduced into New Zealand in the nineteenth century from California and has become the most widely used species in the timber production industry in that country. The potato (*Solanum* sp.) has been uplifted by human beings, from its native home in the high Andes of South America, modified and developed into many varieties, and has been transported around the world because it can be used as a food crop. The plant formerly known as the Chinese gooseberry (*Actinidium chinensis*) was translocated from its native China to New Zealand where an industry was established producing fruit of the plant under the new name of kiwifruit.

We have extended the distribution of some species because of certain useful traits that make the species desirable for use outside of their former known range. For example, willows (*Salix* spp.) have extensive root systems, can grow relatively quickly and are now used in several countries worldwide to stabilise river margins as a flood protection measure. The distribution of willows has therefore been influenced considerably by human use in riparian management.

The effects of introduced species can be many and varied and can include effects on the distribution of other species. For example, the North American grey squirrel (*Sciurus carolinensis*) was introduced into England and has now largely displaced the native red squirrel. The accidental introduction of organisms to new areas may have major pest implications. For example, the South African geranium bronze butterfly (*Cacyreus marshalli*), the larvae of which feed on buds and other parts of geraniums and polygoniums, was accidentally introduced into the Balearic Islands during the last ten years via imported geraniums. In its native South Africa the distribution and abundance of the butterfly are affected in part by a native wasp that parasitises the larvae. In the absence of the parasite wasp on the Balearic Islands the butterfly has now spread to mainland Spain where its rapid spread has been accentuated by trade in garden plants and modern transport. The species has now become a major pest due to the lack of a natural parasite and is now causing great problems for the horticultural industry in Spain.

Human-induced changes in the distribution of some species may result in hybridisation with other species and so have a genetic effect. For example, the North American cordgrass (*Spartina alterniflora*) was accidently introduced to the south coast of England as seeds in shipping ballast in the early nineteenth century (Thompson, 1991). *Spartina alterniflora* hybridised with the European cordgrass (*S. maritima*) and resulted in the production of a new species (*S. anglica*), which in this case is also a major pest plant of estuaries in England where it can form dominant and extensive monospecific swards.

Information about a species distribution (prior to human modification) may be applied in pest control programmes for the introduced species. Studies of the species where it occurs in its native habitat may yield information about the factors that limit or influence its distribution and population dynamics. That information may then be applied in the development of strategies to contain and control the spread of pest species. For example, an understanding of the role of the parasitic wasp in the ecology of the geranium bronze butterfly may yet be applied in control strategies for that species on mainland Spain.

4.7 Ethnobotanical studies

Ethnobotany is the study of the classification, management and use of plants. It is a subject that may involve people from a wide range of academic fields such as botanists, economists, anthropologists, ecologists and linguists. It is centred around local people's perception of the cultural and scientific knowl-

Table 4.2. *Plant categories that are useful to people*

Food and fruit tree crops and their close wild relatives

Forage plants for animal feed and silage

Agricultural and ruderal weeds and other wild plants gathered for food on a regular basis

Trees and bushes used for firewood, housing, boat-building, tools, etc.

Medicinal and drug plants such as stimulants, spices, flavourings, aromatics

Plants used for chemical and/or industrial purposes such as oils, fats, resins, rubber, insecticides, etc.

Fibre plants used for textiles, paper, ropes and nets

Plants used for basketry, furnishing, food containers

Plants used for textile dyestuffs and body ornamentation

Plants used as ornamentals

Plants used for recreation, ritual and religious ceremonies

Based on Given, D. R. & Harris, W., 1994, *Techniques and Methods of Ethnobotany*, The Commonwealth Secretariat. Published with kind permission of the Commonwealth Science Council.

edge of plants. Understanding how plants are managed and used can be useful in studies of biogeography as human activities can influence species distributions.

People are dependent upon plants for a variety of reasons (Table 4.2). Plants may be main food crops (for people and for animals). In many parts of the world fossilised plant material and biofuels provide the only source of energy production. Plant fibre is also used to make paper and many plants have important medicinal uses. Understanding the relationship between people and plants is useful in studies of biogeography, particularly when one is trying to provide explanations for species distributions. There are also various applications to understanding how people interact with plant species: these include the conservation of genetic resources of plant food crops and the exploration for fuel sources derived from plant materials.

There are a very few plant species that form the basic food crops of human beings. Studies of the geographical distribution of some of those plants revealed that they originated in certain well-defined regions of the world. Vavilov, a Russian geneticist, recognised this and subsequently those areas became known as 'Vavilov centres'; many of these are also centres of plant diversity (see Chapter 5). The worldwide distribution of 'Vavilov centres' is shown in Fig. 4.5.

Wild relatives and primative cultivars of species used as food crops have been valuable in the past in the development of crops resistant to diseases and pests that are used today all around the world. The identification of 'Vavilov centres' has provided a focus for conservation efforts because different genetic forms of the same food crops species may be found in these areas. Studies of the biogeography of the food crops of the world and what may prove to be valuable wild relatives of these plants can provide an important regional focus for habitat protection to conserve those genetic resources.

Many sources of fuel such as wood and charcoal are derived directly from living plants as opposed to fuels such as coal which are derived from fossil plant material. Information about the geographical distribution of fuel plants and factors determining their distribution may be used to determine how to make best use of them and to establish whether the resources are sustainable. Information about the former distribution of plants from which coal, peat and petroleum are derived have been applied in exploration for fuel reserves.

The potential for some plant species to be used as biofuels is now being investigated in some parts of the world. For example, in Scotland studies of the geographical distribution of where willow and bracken occur now and where they could be grown in the future can be used to determine their potential as biofuels.

We rely on plant fibre in the production of paper for communication. Studies of the biogeography (and potential distribution) of plant species whose fibre is used to produce paper can be used to locate the most suitable production sites. That information can then be applied in the paper industry so that paper mills are established as close as possible to where the plant material originates and where the product will be used. Studies of the biogeography of plants that have the potential to be used in paper production may be applied in the development of local paper manufacturing industries based on those species.

Plants fulfil many present day health care needs and many pharmaceutical products are derived from plants. For example, salicin is a bitter crystalline compound obtained from the bark of willows (*Salix* sp.) and is used in medicines. Salicylic acid is derived from the willow and is used to make aspirin. Information about the biogeography of medicinal plant species can be used in the development of conservation strategies to protect habitats where those species occur in the wild.

Ethnobotanical studies may also focus on the use of plants in the production of alcohol, in studies of natural history, and in the development of art

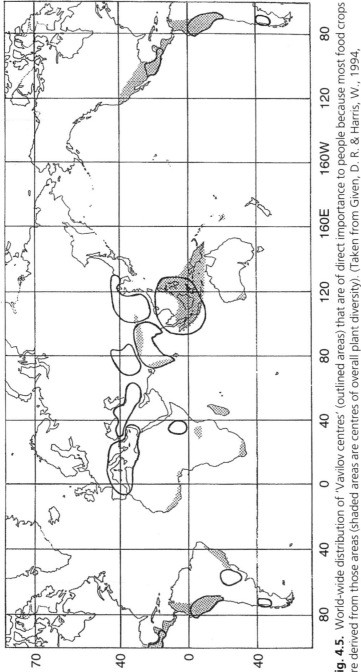

Fig. 4.5. World-wide distribution of 'Vavilov centres' (outlined areas) that are of direct importance to people because most food crops are derived from those areas (shaded areas are centres of overall plant diversity). (Taken from Given, D. R. & Harris, W., 1994, *Techniques and Methods of Ethnobotany*, The Commonwealth Secretariat. Published with kind permission of the Commonwealth Science Council.)

and literature. Human use and management of plants may affect their biogeography and so an ethnobotanical approach to plant biogeography can be valuable when attempting to study and explain plant distribution patterns.

4.8 Cultural impacts on biogeography

Culture has played a role in modifying the biogeography of plants, animals and other organisms. The converse is also true, that the distribution of some organisms can influence and modify local cultures. Culture is a property of a society and is a consequence of the combined values of each of the members of that society, so how does culture affect the distribution of plant, animals and other organisms? Furthermore, how does the distribution of plants and animals influence culture? We will focus here on some of those cultural aspects of biogeography.

4.8.1 Sociocultural aspects of biogeography

Sociocultural aspects of biogeography have involved a wide range of species (Table 4.3) and in some instances the effects have been dramatic. In New Zealand, for example, acclimatisation societies were established and species of plants and animal were introduced to areas where they had not been found previously. This enabled the promotion of revegetation or restoration projects, food production (animals such as goats, horses and pigs) or sport (animals such as mallard duck, rainbow trout and deer). As a result the societies and some private individuals introduced over 130 species of birds, about 40 species of fish and over 50 species of mammals to New Zealand, expanding those species' geographical range.

The biogeography of some taxa has been influenced through activities associated with conservation. People conserve species for many different reasons (Table 4.4) and at present conservation efforts are focused on preventing the extinction of the greatest number of species and conserving the best representative sample of the world's biota. Species that are of greatest conservation concern to people may include any of the following: species whose existence in a particular area is threatened, uncommon species, species found only in one area (an endemic), and 'umbrella' species (upon which the survival of many others is directly dependent). The geographical distribution of all those species can be directly influenced by conservation activities.

Table 4.3. *Groups of species whose geographical distribution may be directly affected by culture*

Species whose existence in any particular area is threatened

National emblems or species regarded as sacred or desired

Charismatic species

Species that occupy protected areas

Species believed to have a damaging impact on 'valuable' species

Species believed to pose a threat to people, e.g. vectors of human disease

Table 4.4. *Groups of species of conservation concern whose geographical distribution may be influenced by conservation management activities*

Taxa whose global, national or regional existence in the wild is threatened and are in danger of extinction

Taxa that are rare (either found at only a few locations or widespread but never abundant)

Taxa for which limited information exists about their geographical distribution or their current status in the wild

Taxa that are only found in one particular region (endemic)

Taxa whose occurrence at a particular place or in a particular region is believed to constitute an important genetic resource

Taxa that are important for the survival of other plant or animal taxa

Taxa that are important to people

World wide there are some plant and animal taxa whose continued survival in the wild is unlikely if the factors causing their current decline continue. The biogeography of those 'threatened species' may be affected by conservation management seeking to protect them and secure their continued survival.

For many years in New Zealand the takahe (*Porphyrio mantelli*) was believed to be extinct (Fig. 4.6). When the bird was rediscovered in 1948 in alpine tussock grasslands of the Murchison Mountains in southern South Island, the country embarked on a conservation programme that continues today. Activities have now modified the geographical spread of the takahe to

Fig. 4.6. The takahe (*Porphyrio mantelli*) – a flightless bird, endemic to New Zealand. (Photograph taken by P. Morrison.)

the extent that the flightless bird now has a disjunct distribution (Fig. 4.7). In the wild it was found only in the Murchison Mountains, despite having been far more widely distributed in the past. The takahe has now been moved to several predator-free islands such as Kapiti, Maud and Mana, where it can be protected most effectively (Fig. 4.7).

Conservation activities can also impact on distribution through the use of some species in revegetation, restoration or rehabilitation projects. For example, in Western Australia the rehabilitation of bauxite mines near Perth in the 1970s involved the planting of eucalypt species from southeastern Australia (such as *Eucalyptus globulus*) rather than species which were native to

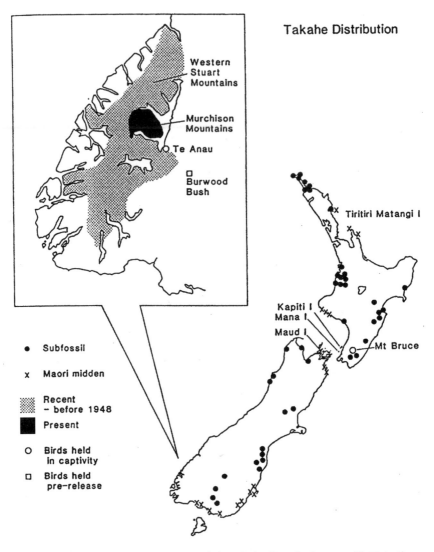

Fig. 4.7. Past and present distribution of the takahe (*Porphyrio mantelli*). Note the bird is now found on Kapiti, Mana and Maud Islands, off New Zealand, the current disjunct distribution being a result of humans moving the bird to predator-free islands where it can be protected most effectively. (Copyright John McIndoe Ltd.)

Table 4.5. *Some examples of sacred trees*

Species	Country	Reference
Karite (*Butyrospermum* spp.)	West African savanna	Harlan, 1975
Banyan (*Ficus indica*)	India	Hartwig, 1872
Pippul (*Ficus religiosa*)	India	Hartwig, 1872
Date palms (*Palmae* sp.)	North Africa, Middle East	Hartwig, 1872
Palmyra (*Borassus aethiopicum*)	India, Ceylon	Hartwig, 1872

From Unruh, J. D., 1994. The role of land use pattern and process in the diffusion of valuable tree species. *Journal of Biogeography*, **21**, 283–295, Blackwell Science Publications. Published with kind permission of Blackwell Science Ltd.

the mined sites. Although policies have now changed so that only local native plants are used in rehabilitation, the use of those non-native plants led to the extension of their geographical range (if only temporarily).

Another group of species whose distribution may be affected by culture are those that are national emblems or regarded by people as sacred. For example, the karite (*Butyrospermum paradoxum*) of West Africa is a tree which is regarded as semi-sacred. As a result, large areas of broadleaved savanna in West Africa are covered in stands of karite (Unruh, 1994). Some other examples of tree species that are sacred are shown in Table 4.5. Information about sacred species is relevant to studies of biogeography because the persistence in the landscape of those species may be the direct result of human attempts to protect them physically or legally.

Some species regarded as sacred or national emblems may be protected by legislation. Plants that are the national flower of a country or the emblem of a district may be propagated and dispersed widely throughout those regions and thus the geographical distribution of those plants may be altered. Species such as the panda are used by conservation organisations (in this case the Worldwide Fund for Nature) as their emblem and in that way become a focus for protection efforts. Traditional use of some species by humans has conferred on those species a level of protection not enjoyed by others. For example, in New Zealand the golden sand sedge (*Desmoschoenus spiralis*), known to Maoris as pingao, is a plant used to highlight patterns in woven articles and decorative panels (Given & Harris, 1994). Investigation of the propagation and cultivation requirements of pingao has led to seedlings being provided for replanting of the species back into the wild and into gardens so that supplies can be secured for continued traditional weaving practices. Again, traditional

Table 4.6. *IUCN categories of protected areas*

Nature Reserve
National Park
Natural Monument/Natural Landmark
Managed Nature Reserve/Wildlife Sanctuary
Protected Landscapes and Seascapes
Resource Reserve
Anthropological Reserve/Natural Biotic Area
Multiple-use Management Area/Managed Resource Area
Biosphere Reserve
World Heritage Site

Adapted from Lucas, P. H. C., 1992. Protected Landscapes. *A Guide for Policy-Makers and Planners*, Chapman & Hall. Published with kind permission of Chapman & Hall.

cultural uses can influence the distribution of plants, animals and other organisms.

Charismatic species are another group whose distribution may be influenced by culture. Some species are perceived by people to be more attractive than others or more appealing. Cultural attitudes may favour the survival or protection of those appealing species and can influence their geographical distribution. For example, all species of whale are now protected under a global moratorium on commercial whaling agreed by the International Whaling Commission in 1988. That moratorium was not because all whales are close to extinction (although the survival in the wild of some whale species may be under threat) but because of a human desire to protect and care for large marine mammals.

The establishment in some parts of the world of many categories of protected area (Table 4.6) has been a direct result of changing cultural attitudes towards the conservation of nature. The geographical distribution of species that occupy protected areas may be influenced by environmental protection mechanisms. Some species, such as the mountain gorilla (*Gorilla gorilla beringei*) of Central Africa, are confined in distribution to one or two protected reserves. The legal protection of those areas has meant that the geographical distribution of rare species such as the gorilla is also protected. That does not mean that the species will continue to exist at that place but demonstrates how protected areas can protect species distributions. Protection of areas of land or sea also provides opportunities for reserved species to colonise or recolonise surrounding areas. That opportunity for colonisation may not have arisen had not the area been designated as protected. Society, by deciding to protect certain areas for the conservation of biological diversity, has therefore influenced the geographical distribution of species of plants and animals.

Some species are believed to have a damaging impact on other species that are perceived to be 'valuable'. Cultural attitudes may influence the geographical distribution of a species if it is a perceived threat to economically important species or one that has some perceived value to society. In some instances a species may be hunted to the brink of extinction because of that perception. In Scotland several birds of prey, such as golden eagles (*Aquila chrysaetos*) and goshawks (*Astur palumbarius*), have been hunted by farmers for allegedly predating highly valued lambs. In North America species such as bald eagles (*Haliaeetus leucocephalus*) and the merganser (*Mergus merganser*) have been hunted and killed because of their apparent impact on resource species such as salmon. Throughout the world, seals have been hunted or culled because of the belief held by some people that they impact significantly on valued fish stocks. In New Zealand the Australian brush-tailed possum (*Trichosurus vulpecula*) is known to carry bovine tuberculosis and may spread the disease to cattle and so threaten the beef industry in that country and for that reason it is hunted and killed in order to protect economic interests.

Culture can also play a role in determining the distribution of species believed to pose a threat to humans such as vectors of human disease. Species that have no apparent value to society or where it is believed that they may pose some danger to society may be the focus of efforts to control or eradicate them. Plants and animals that are poisonous or a threat (such as sharks, spiders, snakes and mosquitoes) are often classified as undesirable. Human efforts to destroy species perceived to be a threat to society can influence and shape species distribution patterns. Some species are implicated in the transmission of human diseases and cultural attitudes towards disease vectors are generally such that humans seek their control or eradication. For example, control may be required for mosquito species that transmit arboviruses such as those that cause yellow fever and dengue fever (see also Chapter 9).

Species distributions may also be affected by people as a result of tourist activities. Some places where particular plants or animals occur are visited repeatedly by people and that regular disturbance can influence whether a species continues to remain at the site and so affect its distribution. For example, in New Zealand the only mainland nesting site of the royal albatross

(*Diomedea epomophora*) is visited by many thousands of people each year. Human disturbance of the bird at that site (and the potential effects on the biogeography of the species) is now minimised through the construction of a hide from which tourists can observe the birds. In some parts of the world there are now policies to control how close people can go to some species such as marine mammals (for example, seals) and nesting birds (for example, penguins and gannets).

4.8.2 Indirect effects of human culture on biogeography

Some organisms may thrive in human-modified landscapes and as a result the geographical distribution of those organisms may change. In western Scotland in the 19th century landowners evicted many farmers from the land in order to establish sheep farms. Until then the farmers had grown crops such as potatoes on much of the fertile land in that region. As a result of that change in land use, bracken (*Pteridium aquilinum*) expanded its range to occupy and in most cases dominate areas that had been left fallow. The survival of species that have spread as a result of human land use practices may affect the future ecological processes that occur in those areas. The evolutionary direction taken by local plant and animal communities may also be modified as a result.

The biogeography of many areas has been changed and even elminated by human land use practices. Throughout the world, wetlands have been drained to create more favourable conditions for agriculture and the range and distribution of many wetland plants have thus been changed and destroyed. In New Zealand, deforestation by fire has created human-dominated landscapes in which, in some places, the cabbage tree (*Cordyline australis*) is now one of the only remaining indigenous tree species. The cabbage tree is able to persist even after fire because, although the existing branches of the tree are readily killed by fire, new branches grow from the protected rhizomes beneath the ground. Fire in that case was a factor that unintentionally led to the persistence on the landscape of one tree species that was able to regenerate.

4.8.3 Cultural change and its impact on biogeography

The distribution of plants and animals and other organisms can be affected by cultural change. For example, cultural attitudes towards species may change. In some cases a species can be perceived to be of economic importance and then prove to be a pest. The Australian brush-tailed possum was introduced to New Zealand late in the 19th century with a view to establishing a fur trade using the animal's pelt. When the international fur trade collapsed, the possum pelts were no longer regarded as valuable. The species did not appear to be of economic value on a world market. The New Zealand government now has a programme of possum control aimed at reducing the impact that the species has on indigenous plant and animal communities. Cultural attitudes towards possums have changed dramatically in New Zealand; they have influenced the geographical distribution of the species such that possums have now been eradicated from many islands off New Zealand.

4.9 The influence of species distribution on society and culture

The worldwide diversity in musical culture has been influenced by biogeography. If you were to travel around the world listening to local musicians you would hear many different sounds and see many different musical instruments. Throughout the world many species of plants, animals and other organisms are used to make musical instruments and the design has been influenced by the local availability of construction materials. For example, panpipes are an ancient, widely dispersed musical instrument found in regions such as Romania, Arabia, Greece, in North America and in several countries of the Andes in South America. Panpipes consist of a series of pipes of various lengths joined together and arranged in order of size from longest to shortest. Throughout the world panpipes are made with materials from a variety of different species. In Georgia, in the USA, panpipes are made out of cane stems, while in other parts of the world they are made from species of bamboo or elder. Before world transport networks were established, musical instrument construction and design was driven by the availability of materials derived from local species. Hence the geographical distribution of species has influenced the development of music in many parts of the world.

Local availability of food crops has also influenced the development of culinary tastes and culinary expertise. In some parts of the world certain drinks are used by the local inhabitants and those drinks have been made from local plant material. Maté is a Paraguayan tea made by an infusion of the leaves of the Brazilian holly (*Ilex paraguayensis*). Kava is a drink made in the islands of Fiji from the root of the shrub *Piper methystichum*. Biogeography has therefore played a role in the development of human dependence on certain kinds of food and drink and on human utilisation of certain species to meet culinary needs.

Architectural design has also been influenced by the distribution of some species that are used locally in the construction of buildings. The design and construction of similar building types in various parts of the world can be diverse due to the effects of people using the construction materials available to them locally. The tent, for example, is a universal design but one that can vary considerably according to geographical location. For example, there is a variety of woody plants used in nomadic building practices in northern Africa where the species more commonly used in building construction elsewhere (oak, cypress and pine) are absent. The plant families most widely used in tent construction by nomadic people in Africa are palms and acacias such as *Acacia raddiana*. In North America the tent design has taken the form of the wigwam and for that buffalo hides are used in their construction. Plants have certain properties that influence the way that they may be used in building construction and their geographical distribution can influence how architectural design evolves.

The design and construction of boats has also been influenced by the availability of materials that can be used in boat construction. The canoe design, for example, has evolved in various parts of the world and the diversity of canoe types reflects the diversity of materials suitable and available locally for construction. The waka of New Zealand made by the Maori was most often built using the totara tree (*Podocarpus totara*). In other parts of the world such as Ecuador materials such as balsa, that can be obtained locally as a forest tree, may be used in boat construction.

The above examples are intended to highlight how people, their survival and culture are directly affected by the geographical distribution of plants, animals and other organisms. Biogeography has had a profound impact on how people live and how cultural diversity has evolved.

References

Barber, K. E., Dumayne, L. & Stoneman, R. (1993). Climatic change and human impact during the late Holocene in northern Britain. In Chambres, F. M. (ed.), *Climate Change and Human Impact on the Landscape*, pp. 225–236. London, Chapman & Hall.

Enright, N. J. & Hill, R. S. (1995). *Ecology of the Southern Conifers*. Melbourne, Melbourne University Press.

Fleming, C. A. (1962). New Zealand biogeography. A paleontologist's approach. *Tuatara*, 10, 53–108.

Given, D. R. & Harris, W. (1994). *Techniques and Methods of Ethnobotany*. London, The Commonwealth Secretariat.

Harlan, J. R. (1975). *Crops and Man*, pp. 69–96. Madison, WI, American Society of Agronomy.

Hartwig, G. (1872). *The Polar and Tropical Worlds: A Description of Man and Nature in the Polar and Tropical Regions of the Globe*. Springfield, MA, Bill, Nichols and Co.

Norton, I. O. & Sclater, J. G. (1979). A model for the evolution of the Indian Ocean and the breakup of Gondwanaland. *Journal of Geophysical Research*, **84**, 6803–6830.

Runcorn, S. K. (ed.) (1962). Continental drift. *International Geophysical Series* **3**. New York, Academic Press.

Smith, J. L. B. (1956). *Old Fourlegs. The Story of the Coelacanth*. London, Longman Green and Co.

Thompson, J. D. (1991). The biology of an invasive plant: what makes *Spartina anglica* so successful? *BioScience*, **41**, 393–401.

Unruh, J. D. (1994). The role of land use pattern and process in the diffusion of valuable tree species. *Journal of Biogeography*, **21**, 283–295.

5

Ecological patterns and types of species distribution

5.1 Introduction

The biogeography of mythical and magical creatures would make a delightful book. There is plenty of information for such a book. There are maps showing the locations of Hobbits in the books by J. R. R. Tolkein and in many other books there are accounts of geographical locations of mythical creatures. A very convincing monograph on the form and life of an unusual group of mammals was published in German in 1957 by Harald Stumpke (published in French in 1962 and in English in 1967 by the University of Chicago Press). That monograph was about the Rhinogrades (or Snouters). Their ecology is very important in determining the biogeography of the group that inhabits the Hi-Iay archipelago. But can we really believe that such a group exists and how valid is the information about their geographical distribution?

We may well question information seen on display in many zoos and botanic gardens. What may seem to be interesting and useful information is perhaps misleading and a gross simplification. For example, the coypu (*Myocastor coypus*), the only member of the Myocastoridae family, is a predominantly aquatic rodent that lives in marshy areas; it is therefore unlikely that it would be found in every part of the shaded areas shown in Fig. 5.1. Despite limited and possibly misleading maps, information about distribution patterns of species and other taxonomic groups have very useful applications in parts of the world where environmental reporting is expected and that information can form the basis for studies into the ecological aspects of biogeography.

Fig. 5.1. Worldwide distribution of coypu (*Myocastor coypus*) a predominantly aquatic rodent that lives in marshy areas. (From Alderton, D., 1996, *Rodents of the World*, Blandford. Copyright Blandford Publishing.)

Even with the simplistic information given in Fig. 5.1 we can ask some interesting questions. What aspects of the ecology of the species affect the size and shape of the shaded area? Has the geographical distribution always been like that? How does that distribution compare with the distribution of other similar species?

The focus in this chapter is on species (and the factors that influence their distributions) and not on other taxonomic groups, of which there are many (Table 5.1). Species are defined components of biological diversity that can be observed and recorded and, because of this, studies of the ecological factors that influence their geographical distribution are made easy in comparison with other taxonomic groups.

The spatial distribution of plants, animals and other organisms has been brought about by evolutionary and geological events and has been influenced by human beings (see Chapter 4), but there are also ecological factors determining species distributions. In this chapter we describe some patterns of species distributions and define some of the terminology used in studies of ecological biogeography. We then describe some of the ecological factors that determine and maintain those distribution patterns, facilitate dispersion of species, and act as barriers to prevent shifting species distribution. Finally, we consider applications.

Table 5.1. *Taxonomic hierarchy for plants and animals (obligate classes are shown in capitals)*

KINGDOM
PHYLUM (Division)
  Subphylum
  Subdivision
CLASS
  Subclass
  Infraclass
  Superorder
ORDER
  Suborder
  Superfamily
FAMILY
  Subfamily
  Tribe
    Subtribe
GENUS
  Subgenus
SPECIES
  Subspecies (lowest category in animal taxonomy)
  Variety
  Form
    Subform

5.2 Patterns in the distribution of species and other taxonomic groups

Whether we look at the worldwide distribution of a species or its local distribution in one country or region, we can observe patterns. There are certain terms that are used to describe patterns in the distribution of species and other taxonomic groups and some are shown in Table 5.2. Taxa that occur throughout the world have a cosmopolitan distribution. The geographical distribution of Myomorpha, for example, is that of a cosmopolitan group of mouse-like rodents (Fig. 5.2). Many bats and birds of prey are cosmopolitan groups of animals, the plantains are a cosmopolitan plant group and the mollusc *Mytilus*, characteristic of rocky shores, is a cosmopolitan genus. A few species of plants and animals such as starlings, plantains and the lichen, *Parmelia sulcata* occur in most countries. *Homo sapiens* and killer

Fig. 5.2. Distribution of a *Myomorpha*– a cosmopolitan genus of mouse-like rodents. (From Alderton, D., 1996, *Rodents of the World*, Blandford. Copyright Blandford Publishing.)

whales (*Orcinus orca*) are two examples of mammals with a cosmopolitan distribution.

Endemics are groups of plants and animals restricted to certain regions (Table 5.2). 'Endemic' is a term that requires spatial qualification, since all species are confined in distribution to a certain area. Some species or taxonomic groups are confined in distribution to a particular continent whilst others are endemic to a single mountain range. Some endemic groups such as the Australian monotremes (platypus and echidna) have evolved in a certain region and therefore have no close relatives. Other groups have become endemic to one region because of extinctions elsewhere (see Table 5.2). The New Zealand lizard-like reptile, the tuatara (see Section 3.4) is a good example of a genus that had a very wide distribution but is now restricted to a few islands.

The pattern in geographical distribution of some species is discontinuous and they are commonly referred to as disjunct (Table 5.2). The grey seal (*Halichoerus grypus*) is an example of a species whose geographical distribution is disjunct due to the relatively large discontinuity between populations of the species in the eastern and western Atlantic (Fig. 5.3).

Some plants and animals are referred to as indigenous and these are native

Table 5.2. *Terms used to describe patterns in the distribution of species and other taxonomic groups*

Type of distribution	Definition
Cosmopolitan	A species or taxonomic group that is distributed widely throughout the world
Primary endemic	A species or taxonomic group is a primary endemic in a particular region if it is native only to that region
Secondary endemic	A species or taxonomic group is a secondary endemic in a particular region if its distribution has contracted so that it is now native only to the region in which it is found
Rare	A species or taxonomic group that is restricted geographically or is widespread but never found in abundance
Disjunct	A species that occupies areas that are widely separated and scattered (species with a discontinuous distribution)
Indigenous or native	A species that originates in a particular place or which has arrived there entirely independently of human activity

or occur 'naturally' in a region; generally speaking they originate from that place. The term 'naturally' usually implies that the species does not occur in a region as a consequence of human activity. 'Indigenous' requires additional qualification when used to describe the pattern of distribution of a species, so that the geographical area to which the species or taxon is indigenous must also be described. The southern right whale (*Eubalaena australis*), for example, is indigenous to the oceans of the southern hemisphere and the mountain gorilla is indigenous to the Virunga mountains of Central Africa on the border of Rwanda, the Democratic Republic of Congo and Uganda.

5.3 Distributions of species or other taxa that have changed

The range of some species may change due to natural processes or as a consequence of human activities. There are various terms used to describe species whose ranges have changed or are still changing (Table 5.3). In some

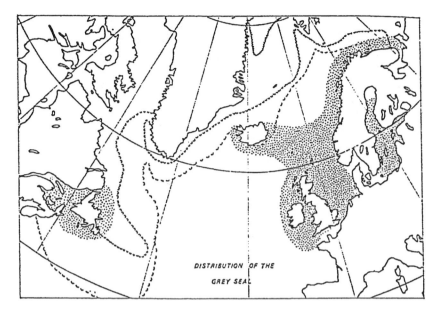

DISTRIBUTION OF THE

GREY SEAL

Fig. 5.3. Disjunct distribution of the grey seal (*Halichoerus grypus*). Note the discontinuity in distribution between populations in the western and eastern Atlantic. (From Hewer, H. R., 1974, *British Seals*, Collins. Copyright H. R. Hewer.)

cases terms such as 'adventive', 'exotic' and 'introduced' are used interchangeably to describe species and often that is not a problem. However, we have to distinguish between species that have been purposefully introduced by people (an introduced species), those that have expanded their geographical range by natural means (a naturalised species) and those that have been transported to a new location and have become established there as a consequence of human activity (alien). Each term can imply different things and can have implications for how people manage those species. In some parts of the world native or indigenous plants and animals are protected, while exotics, aliens and adventives are managed or eradicated.

Humans often introduce species to new areas to achieve a particular objective (such as to establish a commercial enterprise based on that species) and therefore classification as an introduced species implies that there is a good reason for its presence in a particular place. The control of exotics or alien species is usually undertaken when the organism has the potential to impact on the survival of indigenous species, the health of humans (such as vectors of human diseases), or species of direct economic importance to humans.

Table 5.3. *Some terms used to describe species whose ranges have altered due to natural processes or as a consequence of human activity*

Term	Definition
Alien	A species that has reached an area as a consequence of the activities of neolithic or post-neolithic human beings or of their domestic animals
Adventive	A species or taxonomic group that has arrived and established in the wild outside its former known geographical range either as a consequence of human activity or entirely independently of it
Naturalised	A species or taxonomic group that has expanded its range entirely independently of human activity and has now become established permanently in a new area
Exotic	A species or taxonomic group that occurs (but is not necessarily established in the wild) outside its former known geographical range
Introduced	A species or taxonomic group whose range has been purposefully expanded as a consequence of human activity
Invasive	An alien species the distribution and/or abundance of which in the wild is in the process of increasing
Vagrant	A species that has expanded its range entirely independently of human activity but has not necessarily established permanently in new areas

5.4 Patterns in distribution of species abundance in space and time

If the distribution of every species in the world were known and it were possible to overlay maps of their distributions it would become apparent that some regions of the world support far more species than others. Species richness is the number of species present in any given area and varies from place to place. Some species occur together in communities, assemblages and guilds. They do that for a variety of reasons and consequently share the same spatial distribution. Species may aggregate and occur together because (1) they share preferences for a particular habitat type or climate, (2) they depend upon one another for survival, (3) they have arrived at the same place at the same time by accident, (4) they occur there as a consequence of human activities, or (5) individuals of those species share similar biological attributes. Whatever the reason for species aggregation, the end result is that patterns have been observed in the distribution of species richness throughout the world.

Three phenomena that have been observed are latitudinal, altitudinal and peninsular gradients in species richness. One example of a latitudinal gradient in species richness is from Europe where the numbers of reptile species (excluding marine tortoises and introduced species) decrease with increasing latitude. In that case there are between 0 and 2 species in northern Scandinavia and Iceland, while in Morocco in North Africa there are 72 species. There is often no simple explanation for gradients in species richness as it can be different for different groups of species.

5.5 Patterns in distribution of other levels of biological organisation

Patterns have been observed in the distribution of all levels of biological organisation, including communities, assemblages and guilds of species, and also biomes. The worldwide distribution of the plant community known as paramo is shown in Fig. 5.4. The pattern of distribution of the paramo plant community is such that it is restricted to high mountains in the tropics and supports a rich flora of species with particular life forms that are found only in tropical alpine regions.

5.6 Patterns of species distributions in relation to abiotic and biotic factors

Evolutionary, geological and human factors that have shaped biogeographical patterns are discussed in Chapter 4. There are, however, some principal ecological factors that influence plant and animal distributions. Each one of these factors may operate at a different spatial scale and its importance may vary according to the species in question. We look here at some examples of species of plants and animals whose distributions are determined by various ecological factors at a variety of spatial scales.

The geographical distribution of an organism depends to a large extent on the organism itself, including such factors as the size of an organism, its ability to reproduce and its ecological requirements. The environment that supports the organism can also influence its distribution. In every environment there are many combinations of abiotic (non-living) and biotic (living) variables. In some locations certain combinations of those variables may meet the

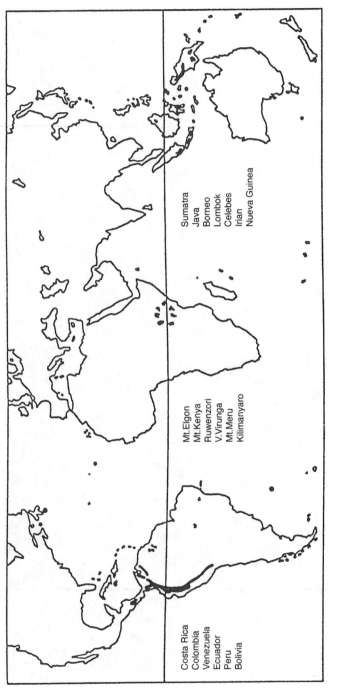

Costa Rica
Colombia
Venezuela
Ecuador
Peru
Bolivia

Mt.Elgon
Mt.Kenya
Ruwenzori
V.Virunga
Mt.Meru
Kilimanyaro

Sumatra
Java
Borneo
Lombok
Celebes
Irian
Nueva Guinea

Fig. 5.4. Worldwide distribution of paramo regions – a plant community restricted to tropical high mountains. (From Lauer, W., 1981, Eco-climatological conditions of paramo belt in tropical high mountains. *Mountain Research and Development*, **1**(3–4), 209–221. Published with kind permission of University of California Press.)

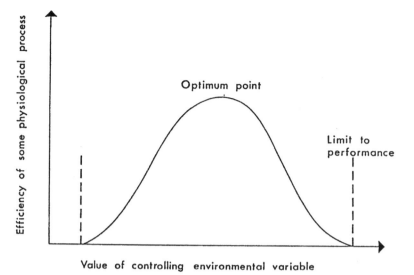

Fig. 5.5. An example of a species tolerance curve showing the limits to performance of physiological processes for any given species. (From Putman, R. J. & Wratten, S. D., 1984, *Principles of Ecology*, Croom Helm Ltd. Copyright Croom Helm Ltd.)

requirements of more than one taxon and as a result some taxa share the same geographical distribution. The interactions of organisms with their environment and associated species can also affect their geographical distribution. Some organisms (such as species of ants) modify their environment and in that way influence their own distribution.

Every living species has evolved to live within certain limits of certain abiotic factors, although those limits may not be very precise. The extent of the distribution can be viewed conceptually as Shelford's law. In 1913 V. E. Shelford suggested that organisms have ecological minimum and maximum limits of tolerance (with a range in between). That law helps us to understand the distribution of organisms. A species tolerance curve depicts (for any physiological process) the efficiency of operation of that organism (Fig. 5.5). This curve is typically bell shaped, its peak representing the optimal conditions for a particular physiological process. Some species have narrow limits of tolerance to some abiotic factors (stenotopic) and others have wide limits of tolerance (eurytopic). It would be expected that fewer individuals of any given species, given a choice, would occupy environments in which the efficiency of their physiological processes is reduced. The geographical limit would be reached at the limit of performance of the species for a particular environmental variable (such as a temperature range or annual rainfall).

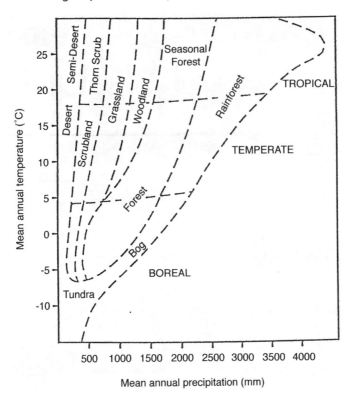

Fig. 5.6. The correlation between the distribution of the world's major biomes, mean annual precipitation and mean annual temperature. (From Watson, R. T., Zinyowera, M. C. and Moss, R. H. (eds.), 1996. *Climate Change 1995: Impacts, Adaptations and Mitigation of Climate Change: Scientific-Technical Analyses*, Cambridge University Press. Published with kind permission of the Intergovernmental Panel on Climate Change.)

Abiotic factors affect not only the distribution of populations but also the distribution of other levels of biological organisation, such as communities. The world's major biomes are also based in part on abiotic factors such as mean annual temperature and mean annual precipitation (Fig. 5.6).

5.6.1 Plants

The geographical distribution of plants is determined largely by edaphic factors (such as soil nutrients and moisture), climate, the presence or absence

Table 5.4. *Factors that determine the geographical distribution of plants and animals*

Climate
Availability of suitable or potential habitat
Availability of water
Edaphic factors (soil moisture and soil minerals)
Influence of herbivores (vertebrate and invertebrate)
Influence of animal and plant competitors
Influence of animal predators
Availability of prey for animals
Availability of habitat to permit migration or to allow species to shift location
Historical factors

of other plants, and the effects of grazing animals (invertebrate and vertebrate herbivores; see Table 5.4). The effects of herbivores on the distribution of plant species can be considerable, particularly if grazing of the plant communities is selective. That can alter species composition of those plant communities over time.

Some plant species have developed ways to regulate their environment and in so doing influence not only their distribution but also the distribution of others. Other plants exhibit what is known as allelopathy. An allelopath releases compounds that are toxic to other species. In so doing the allelopath may gain a competitive advantage over other species and may influence the distribution of its competitors. For example, bracken (*Pteridium aquilinum*) can act as an allelopath by releasing toxic compounds.

5.6.2 Animals

The distribution of animals is affected mainly by abiotic factors and by other organisms (Table 5.4). In general, animals can be divided into two groups – endotherms and ectotherms – and of these the endotherms have greater independence over environmental conditions.

As for all abiotic factors, there is a range of temperatures at which physiological and behavioural processes are at optimum (see Fig. 5.5). For animals that applies to everything from rates of digestion to visual acuity. It is

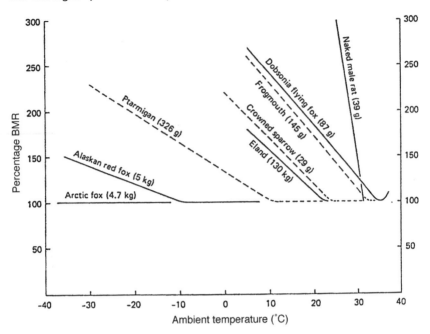

Fig. 5.7. The responses of the metabolic rate of various species of birds and mammals to environmental temperature. Lines (broken for birds and solid for mammals) show the species thermal neutral zone and how species basal metabolic rate (BMR) is affected by changes to ambient temperature. (From Gordon, M. S. (in collaboration with G. A. Bartholomew, A. D. Grinnel, C. Barker Jorgensen and F. White), 1982, *Animal Physiology: Principles and Adaptations*, 4th edn, Collier Macmillan Publishers. Reprinted with permission of Prentice-Hall Inc., Upper Saddle River, NJ.)

advantageous therefore for animals to maintain body temperature at the level most suitable for the essential physiological processes. The way temperature limits animal distributions depends on their thermal physiology; that is, whether it is ectothermic or endothermic.

Ectothermic organisms regulate their body temperature largely by use of external heat sources. They include invertebrates, amphibians, reptiles and fish. Endothermic organisms are those which have evolved high levels of metabolism and can generate body heat by physiological means. They include birds and mammals. To a certain extent their distribution can be independent of temperature but it is related to the temperature–energy relationship (Fig. 5.7) (including the level and width of the thermoneutral zone). For example, the Arctic fox (*Alopex lagopus*) has a low, wide thermal neutral zone (the flat black line in Fig. 5.7). This means the fox can survive in ambient temperatures as low as – 38 °C without having to increase its metabolic rate. By way of contrast the thermal neutral zone of the white-tailed ptarmigan (*Lagopus leucurus*) extends to 10 °C and the bird has to double its basal metabolic rate in order to survive temperatures as low as − 30 °C. The ability of organisms to generate body heat has important implications determining their geographical distribution.

Both the Arctic fox and the white-tailed ptarmigan are able to survive over a wide range of temperatures because not only are they endotherms but they are also very well insulated. The emperor penguin (*Aptenodytes forsteri*) of Antarctica not only has a distribution in one of the most harsh environments in the world but also breeds there during the worst conditions imaginable. It breeds on the edge of the Antarctic continent, on sea-ice, during the depths of the harsh Antarctic winter, a feat made possible because of a wide, low thermal neutral zone, very effective insulation and in particular its body shape (low surface area and high mass).

The geographical distribution of some species seems to be affected by certain limits of climate. For example, in England the distribution of the reed warbler (*Acrocephalus scirpaceus*) does not occur north of the 16 °C July isotherm (Fig. 5.8). There seems to be a clear link between the limit of distribution and temperature, but is there cause and effect? Is the explanation for the species distribution as simple as that? A more detailed analysis may reveal that other factors (such as annual rainfall) influence the survival (and therefore the distribution) of the reed warbler. One should be wary of apparently simple links between abiotic factors and geographical distribution.

Ectothermic organisms regulate their body temperature largely by behavioural means and in general their distribution is limited by external temperature conditions. Their body temperature rises and falls with ambient temperature conditions but, over a limited range and depending on environmental conditions, they can maintain a body temperature independent of the ambient temperature. Their level of metabolism behaves in a similar way; in general the level of metabolism rises and falls with temperature but for some species there may be a point at which the level of metabolism seems to be independent of external temperature. For ectotherms, temperature is the most important limiting factor. However, some ectothermic species have evolved mechanisms to allow them to extend their geographical distribution into what would normally seem to be unsuitable conditions. The North American garter snake (*Thamnophis sirtalis*) is a good example. There are two subspecies, a southern species and a northern species: the northern subspecies appears to have a physiological mechanism that operates at lower temperatures, allowing it to extend its activity during cold conditions.

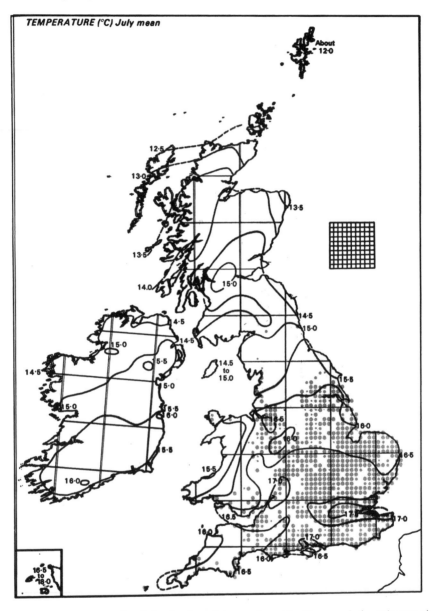

Fig. 5.8. The geographical distribution of the reed warbler (*Acrocephalus scirpaceus*) (indicated by the grey shaded area) showing how the species does not occur north of the 16°C July isotherm. (From *The Atlas of Breeding Birds*, 1976. Compiled by J. T. R. Sharrock and published with kind permission of the British Trust for Ornithology.)

5.6.3 Associations of plants and animals

The biogeography of some organisms is influenced by the distribution of other organisms, quite apart from the abiotic influences of climate. Interactions and associations of some species with others have a role in determining their geographical distribution. There are various interactions which can influence species distributions and these include plant–plant, plant–animal and animal–animal types.

Parasites are a group of organisms whose distribution is influenced by interactions with other species. The biogeography of parasites is determined by host suitability and host availability and therefore by the geographical distribution of their host species. Mistletoe and 'root parasites' are two groups of plant parasite whose distributions are determined by their association with other organisms. In the UK, southern Scandinavia and central and southern Europe, the mistletoe (*Viscum album*) is a hemiparasite (deriving only part of its nourishment from its host) of deciduous trees and in some cases pine and fir trees. In New Zealand, the red-flowered mistletoe (*Peraxilla tetrapetala*) (Fig. 5.9) is also a hemiparasite and has several host trees and shrubs including species of beech (*Nothofagus* sp.). The geographical distribution of current and potential host species of *Viscum album* and *Peraxilla tetrapetala* will define the maximum potential distribution of the parasite. Not all potential hosts will necessarily be parasitised as there are often other ecological factors that determine whether the association will occur between parasite and host. The ecological factors that determine the distribution of parasite hosts therefore also determine the potential distribution of the parasites themselves.

Another association occurs between epiphytes and their supporting hosts. An epiphyte is a plant that grows upon another but is not organically connected to its host. Examples of epiphytes from the plant world include ferns, bromeliads and orchids. The geographical distribution of epiphytes, as for parasites, is therefore influenced by the availability of habitat on suitable host organisms as well as the other ecological factors that determine or limit its own distribution (Table 5.4).

Some organisms exhibit a symbiotic relationship, which means that there is an association between species whereby the metabolic dependence of the associates is mutual. That association differs from the parasite–host relationship in that the benefits are derived by each species and so a symbiont will not cause the death of its associated organism. As with parasites and epiphytes, the geographical distribution of a symbiont will be determined

Fig. 5.9. The red-flowered mistletoe (*Peraxilla tetrapetala*) – a hemi-parasite endemic to New Zealand whose host species include *Nothofagus* sp. (Photograph kindly provided by John Smith-Dodsworth.)

by the ecological factors that determine its own survival and that of its associate.

Plant–animal associations can have implications in studies of biogeography. Some insects for example are wholly dependent (obligate feeders) on certain plant species and their distribution is therefore determined in part by the distribution of the species that they require as food. In New Zealand this is true of the speargrass weevil (*Lyperobius huttonii*), a nationally endangered animal that lives and feeds exclusively on the speargrass plant (*Aciphylla squarrosa*). The geographical distribution of animals such as the speargrass weevil is determined to some extent by the distribution of its host and food source.

Some birds are associated with a fauna of insects, such as lice, that live permanently on the bird. That form of animal–animal association partly determines the geographical distribution of the insects, particularly if the insect can live only on certain species of animal. Understanding associations between organisms can therefore be valuable in studies of ecological biogeography to help to explain some species distributions.

5.7 Applications

Information about the ecological factors that influence or determine the geographical distribution patterns of individuals, populations or communities of species and other taxa may be applied in various ways. Some of those applications include (1) choice of environmental indicator species (2) conservation management (including survey for threatened species, species recovery programmes and choice of areas worthy of protection to conserve biological diversity) and (3) pest management.

5.7.1 Indicators

Every plant and animal requires certain conditions for their own growth and survival at any particular place. The presence of some species or groups of species, therefore, may be used to 'indicate' the state of the environment in which they occur. The presence of some plants and animals can be used to indicate certain conditions such as the quality of water, local climate and soil. Some plant species have been used as indicators in the location of many minerals including gold and copper. In England, the National Rivers Authority use the presence of certain aquatic invertebrates such as mayflies (the insect group Ephemeroptera) as indicators of certain levels of water quality. The aquatic larvae of some species of mayfly are very intolerant of organic enrichment so the presence or absence of mayflies is a useful biological indicator.

Lichens have been used widely as indicators of air quality. They are an outstandingly successful group of symbiotic organisms that exploit a wide range of habitats throughout the world. Climate, topography, and habitat management may all affect lichen distributions. However lichens are also a practical indicator of air quality owing to the sensitivity of some species to sulphur dioxide (SO_2). For example, in England and Wales the presence of the lichen *Pleurococcus viridis*, when confined to the base of trees with moderately acidic bark, was found to be an indicator of a mean winter atmospheric concentration of SO_2 of over 170 micrograms per cubic metre.

Some caution is required when using indicator species because throughout a species range there can be some variation in the environmental tolerances of individuals or populations of species. Some species commonly associated with clean water may be able in some regions to survive a certain degree of pollution or may persist for a while after a pollution event. Those species may not be useful as indicators of pollution. Furthermore, over time, some species may adapt and become tolerant of the pollutants that first caused them to disappear. Species that recolonise places from which pollution had originally caused their disappearance may not be suitable environmental indicators. There are factors other than the presence of pollutants that can influence whether a species will occur at a particular place and they must be considered when one is interpreting the presence or absence of indicator species.

Another application of indicators is in the selection of areas worthy of protection to conserve biological diversity. Some species or groups of species are believed to be indicative of a particular habitat, vegetation association or lack of disturbance. The presence of some species has been used to indicate the existence of pristine unmodified wildlife habitats which justify top priority for conservation of biological diversity. In the UK Peterken (1981) has identified plant species such as *Luzula sylvatica, Carex pendula* and *Galium odoratum* as having a strong affinity for ancient natural woodlands in central Lincolnshire. In that region the presence of those species may be used as an indicator of ancient woodland. Some species may also be indicative of habitats that are particularly species rich or are suitable for rare or threatened species.

5.7.2 Conservation management

The fact that some parts of the world have more species than others has been used in environmental protection initiatives. Some areas that are especially species rich have become the focus of conservation efforts. For example, there are many centres of plant diversity throughout the world including the Yucatán peninsula in Central America, and the tropical rain forests of Brazil (see Section 7.6 for criteria for selection of protected areas). Many of these areas have been identified by the World Conservation Union in its Centres of Plant Diversity project (Box 5.1) and some are shown in Fig. 5.10.

Studies of the worldwide geographical distribution of endemic birds has also been used in environmental protection initiatives. The International Council for Bird Preservation (now Birdlife International) undertook a study to identify Endemic Bird Areas (ICBP, 1992). Those are areas within which birds with restricted ranges occur. A bird with a restricted range is one whose breeding range is below 50 000 square kilometres. A total of 221 Endemic Bird Areas were identified, within which 2484 species occur (that is 95 per cent of all the restricted-range birds). Figure 5.11 shows the worldwide distribution of the world's Endemic Bird Areas. Such a map identifies the

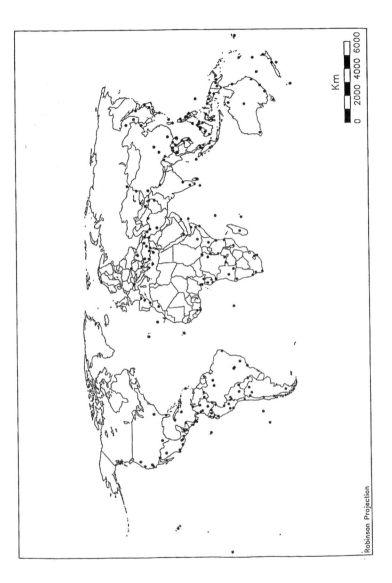

Km

0 2000 4000 6000

Robinson Projection

Fig. 5.10. The global distribution of centres of plant diversity (data compiled as part of the IUCN's Plant Conservation Programme). (Taken from *Global Biodiversity: Status of the Earth's Living Resources*, 1992. A report compiled by the World Conservation Monitoring Centre and edited by B. Groombridge. Chapman & Hall. Published with kind permission of the World Conservation Monitoring Centre.)

Box 5.1. The Centres of Plant Diversity Project of the World Conservation Union

The objectives of the international Centres of Plant Diversity project were:

To identify areas which if conserved would safeguard the greatest number of plant species.

To document the many benefits, economic, and scientific, that conservation of those areas would bring.

To develop a strategy for the conservation of centres of plant diversity worldwide.

Centres of plant diversity were:

Botanically rich areas that could be defined geographically.

A geographically defined area with high species diversity or endemism.

A vegetation type of exceptionally high diversity.

Approximately 250 areas and regions were selected worldwide for consideration as centres of plant diversity (see Fig. 5.10). Information was then compiled about the geography, vegetation, flora, useful plants, other values, threats and conservation for each of those places using standardised data sheets.

The first phase of that project is now completed and several volumes of a directory of centres of plant diversity have been published. Some examples of centres of plant diversity include the Amazon rain forests, the Atlantic forests of Brazil and the Atlas mountains of Africa.

---

places in the world where bird conservation initiatives should be focused if they are to maximise the protection of birds with restricted geographical ranges which are often of conservation concern in the places where they occur.

Information about the ecological factors that determine the geographical distribution of species may be valuable when decisions are being made about whether to move individuals of a species to a new location or to an old location where that species used to occur. There are various reasons why people may want to move a species. First, for conservation purposes a species may be translocated to a more secure location or back to a place from which it has previously become extinct. Secondly, a species may be moved for economic reasons to be used at the new place as an economic resource. Thirdly, a species may be moved to act as a biocontrol agent to limit another species (such as a pest plant or animal).

Understanding the factors that determine species distributions may be used to determine what species should or should not be introduced as biocontrol agents, as economic resources or as a conservation measure. That may mean some organisms may not be considered appropriate for introduction to a region if the introduction is unlikely to succeed or will potentially impact detrimentally on the native plant and animal life. In England it was concluded from the data from the Common Bird Census of the British Trust for Ornithology that the distribution of the red-legged partridge (*Alectoris rufa*) was determined to a large extent by annual rainfall. The adopted range of the game bird coincided with areas that receive an annual rainfall of less than 89 centimetres. While there are other factors influencing the survival of the bird, such as lower precipitation in the breeding season affecting chick survival, information about the correlation between bird survival and annual rainfall can be used to optimise efforts to introduce the bird to new areas. In fact, attempts to establish the bird in areas of high rainfall have largely failed. Figure 5.12 shows the distributions of the red-legged partridge in the UK, together with areas of rainfall.

The same is true for introductions of threatened species to a new site (or reintroduction to an old site). An assessment of the suitability of a species introduction can be made on the basis of information about its ecological requirements. Such an assessment is important if endangered plants and animals are to be placed at new sites so that the success of the introduction can be ensured. Biogeography can therefore be applied in the development of species recovery programmes for plants and animals whose existence in the wild is threatened and whose translocation to new sites is necessary.

5.7.3 Pest management

An understanding of the ecological factors that determine the distribution of species may also be used in pest management. Pest species with an ability to expand their range in order to occupy new large areas may be identified as priorities for pest control ahead of species that already occupy their entire potential range. Factors that determine the geographical distribution of pest species (such as vectors of communicable diseases) may also be used for preventing or halting their spread (see Chapter 9). The response to an invasion of such a pest species may be improved if information is available about factors that influence its distribution.

Pest plants that are limited by low light intensities may be eradicated or controlled by growing species that will outcompete and shade the pest species.

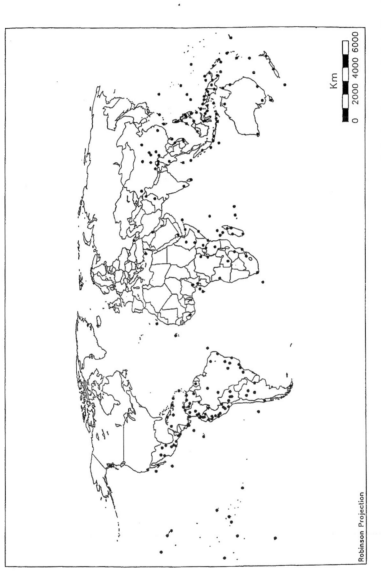

Fig. 5.11. The global distribution of Endemic Bird Areas (data compiled by Birdlife International). (Taken from *Global Biodiversity: Status of the Earth's Living Resources*, 1992. A report compiled by the World Conservation Monitoring Centre and edited by B. Groombridge. Chapman & Hall. Published with kind permission of the World Conservation Monitoring Centre.)

Robinson Projection

Km

0   2000 4000 6000

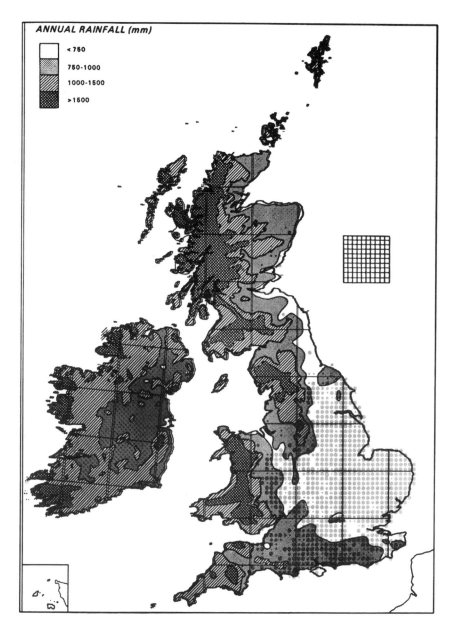

Fig. 5.12. The geographical distribution (indicated by the grey shaded area) of the red-legged partridge (*Alectoris rufa*) in the UK coincident with areas of rainfall. (From *The Atlas of Breeding Birds*, 1976. Compiled by J. T. R. Sharrock and published with kind permission of the British Trust for Ornithology.)

Limiting factors may also be used when evaluating whether a certain organism should be introduced to a region as a biocontrol agent. Information about the ecological factors that influence species distributions, therefore, has a role to play in the development of pest control strategies.

The distribution of some organisms (such as parasites) is determined largely by the distribution of other species (the parasite host). That information can be applied by field biologists when carrying out targeted field surveys for parasite species (such as mistletoes). Field surveys may be undertaken only in areas where mistletoe hosts occur and so prevent effort wasted in surveying elsewhere.

References

ICBP (1992). *Putting Biodiversity on the Map: Priority Areas for Global Conservation.* Cambridge, International Council for Bird Preservation.

Peterken, G. F. (1981). *Woodland Conservation and Management.* London and New York, Chapman & Hall.

6

Biogeographical information: collection, retrieval and application

6.1 Introduction

On a windswept moor in the south of England (not unlike one in *The Hound of the Baskervilles* by Sir Arthur Conan Doyle, the creator of Sherlock Holmes), a biogeographer has carefully edged out onto the unstable and dangerous surface of a bog (Fig. 6.1). A long, thin tube is pushed metres deep into the ground and withdrawn with great effort. From that tube is extracted a cylinder of mud. What has this dangerous mission onto the unstable surface of a bog to do with biogeography? The contents in the core of mud extracted from the swamp may tell a story. From that material it may be possible to use information which helps to establish a picture of the past abundance and distribution of plant communities, in particular the changing picture of tree species that has evolved over many years. The biogeographer was a specialist in palaeoecology (the study of the ecology of fossil biological communities) and he was looking for peat with deposits of pollen. Over the ages pollen from trees has fallen on the swamp and slowly layers of pollen have become embedded in the mud sediments. We have access to many kinds of material which have often helped scientists to study the geographical distribution of biota that lived in the far distant past.

From where do we glean information about the geographical distribution of biota? There are two sources: the organisms themselves (or their remains or evidence of their behaviour) and information already collected by someone else (see Table 6.1). In this chapter we review briefly some methods used for the collection and analysis of data on the spatial and temporal distribution of biota. We do not discuss the detailed aspects of sampling equipment, of which there

Fig. 6.1. Evidence from the past. *Above*: Coring a bog in the New Forest, England. *Below*: A freshly exposed core of sphagnum peat. (Photographs kindly provided by Keith Barber.)

is a huge variety for air, sea and land. Rather we comment briefly on the usefulness of data collection and analysis.

6.2 Collecting information direct from biota
6.2.1 Data from the past

The fossil record in geological terms is very tiny and fragmented, but nevertheless it does provide us with a rich picture of where some organisms were at particular times of geological history. But the fossils not only give us glimpses of life as it was in the far distant past, they also give indications of their past behaviour. Footprints of dinosaurs have often been discovered; not just the occasional footprint but several tracks preserved in the rocks have revealed stories about the animals' geographical distribution and behaviour.

Sediments in some lakes have accumulated deposits of diatoms, or at least their remains. Diatoms are microscopic, unicellular or colonial algae (phylum Chrysophyta) and many deposit silica in their cell walls. The many different species are distinguished from each other by the shape, structure and architecture of the silicified walls. Different species of diatoms live in different conditions and deposits of diatoms in lake sediments have been used to build up a picture not only of past patterns of distribution and abundance of algae but also of the past lake environment.

Archaeological sites have often proved to be a rich source of biological material that has told us something about the biogeography of plants and animals from distant ages. Ancient human remains, notably the astonishing discovery in 1991 of the so-called 'Iceman' in Europe has added intrigue to our knowledge of land uses of about 5000 years ago. The seeds, pollen and fragments of vegetation found with the Iceman have all been used to establish a picture of the landscape in the late Stone Age.

Pollen analysis (see Section 6.1) extracted from peat deposits in bogs (Fig. 6.1) has been used to reconstruct the nature and extent of human impacts in many parts of the world. A picture of the impact of the Romans on the landscape and biological communities in the north of England has emerged from pollen studies and a certain amount of 'palaeo-hypothesising'.

6.2.2 Data from the present

Imagine you are a biogeographer standing on top of a hill overlooking a woodland or overlooking a rocky coastline. You are asking yourself 'What's there, where is it and when does it occur?' You are thinking about how to obtain information on the organisms in the area, where they occur and at what times of the, say, season or year. Direct observation, or a written or photographic record together with information of environmental conditions at the time, is the most simple method of obtaining data. What you see and record could be the organism itself or the noise it makes or the product of its behaviour. You could be using a bat detector to record unseen bats or you might have noticed the footprints of a mammal.

From the top of that hill, you will not be able to see all the organisms and therefore you will need to explore the area and take a closer look. Data on the biota could be collected in a random manner by walking in the area, or a more systematic approach could be adopted. By dividing the area into spatial units, using quadrats of varying sizes, it is possible systematically to record the organisms. For example, a standard method of surveying ground dwelling plants is to use quadrats of about 1 metre square. These are placed randomly throughout the area and the species composition in each quadrat is recorded. Different-sized quadrats could be used depending on the scale of the survey being undertaken.

A quadrat, because of its known area, provides a way of quantifying the data in terms of abundance. Other sampling methods such as using a net to collect marine organisms in a rock pool can provide information only on what is there and not what abundance there is of it.

Some organisms will not be visible to you and some may occur at times when you are not there. For invertebrates there are many and varied methods of sampling. These include light traps for night-flying insects, pitfall traps for ground-dwelling invertebrates and suction traps for aerial invertebrates. Some traps are coloured, coated with sticky material or even given a scent or pheromone in a bid to attract organisms to the trap.

Remote sampling has reached its ultimate in the form of modern techniques for remote sensing; that is, using a sensor or camera to record images of the ground. Satellites are commonly used today as platforms for remote sensing devices for surveying land use patterns and vegetation communities. They are also used for tracking organisms wearing radio transmitters and for modern global position systems. Geographical Information Systems or GIS have now brought advanced technological methods to the aid of biogeographers (see

Section 6.7).

The range of movement of individual animals can be tracked using radio transmitters. Individuals can also be identified by natural features or marking and by the addition of visual tags or radioactive tags. For many decades, fish, seals and game and other birds have been ringed or tagged as part of studies of the movement of those animals and the locations inhabited by them. Even butterflies have not escaped having ink on their wings as part of biogeographical studies. All methods used to observe, record or mark an organism have their limitations and it is important in analysis of data not only to recognise these limitations but also to quantify them where possible. The presence of an observer may be enough to change the behaviour of an animal, the use of a pitfall trap may be biased towards certain individuals and, when an organism is marked, that may alter its behaviour. Having the taxonomic expertise accurately to identify the organism is an essential prerequisite. Confirmation of the identification may be necessary at times and that is a good reason for ensuring rigorous and careful recording.

Surveys and sampling may require permission of landowners; to enter and take photographs in an area of high conservation, cultural or landscape importance may require a licence. Licences may have to be obtained to capture or even approach some animals. Above all, there is a responsibility to be undertaken by all who survey and sample biota. There is a responsibility to ensure that least damage and least harm is caused to the environment and of course to the organisms.

Much of the basic sampling and surveying undertaken for biogeographical studies is at the species level. However, there are occasions when it is important to know the distribution of a family or an order. Surveys being undertaken as a basis for establishment of protected areas may require data not only on species but also on other taxonomic levels. This is to ensure that there is conservation of the greatest taxonomic diversity.

Not surprisingly, most groups of organisms have not been the subject of biogeographical surveys. This has come about simply because the groups considered to be more attractive or more easy to see have usually been the target of these studies. Consequently there is not only a lack of expertise about the vast majority of taxa but there is very little information about their distribution. Birds, butterflies, large mammals and flowering plants have been the subjects of most biogeographical studies. As a justification, some would say that you need only survey birds. Those surveys and any subsequent establishment of protected areas will conserve other taxa. So why bother with earwigs and mosses or any other group?

Table 6.1. *Sources of biogeographical information. Existing information about geographical distributions of plants, animals and other organisms is available from various sources*

A. Verbal and unwritten

B. Record (written, mapped, specimens)
Herbariums
Museums and collections
Natural History Society records
Illustrations: paintings (ancient and modern) and photographs
Books: atlases, travel books
Diaries
Student theses and dissertations
Scientific reports
Species recovery plans

C. Digital
Computer databases
Internet and World Wide Web (WWW)

6.3 Information retrieval

The geographical distribution of some taxa may be determined without a survey or without using any of the techniques described earlier. That is because a large amount of information already exists about the distribution of certain taxa. Existing sources of information can be verbal or recorded (Table 6.1). Some indigenous knowledge includes verbal accounts of distributions of biota handed down by word of mouth. Recorded information can be in three forms: written, illustrative and digital.

6.3.1 Herbaria

A herbarium is a place where information is stored about plant biogeography. Collections in herbariums may be biased towards easily collected taxa, so biogeographers can expect to find more information about these plants in the herbarium. The information is held in the form of 'vouchers'. Most vouchers consist of a dried specimen of a species of plant attached to a sheet of card (Fig. 6.2). Other material is preserved. The voucher will generally have the

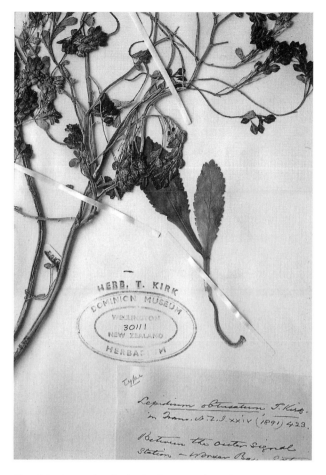

Fig. 6.2. Example of a herbarium voucher, depicting a voucher specimen of *Lepidium obtusatum* – a coastal herb of New Zealand that is now believed to be extinct. (Photograph kindly provided by Jeremy Rolfe.)

following information written on it: the name of the plant family and species that is attached to the card, where and when the plant was found, the name of the person or persons who collected the plant material, and the name of the person who identified the species. Some vouchers may also have recorded on them details of the habitat or plant association from which the specimen was collected. The voucher may be plant material that is dried or preserved by other means, such as dried seed.

The amount of information recorded with specimens varies and depends on who collected the specimen, who prepared the specimen and often in what year the specimen was prepared. Many vouchers from the last century tend to record only a few details of where and when a plant was collected (see Fig. 6.2). The value of data on vouchers may be limited because there is not enough information to determine where and when the specimen was collected (see also Section 6.4). Historical records often did not mention accurate reference points such as grid references for maps, although these are in use today. Some herbarium vouchers are several hundreds of years old and modern maps may not have been available when the specimen was found. Many specimens were collected at a time when it was not realised that detailed information (about where and when a species was found) would be of use in studies of the species distribution.

6.3.2 Museums and collections

Museums are sources of information about the geographical distribution of plants, animals and other organisms. The information accompanying the specimens is typically very detailed (Fig. 6.3), with notes on the classification, who collected the material and where it was collected. Many of the limitations with existing information stored in a herbarium apply to information from museum collections and collections of fauna. Collections are less likely to have information about the distributions of species that are difficult to find or collect, or that occur in remote places. Museum staff, as part of their work, appraise the accuracy of identifications of species, and visitors to the museum also check the accuracy of records.

6.3.3 Society records and biogeographical journals

The publication of many natural history groups, learned societies and academic institutions are sources of biogeographical information. Those publications range from the long-established journals of the Linnean Society (the Society was established in 1788 and produced its first journal in 1791), to more recent arrivals such as the *Newsletter of the New Zealand Botanical Society* (1985 to present). There are various journals that contain biogeographical information and some of those have an editorial policy that encourages biogeographical reports. Some examples of journals of that kind include: the *Journal of Biogeography* (Blackwell Science), the journal of the Linnean Society (Academic Press); *Global Ecology* and *Biogeography Letters* (Blackwell Science) and *Biodiversity Letters* (Blackwell Science).

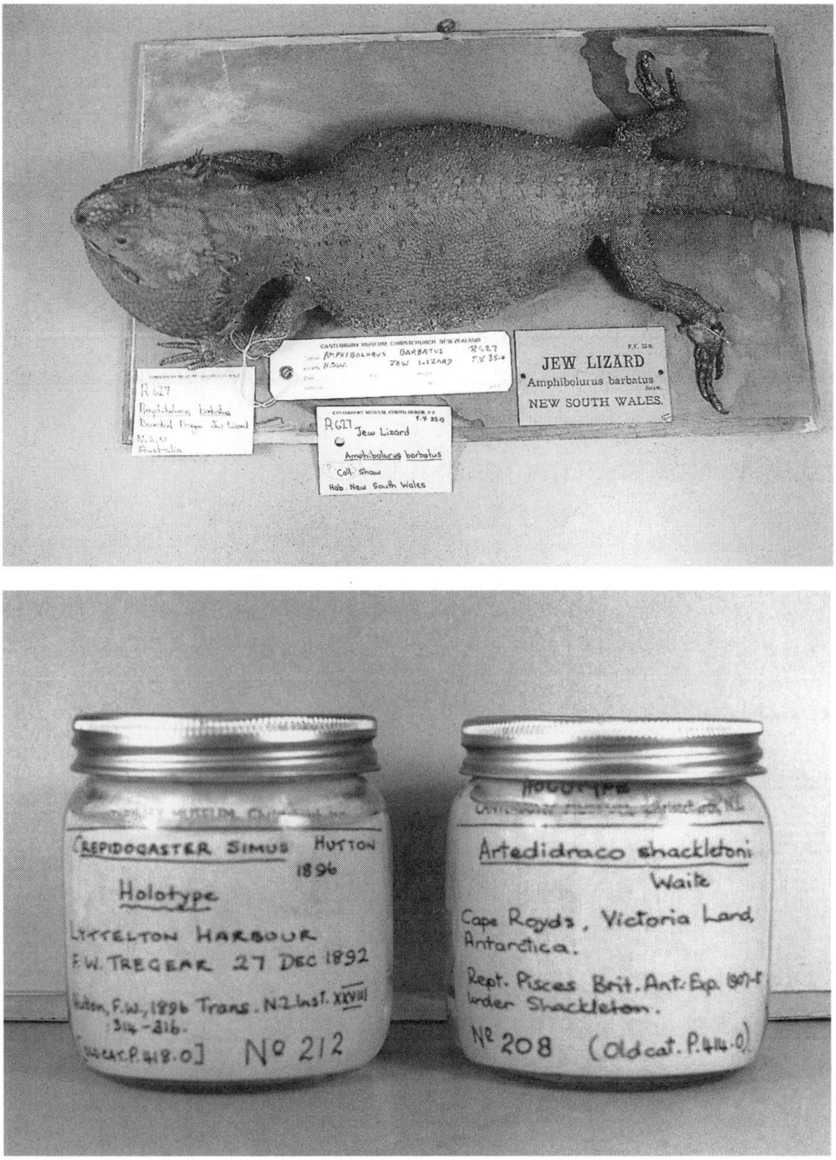

Fig. 6.3. Examples of museum tags. The tags or labels on specimens held in museums contain variable biogeographical information. *Above*: four tags for an old specimen of the lizard *Ampibolurus barbatus* in which the locality is simply given as New South Wales (far more detailed locality information is required today). Below, historically, taxonomically and biogeographically important specimens. These are holotypes or the type specimen used by the original author at the time of publication about the species. One of these is from the British Antarctic Expedition of 1907–1909. (Photographs taken by Ian F. Spellerberg, with permission of the Canterbury Museum.)

Many natural history societies specialise in particular groups of organisms and a large amount of information can be collected about where and when species have been found from researching papers held by those societies in newsletters, bulletins and society journals. For example, in the UK the Royal Society for the Protection of Birds (RSPB) promotes the conservation of birds and their habitats. In New Zealand the Wellington Botanical Society promotes the study and conservation of New Zealand's native plants. Other natural history societies such as the Dorset Natural History and Archaeological Society in the UK collect information only about a particular region. In addition, members of those societies may be able to provide information about species distributions based on their own observations.

6.3.4 Illustrations: paintings and photographs

There are some other unlikely sources of existing information about the geographical distribution of biota. Artwork can provide a record of species distributions. For example, cave drawings have provided us with a documented record that some species occurred at a particular period in time and location. Paintings or sketches by artists can be a source of information about the distribution of some species. Likewise, photographs can be a source of information about species distribution. With both paintings and photographs identification is not always easy and one must be wary of distribution information derived from such illustrations. Some artists may have embellished their pictures such that a biogeographer cannot rely on the accuracy of their paintings. The imagination of some artists, in particular early illustrators, led to rather strange depictions of creatures that appear almost mythical. Sometimes artists transferred features of one species to another, thereby creating images of species that never existed; occasionally features of some species were exaggerated or entirely ignored for the purpose of the illustration. In some mediaeval manuscripts peacocks are drawn without crests, finches are drawn with long beaks or long tails and occasionally the bustle-like secondaries of the crane were transferred to other birds such as storks.

6.3.5 Books and diaries

Information already exists about the global distribution of some species. For example, in world atlases of species there are maps that illustrate the geographical distribution. That information is often based on the recorded presence of a species in a particular country or region. Maps of this kind are limited because they can give a false impression of species distribution. Species are rarely found throughout an entire country or an entire ocean. The geographical distribution of a taxon in any country is normally localised, depending upon the availability of suitable habitat.

Some travel books or travel journals can be sources of information about the distribution of species. One of the most famous examples is the diary of Charles Darwin from his voyage on *HMS Beagle* (Barlow, 1945). Darwin spent five years recording his daily activities aboard ship and his observations provide a wealth of information about species and their distributions. The travel diaries of Sir Peter Scott from his journeys to Australia, Africa and Antarctica (Scott, 1983) comprise another example of written works containing information about species distributions. Ships' log books may also provide information about the distribution of marine mammals or sea birds. For example, whaling ship records have been used to map the geographical location of several whale species beside the Antarctic ice shelf. Information in travel books may have limitations because it is sometimes not clear where the records were made or when. Also, the accuracy of the records depends on the expertise of the writer in identifying species correctly.

Another source of information is the diaries of naturalists. For example, Gilbert White (1720–1793) recorded his meticulous observations of the natural history of Selbourne (Box 6.1).

6.3.6 Scientific reports and journals

Scientific reports and journals contain information about the geographical distribution of taxa. The distribution of many kinds of taxa (bees, birds, insects, fish, vascular plants) have been published in specialised atlases. Some are devoted entirely to the geographical distribution of one species. For example, in Australia an atlas has been developed by the Australian Koala Foundation that describes the distribution of the koala (*Phascolarctos cinereus*) and its habitat. Other atlases have been published that describe the geographical distribution of a number of species. For example BirdLife International have published books that describe the distribution of many birds, including those that are rare and endangered and those that are migratory. In Australia, as in many other countries, various atlases have been published for various groups of species such as birds, mangrove species, elapid snakes and the 75 species of Australian banksia plants.

Species monographs are scientific publications about a particular species.

Box 6.1. This is an entry from Gilbert White's *Diary* or *Calendar of Flora* dated 1766. The diary is a wonderful example of natural history recording with its detailed observations of events (phenology) and it is also an important piece of biogeographical information. Gilbert White was the Curate of Selbourne in the south of England. (This entry is from *A Nature Calendar by Gilbert White* edited by Wilfred Mark Webb, F. L. S., and published in 1911 by the Selbourne Society, London. Published with kind permission of the Selbourne Society)

1766. *15.*

April 20. The Cuckow, cuculus, returns, & sings.

White bryony, bryonia alba, shoots.

Greater stichwort, caryophyllus holosteus arvensis glaber flore majore, blossoms.

Privet, ligustrum, in full leaf.

Round-podded, lunar violet, vul: Honesty, lunaria siliculis subrotundis, blows.

21. Young Ravens, corvi, are fledge.

Young Geese.

The berries of Ivy, Hedera, ripen: it flowers in October; & is the last flower the bees, & flies feed on.

Pile-wort, Chelidonium minus, every where in high bloom.

Quince-tree, malus cydonia, leafes.

Dwarf elder, or Dane-weed, or wall-wort, sambucus humilis, seu ebulus, emerges.

22. Garden-strawberry, fragaria, buds for bloom.

Black-beetle appears on evenings.

Wild black-cherry-tree cerasus sylvestris fructu nigro, begins to blow.

The Cypress, cupressus, blows.

Publications of that kind often contain information about distribution. Wildlife monographs (published by the US Wildlife Society), such as the field study by Richard Clark of the short-eared owl (*Asio flammeus*) in North America, is one example (Clark, 1975). In that case a map is provided of the geographical distribution of areas of permanent residence of the owl.

6.3.7 Species recovery plans

Recovery plans are publications that describe what actions are needed to protect a particular species, perpetuate good habitat for that species, or restore the habitat. The plans are generally prepared for species that are of special conservation concern and whose presence in a particular country is threatened. Species recovery plans have been written in many countries throughout the world including the USA, the UK, Australia and New Zealand. Species of special concern for which plans are developed invariably have a restricted geographical distribution that makes them most vulnerable to disturbances. Included in most species recovery plans is a map that describes the geographical distribution of the species for which the plan was prepared. Figure 6.4 is a map of the distribution of the orange-bellied parrot (*Neophema chrysogaster*), one of Australia's most endangered birds, and was taken from a conservation statement (a version of a species recovery plan prepared by the Royal Australasian Ornithologists Union).

6.3.8 Computer databases that store existing information

There are many agencies and individuals that store existing information about the geographical distribution of species but only one international agency, the World Conservation Monitoring Centre. This is based in Cambridge and Kew Gardens, England, and was established to provide research, information and technical services so that decisions affecting the conservation and sustainable use of biological resources may be based on the best available scientific information. The Centre can provide information on the conservation and sustainable use of species, in particular those species of conservation concern. That is achieved in part through the use of information about the geographical distribution of some species.

A biological diversity map library has been developed by the WCMC; it has information on the distribution of many of taxa. One major database managed by the WCMC map library is the plants database, which holds

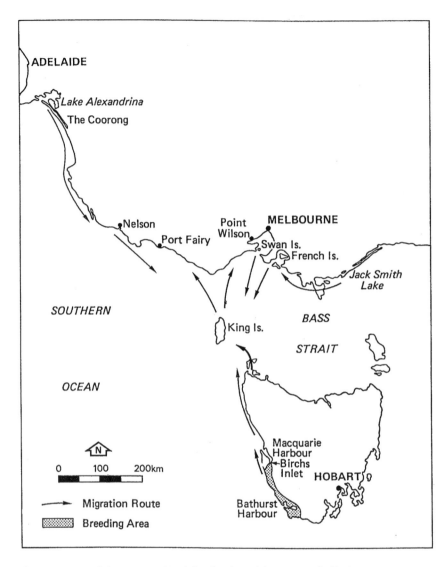

Fig. 6.4. Map of the geographical distribution of the orange-bellied parrot (*Neophema chrysogaster*) in Australia. (Taken from a Royal Australian Ornithologists Union Conservation statement prepared by Brown, P., Wilson, R., Loyn, R., Murray, N., and Lane, B., 1985. RAOU Report No. 14. Melbourne. Copyright the Royal Australian Ornithologists Union.)

computerised data (in a Geographic Information System – see Section 6.7) on over 80 000 plant taxa. The biological diversity map library also holds digitised maps of several biogeographical classifications, including maps of the biogeographical provinces of the world (Udvardy, 1975) and the Ecoregions Map of the continents (Bailey, 1989).

Information about the geographical distribution of some species is available for certain regions of the world from the databases set up by government agencies. In the USA, for example, the Montana Natural Heritage Program (MTNHP) has been established. State-wide distribution maps are available for species of special concern, such as threatened, endangered or sensitive plants, animals or plant communities. MTNHP has acknowledged that the distribution maps that have been produced are not definitive; that is, there are still areas of Montana that have not been adequately surveyed for particular species. The maps so far are limited, therefore, because they do not identify areas that have not been surveyed.

Some natural history societies store information on their own databases about where particular species have been found. For example, the Wildfowl and Wetlands Trust (established in 1946 in the UK) along with the British Trust for Ornithology manage a scheme to monitor waterfowl population numbers and trends in those numbers. This wetland bird survey aims to provide a scientific basis for the conservation of waterfowl in the UK and as a result a large amount of information is stored about the geographical distribution of a great many species of wetland birds such as divers, grebes, swans and ducks. The New Zealand Native Orchid Group have a database on the distribution of all species of orchid that are indigenous to the New Zealand botanical region (St George *et al.*, 1996).

6.3.10 Internet and the World Wide Web

Existing information about species distributions is available through the Internet on the World Wide Web. One example of how the World Wide Web can be used to obtain information about species distributions is from Australia. At a national level the Australian Environmental Resources Information Network (ERIN) is available on the World Wide Web. That network provides information on the national distribution of many species of plant and animal. At present, the focus is on terrestrial species and in particular the major land cover trees. The spatial information used in ERIN to generate the maps has been taken from the Australian Surveying and Land Information Group

(AUSLIG). That system allows for searches to be made for information about the national distribution of certain species. There are limitations with the system. For example, it is not clear whether the species distributions that are described are 'real'. That means there is no information about areas that have not been surveyed for particular species. It is not clear, therefore, whether the presented map is an accurate representation of the species actual distribution. Also in Australasia, the Tasmanian Parks and Wildlife Service has provided a set of maps on the World Wide Web that illustrate the known and predicted distributions of wildlife for Tasmania.

6.4 Limitations of existing sources of information

Some existing information can be difficult to understand or the Latin names of some species may have changed. To find existing distribution information for some species you have to search using the species' other names (synonyms). For example, the jersey fern (*Anogramma leptophylla*), a small annual fern found in temperate regions throughout the world from the British Isles to New Zealand, has also been called *Polypodium leptophylla* and *Grammitis leptophylla*.

Sources of information may be inaccurate and so may require verification. For example, the species may have been identified incorrectly, or the time and place may have been recorded inaccurately. Therefore, existing records are more valuable to a biogeographer if they can be verified. Verification can take many forms depending on the species in question and the technique used to collect the information. Plant occurrences may be confirmed if a herbarium voucher exists (see Fig. 6.2). The existence of a berbarium voucher is verification that a particular plant was found at a particular time and place. That voucher may have been identified incorrectly. Without the voucher it would be impossible to say whether the collector had identified the species correctly. For rare species and/or species subject to collection by collectors, some institutions have a policy of not releasing information about where that species was located. Some institutions modify the information to make it impossible to use the information to relocate the species. In this way the institution maintains data security for some species. Other methods of verification may be used for other species. Photographic evidence is usually sufficient for most animals. Invertebrates are often collected to verify sightings. For marine animals sound-recording equipment such as hydrophones or remote cameras may be used to provide proof that the species in question was located.

There can be a problem if materials held by museums or the data recorded are hoaxes. One of the most famous examples of a deliberate hoax was that of the jaw and skull fragments of 'Piltdown Man', which were found between 1908 and 1913 in an old gravel bed in Sussex, England, by Mr Charles Dawson, an amateur geologist. The material was subsequently lodged at the British Museum. In the 1950s detailed examination of the material demonstrated that it had been faked. There can also sometimes be hoax material in the literature. In 1975 Peter Scott and Robert Rines published an article about naming the Loch Ness monster and suggested a scientific name for that species (*Nessiteras rhombopteryx*). Was the suggested name for the monster a hoax (rearrange the letters of the latin species name and see what you think)?

Places referred to on existing information may have changed name. The name used to describe the place where the species was observed may be a local name that is not used on maps or there may be several places with the same name; it may be difficult, therefore, to determine where the species was found. For example, in New Zealand there are many records of plants having been found at 'Ocean Beach'. However, there are many places in New Zealand named 'Ocean Beach' and it may be impossible to determine where exactly the species was found.

Existing information about species distributions can be scattered widely. Information about the distribution of species in one country is sometimes stored in herbariums, museums or in the publications of another country. It can take a considerable amount of time to collect that information and therefore prove expensive.

6.5 How 'real' is the distribution?

The information about the distribution of some species may not be 'real' or accurate. This may be because of incomplete field data about the taxon in question. For example, some taxa have not been observed or collected from the whole of their range, because they are difficult to find (cryptic) or occur in inaccessible areas, or because they are difficult to observe or collect. For example, nocturnal species that live in tropical rain forests are not recorded or collected very often but that does not mean that they are not abundant and not widely distributed throughout their habitat. Distribution maps actually show the distribution of the people collecting the information. To describe accurately the geographical distribution of a species, more than one source of information should be used. It is unlikely that a species distribution determined solely from herbarium vouchers or museum collections will be 'real'.

Information about the distribution of mobile species can be misleading. Some species do not occupy their total range or required habitat all the time. Some species occupy different ranges or habitats at different stages in their life cycle. Some species shift their range over the course of time. Some species are 'vagrant', and may occupy places only temporarily, so their occurrence at a particular area may be an exception rather than the rule. For example, many species of migratory birds wander widely across the globe. The presence of a species does not always mean that the species is found there throughout its life cycle. In some cases birds have been known to stray outside what would be called their 'normal' range. In addition, mobile species may not occupy their required range all the time. Species ranges are also in a continual state of flux and are expanding and contracting in response to abiotic or biotic factors such as environmental changes or competition for resources.

6.6 How to present information about a species distribution

The distribution of a species can be illustrated in a variety of ways for a variety of uses. Some types of map include dot distribution maps, grid-based maps, hybrid dot distribution and range maps, and range maps (see Fig. 6.5–6.8). Maps can also be drawn to a number of different scales. For example, an atlas may be drawn using a small scale whereas a map showing the distribution of a species in a small woodland may use a much larger scale. What map type should be used depends very much on what the map is to be used for.

Dot distribution maps are used to illustrate that a species was present at a particular place. Figure 6.5 shows the distribution of the endangered divaricating shrub *Teucridium parvifolium* in the lower part of North Island, New Zealand. Dot maps are particularly valuable for less mobile species that are unlikely to move after the record was made. However, dot maps illustrate only where a species occurs or has occurred in the past. Dot maps do not show where the species does not occur. Blank areas on dot maps do not indicate that a species is absent but they indicate that no records have been made of the species at those sites. Dot maps can be modified to identify areas that were surveyed for a species but where that species was not found.

Dot maps are limited if they are created using historical information. It is not always useful to know that a species was recorded at a certain place many years ago if human disturbances or environmental change (for example, plant succession) has led to its disappearance from that site. Historical information

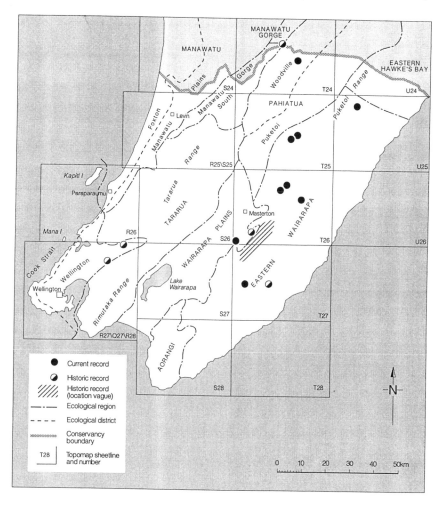

Fig. 6.5. A dot map of the distribution of the divaricating shrub *Teucridium parvifolium* for the lower North Island, New Zealand. The dots indicate that populations of that plant have been recorded at those places. (Taken from Townsend, A., Beadel, S. M., Sawyer, J. W. D., de Lange, P. J. and Shaw, W. B., 1998, Plants of National Conservation Concern in the Wellington Conservancy. Department of Conservation, Wellington, New Zealand.)

about the distribution of highly mobile species such as birds may also mislead people when that information is used to generate dot maps.

A grid-based map is generated using information about the presence or absence of a species in a geographically defined unit. That unit can be political (country or state) or can be generated by dividing a defined area into cells of equal size to generate a grid (see Fig. 6.6). Again a grid-based map does not always show which grid squares have been surveyed for a particular species but merely where that species has been found. Kirkpatrick *et al.* (1980) mapped the geographical distribution of threatened plants in one area of Tasmania and on those maps showed not only the grid squares within which the plants were found but also which squares were surveyed but where the plants were not recorded. Figure 6.6 is an example of a grid-based map from that survey and shows the geographical distribution of grid squares in which the plant *Cyathodes pendulosa* was found.

A range map illustrates the range of a species based on where that species has been recorded. However, the localities at which the species was found are not shown on a range map. Figure 6.7 shows the range areas in which larvae of the common European eel (*Anguilla vulgaris*) were found.

A hybrid dot distribution and range map shows the locations where a species has been recorded but also encloses these dots within a boundary that is intended to indicate the range of the species. Figure 6.8 is an example of a hybrid dot and range map for *Tamiasciurus hudsonicus loquax*.

Both range maps and hybrid dot and range maps have limitations. Unsuitable habitat for a species is included within the distribution range shown on the map. Although the range is shown, a species can be expected to be found in suitable habitat only within this range. One should be wary of the generalised view of a species range that may be shown on some range maps.

6.7 Some modern methods for mapping species distributions

There have been some recent developments in how to map the distribution of a species. Most of the advancements have been in the methods for generating maps and the techniques used to interpret maps. The organisation of spatial information has been improved with the advent of Geographical Information Systems (GIS). A GIS is a computing system for the storage, display and analysis of digitally stored spatial data. GIS are useful in the study of the geographical distribution of species in space and time because they can be used to store and access large amounts of data about species distributions. GIS can be used to generate species distribution maps relatively quickly and can be used to analyse several spatial data sets at the same time, including species distributions (see Section 2.5). A GIS can be used to overlay maps of species distributions and maps that show other information such as soil type and

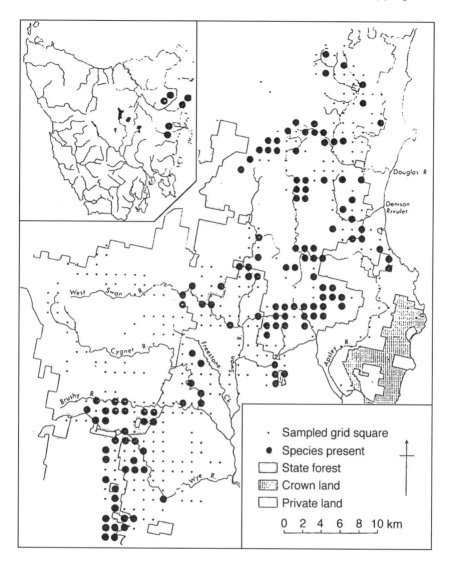

Fig. Fig. 6.6. A grid-based map of the distribution of *Cyathodes pendulosa* in east coast Tasmania. The large black dots indicate that the species was observed in the area defined by the grid square. (Taken from Kirkpatrick, J. B., Brown, M. J. and Moscal, A., 1980, *Threatened Plants of the Tasmanian Central East Coast*, Tasmanian Conservation Trust Inc. Published with kind permission of J. Kirkpatrick.)

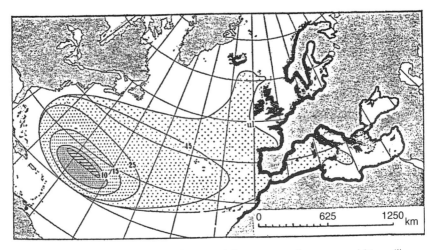

Fig. 6.7. A range map of the distribution of the common European eel (*Anguilla vulgaris*) during its various stages of development. (Taken from Hardy, A., 1956, *The Open Sea, Its Natural History*: Part 1: *The World of Plankton*, Collins. Copyright A. Hardy.)

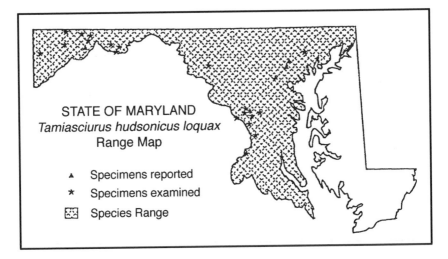

Fig. 6.8. A hybrid dot distribution and range map of the distribution of *Tamiasciurus hudsonicus loquax*. (Taken from the wildlife monograph by Scott, J. M., Davis, F., Csuti, B. *et al.*, 1993, *Gap analysis: A Geographic Approach to Protection of Biological Diversity*. Wildlife Monographs, **123**. Supplement to the *Journal of Wildlife Management*, **57**(1). Published with kind permission of the Wildlife Society who hold the copyright.)

climate. In that way a GIS can be an aid to environmental modelling (see also Section 9.9).

Computer databases are now widely used to store information about species distributions. However, not all people in all countries have access to computers. Where computers are used it can be beneficial to standardise the way information is stored. If information about where and when species have been recorded is stored in a standardised way then it will be possible to collate that information more easily and share information. One example of computer database standardisation is the International Transfer Format used for records held by botanic gardens for the storage of information about what plants are grown by the garden and from where they were obtained. There is some information that, if standardised when it is recorded and stored, would make biogeography much easier. This includes the name of the species, the time and place the species was found or recorded, and the name of the person who took the record and identified the species.

6.8 Open access to information

A problem that is shared with all methods for storing information about species distributions is that of information security. In particular computer databases and the World Wide Web are making information ever more accessible, but is that a problem? There are advantages and disadvantages in making information about species distributions openly available. In some cases the more people that can access the information the better. For example, if planners have access to that information they may avoid the development of sites where rare species of plants and animals occur. Ecologists may use information in the design of ecological restoration projects. Land owners also may use information about species distributions in the design of farm management plans to identify areas most suitable for soil and water conservation. Scientists may be able to use the information that is available to provide ecological explanations for observed distribution patterns.

However, access to information about the distribution of some species may have disadvantages. For example, information about the distribution of rare or threatened species may be used by people wanting to collect those species and as a result populations may become extinct. Populations of some species may be destroyed simply as a result of people visiting the site where the species occur, particularly those species that survive in fragile environments.

6.9 How to maintain up-to-date biogeographical data

There is no such thing as a definitive distribution map for a species and it would be impractical to maintain up-to-date maps for all species all of the time. One must be aware of the need for up-to-date biogeographical information and to recognise the limitations of old data. Therefore, records on the distribution of species must be reviewed from time to time as they can quickly become out of date, but how frequently should that review take place? On what basis should some species distribution maps be updated more frequently than others? In different parts of the world organisations are continually updating biogeographical data sets. However, limited resources often make it impossible to do that for all species. Some factors that influence how frequently biogeographical data sets should be updated for a particular species include the degree to which the species is extinction prone, the extent to which the species distribution fluctuates in space and time, the current or potential threat to the habitat of the species, and the degree to which humans utilise the species for their own needs.

References

Bailey, R. G. (1989). Ecoregions map of the continents. *Environmental Conservation*, **16**, (4).

Barlow, N. (ed.) (1945). *Charles Darwin and the Voyage of the Beagle*. London, Pilot Press.

Clark, R. J. (1975). A field study of the short-eared owl *Asio flammeus* (Pontoppidan) in North America. *Wildlife Monography 47*.

Kirkpatrick, J. B., Brown, M. J. & Moscal, A. (1980). *Threatened Plants of the Tasmanian Central East Coast*. Tasmanian Conservation Trust Inc.

Scott, P. (1983). *Travel Diaries of a Naturalist*, ed. Miranda Weston-Smith. London, Collins.

St George, I., Irwin, B. & Hatch, D. (1996). *Field Guide to the New Zealand Orchids*. Wellington, New Zealand Native Orchid Group.

Udvardy, M. D. F. (1975). *Biogeographical Provinces of the World*. Morges, Switzerland, IUCN Occasional Publication.

7

Habitat fragmentation

7.1 Introduction

In western Brazil, in the district of Rhondonia adjoining Bolivia, two children have walked to the end of a newly made dirt road overlooking a landscape which extends to the horizon. Instead of vast forests stretching as far as the eye can see, the view before them consists of small forest fragments amidst smouldering remains of much larger forests. Thousands of kilometres away in southern England two more children have found a small fragment of isolated woodland in the mist of an agricultural landscape. They have found a woodland haven to play in but that small area of woodland (Fig. 7.1) is but a trace reminder of the larger expanses of woodlands which once existed throughout England and much of Europe. The environments in which both sets of children find themselves have been affected by human induced processes which have brought about the reduction in area and the fragmentation of biological communities and the habitats of species and populations in those communities.

Over time, biological communities and habitats are transient and naturally change in area, shape and spatial arrangement in the landscape. Therefore, in most landscapes there is some level of spatial heterogeneity or patchiness of the biological communities. Most species have indeed evolved to live in several patchy environments. There are very few examples of species where there is naturally only a single population in one place.

The impact of humans and the growth of land used for agriculture, forestry, cities and roads has resulted in a rapid increase throughout the world of habitat modification, loss and fragmentation. Biological communities

Fig. 7.1. Woodland fragments in a European rural landscape.

everywhere are changing and becoming smaller and smaller, sometimes leading to the geographical isolation of plant and animal populations. This process of habitat reduction and fragmentation change, sometimes referred to as insularisation, poses the greatest threat to the many levels of biological diversity. The other major threats come from direct exploitation, pollution and from the effects of introduced, invasive species.

The fragments of biological communities and habitats which remain have often been likened to islands (island habitats) because the fragments appear to be discrete entities and may be surrounded by conditions which make dispersal between fragments difficult for some forms of plants and animals. It is because the process of insularisation poses the greatest threat to nature that it is not surprising that many biogeographers, ecologists and conservationists have researched the effects of habitat fragmentation by way of direct observation and via theories. In this chapter we briefly consider the theory of metapopulations, the role of island biogeographical theories in conservation, the ecology of some kinds of habitat fragments, conservation strategies for habitat fragments, and finally methods of analysis used in research on the effects of habitat fragmentation.

7.2 Biogeography of fragmented habitats

The distribution of many species and other levels of taxonomic organisation have been fragmented by movements of continents, sea level changes, periods of glaciation and changing climate (see Section 4.0 for examples and Section 5.5 for the paramo). Consequently some species naturally have a geographical distribution made up of fragmented and sometimes isolated populations. Fragmentation has also been caused by humans. The impact of humans has been such that many biological communities are now no longer intact, are greatly reduced in size and are often no more than scattered fragments.

The scale of fragmentation can be considered in terms of the extent and the time scale. Spatial scales may range from large geographical areas to merely hundreds of metres. Typically, fragmentation of forests is described as the remaining fragments within areas of some hundreds of hectares. At a smaller scale, fragmentation may occur within a few hundred square metres, such as in some grasslands where the original plant communities exist as fragmented clumps or tussocks. In terms of time scales, forests in temperate regions have long been subjected to large-scale fragmentation. In the past few decades and particularly the past few years, there has been a rapid increase in the rate of forest fragmentation in tropical areas. This has come about largely because of logging and forest clearance for agriculture. Often forested areas have been burnt indiscriminately. In 1997, fires destroyed vast areas of forest in Indonesia and the smoke from those fires lay over much of Southeast Asia for weeks, causing widespread disruption to human life and health. The scale of the loss of the forest wildlife communities has been huge and perhaps one of the worst environmental disasters in recent years.

For species, we would generally expect the immediate effects of fragmentation to result in extinctions, caused largely by loss of habitats and changes in microclimate. Long-term effects would probably include colonisation by edge species and later the effects of those edge species on the organisms which had previously dominated the interior of the communities.

But what effect does fragmentation have on the populations and individuals of a species? What processes are likely to lead to extinction? What are the best conservation and restoration options? These are just some of the questions prompted by study of fragmentation of communities and habitats.

Such questions have been researched by direct observation, by recording movements of individuals between habitat fragments, and there have also been some theories put forward to try to help us to understand the processes involved. Examples of the latter include the theory of metapopulations and various theories about island biogeography.

7.2.1 Metapopulation theory

A metapopulation is a group of populations that are possibly but not necessarily interconnected. It is a theory that deals with individuals of species and the rate or incidence at which individuals move (usually infrequently) from one place (a population) to another, typically crossing habitat types which are not suitable for their feeding and breeding activities, and often with substantial risk of failing to locate another suitable habitat patch in which to settle. The processes of colonisation and extinction are central to the concept of metapopulations and it is a reminder of the MacArthur and Wilson Equilibrium Theory of island biogeography. However, the latter is based on the rates of colonisation and extinction of several species and the former on individual species (see Section 3.5). Metapopulation theory has become the paradigm for single-species populations (Harrison, 1994).

There is another important difference between these theories: the source of colonisation for islands is the mainland, which does not suffer from extinction and it is only on the islands where there is turnover. In metapopulations, the source of the colonists is the existing set of populations which is in a constant state of turnover and which may itself become extinct.

The theory of metapopulations has its origins in the work of some of the early ecologists (see Section 1.4). The term was used in 1970 by Richard Levins to refer to a population of populations which go extinct locally and recolonise. From then on the theory was used commonly in the conservation biology literature to describe a population of populations and as a basis for modelling the dynamics of metapopulations. Populations in an ecological sense are groups of individuals of the same species living in a certain area. Metapopulations are groups of interacting populations (of different sizes in different-quality habitats) with a finite lifetime (expected time to extinction). The concept of metapopulation is therefore closely linked with the processes of population turnover (see Section 3.6), extinction and the establishment of new populations. The study of metapopulations is essentially the study of interacting populations: some become extinct; some colonise new and vacant patches.

For conservation, the metapopulation theory provides a framework for understanding threats faced by species in fragmented habitats (Harrison, 1994). It gives emphasis to the need to maintain a balance between extinction and colonisation. It is not surprising therefore that there has been much research on how best to manage fragmented habitats (sometimes as networks of patches) to ensure that dispersal is facilitated between populations and that there is a flow of genes between populations. (See Section 7.4 for designation of nature reserves and Chapter 8 on linear landscape features). The integration of such genetic and biogeographical aspects has been termed population vulnerability (or viability) analysis (PVA).

Although the theory may have little value as a generalisation in conservation biology, it does have a value as a basis for testing ideas and for analysing processes. Furthermore, although it seems that it has been difficult to find species whose ecology and biogeography fit the classic metapopulation theory, there are some species which appear to exist as networks of populations. For example in Belgium, Neve *et al.* (1996) describe a metapopulation structure for a vulnerable butterfly species, *Proclassiana eunomia*. Their research seems to show that this butterfly has nested metapopulation structure, with movements between habitat patches. The authors suggested that a network of suitable habitat patches is necessary for the long-term conservation of the species.

7.2.2 Island biogeographical theories and conservation

Protected areas (of which there are many types) provide us with a major way of conserving nature. These protected areas may be owned or leased by government or conservation agencies, or be owned privately. No matter who owns them there is always a cost in terms of acquisition and management of the area. There are limited resources available for purchasing and management of protected areas and therefore we should ask how best that money can be spent. If there are options, is it best to have as large an area as possible, or is it best to have many small protected areas or a few large ones? These and other questions have led to much discussion about the possible application of island biogeographical theories to habitat fragments.

Fragmented habitats may appear to be 'islands' in the landscape. Indeed a small fragment of a woodland in a 'sea' of agriculture does seem rather like an island (see Fig. 7.1). We could assume therefore that the biogeography of that habitat fragment would be similar to or the same as a real island. We might also consider that large habitats have more species (of a certain taxonomic group) than small habitats. As early as 1913, research on the numbers of species on mountain peaks indicated a species–area relationship. At the time it was suggested that 'a possible law appears justified; the smaller the disconnected area of a given zone ... the fewer the types which are persistent therein'. Since that time there have been numerous reports of species–area curves for fragmented habitats, ranging from birds in woodlands to primates in Amazon rain forests. It was this kind of thinking which led to some ideas being put forward about the shape and location of potential designated areas for nature conservation.

In 1975, Jared Diamond, a notable field ecologist, published a paper in *Biological Conservation*, with the title 'The island dilemma: lessons of modern biogeographical studies for the design of natural reserves'. In that article, he suggested a set of design principles to minimise extinction rates in nature reserves. Those principles included the following:

> A large reserve can hold more species at equilibrium than a small reserve.
> A reserve located close to other reserves can hold more species than a remote reserve.
> A round reserve will hold more species than an elongated one.

Five years later, The World Conservation Strategy (WCS) (published by the International Union for the Conservation of Nature, with cooperation from the World Wide Fund for Nature and the United Nations Environment Programme and in collaboration with the United Nations) addressed the issue of biogeography of protected areas. This first world conservation strategy was a 'milestone document' and it was also both prestigious and influential. Many nations throughout the world prepared national responses to the WCS and those responses have led to many important conservation initiatives.

One small section of the WCS dealt with suggestions about the geometric principles for nature reserves based on Diamond's paper (Fig. 7.2). Like other publications before it, here was an attempt to relate some aspects of island biogeography to the selection and design of nature reserves. It was suggested that, where there is a choice, it is best to have a large single compact area for a nature reserve. If a few smaller areas is all that is available then it is best if they are close together and somehow linked. The worst case seems to be a single, small, sausage-shaped nature reserve. Can these suggestions be supported? Even more important, are we asking the right questions? In the following sections we describe some aspects of the biogeography of habitat fragments and draw conclusions about the relevance of island biogeography to conservation strategies for fragmented habitats.

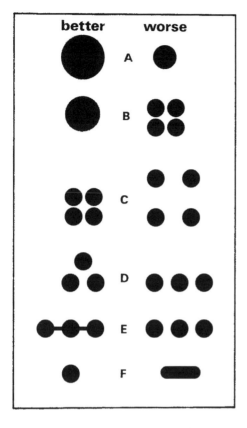

Fig. 7.2. This figure is from the World Conservation Strategy of 1980 and description was as follows: 'Suggested geometric principles, derived from island biogeographic studies, for the design of nature reserves. In each of the six cases labelled A to F, species extinction rates will be lower for the reserve design on the left.' (From the World Conservation Strategy, 1980, IUCN, UNEP, WWF.)

7.3 Heathland islands or heathland fragments?

In some regions of western Europe, heathlands have long been part of the landscape. Heathland communities are dominated by low-growing shrubs and tend to be plant species poor. Much of the expanse of heathlands which existed for some hundreds of years has now disappeared, leaving behind only a few small fragments. Although these heathlands are poor in plant species, they are unique and considered to be endangered biological communities. There are many protected species of invertebrates, reptiles, amphibians and birds that are largely dependent on the remaining heathlands for survival.

In England, the loss, fragmentation and isolation of heathlands has been as serious as has been the loss, fragmentation and isolation of some tropical forests in other parts of the world. Agriculture and forestry have been the main impacts. Some of these remaining fragments have been used as 'outdoor laboratories' where the impacts of fragmentation on biological communities have been researched. In 1979 the Institute for Terrestrial Ecology in England was contracted by the Nature Conservancy Council (now English Nature) to look into the effects of heathland fragmentation on the invertebrate communities and to make recommendations for the conservation of the remaining heathlands.

The field work was undertaken over one year: samples of beetles and spiders were collected from 22 heathland fragments (representing the full range of fragments from 0.1 ha to 500 ha) every two months during that year. A huge collection of material was assembled and a vast amount of data was obtained. During the intensive surveys, some additional interesting discoveries were made. For example, a rare spider (Fig. 7.3) the ladybird spider (*Eresus niger*), which had not been recorded for 70 years, was found on one of the heathland fragments. It was unlikely that this discovery would have been made but for the intensive field surveys. This demonstrates the need to have more extensive biological databases supported by extensive field surveys.

At the time of the research, there had been much said in the biogeographical literature about species–area curves (for both island and habitat fragments). There was, not surprisingly, some expectation that the results from these heathland surveys would show that there were species–area relationships between the numbers of spider and beetle species and the area of the heathland: the larger the area, the greater should be the number of species.

As it turned out there was a surprise for everyone involved. At first few could believe the results (Fig. 7.4). No simple relationship was found between area size and the abundance of invertebrate species. For the beetles, the number of species tended to decrease with increasing area and for the spiders (158 species) there was no clear relationship. For a subset of those spiders (60 species) that was considered to comprise typical heathland species, there was a weak positive relationship between number of species and size of area.

So what was the explanation? Why the variation and why no clear species–area relationships? The heathland fragments seemed like 'islands' and of course heathland 'island' fauna must have a source; it must come from somewhere and that source would not only be the heathlands themselves. In this case the source for the fauna found on heathland fragments was both the heathlands and the surrounding land which was used for many purposes such as agriculture and forestry. Clearly it was nonsense to think of the heathland

Fig. 7.3 A male of the very rare ladybird spider (*Eresus niger*). This species was once thought to have become extinct in Britain early in the 20th century, but during extensive heathland surveys in the late 1970s it was found on some fragments of heathland in southern England. The abdomen of the male is scarlet with large black spots. (Photograph kindly provided by Nigel Webb, Furzebrook Research Station, Institute of Terrestrial Ecology, England.)

fragments as islands and equally clear was that the surrounding land would have an effect on the heathland beetles and spiders. But what was the extent of that effect? To investigate this was the next step in the research.

Previous examination of the heathland fragments of Dorset had shown that the area of the fragments and the extent to which they are surrounded by other heathland only partly explained variations in observed species richness and species composition. A subsequent step in the research was to investigate the species richness in terms of the vegetation types surrounding the heathland fragments. Invertebrates were sampled on the 22 heathlands and the extent of nine vegetation types adjacent to the fragments was analysed. The results showed that, where structurally more diverse vegetation was adjacent to a piece of heathland, there was a tendency for invertebrate species richness to be greater. Few changes in invertebrate species richness were found where the heathland was surrounded by vegetation of low structural diversity (Webb *et al.*, 1984).

Undoubtedly, heathland fragments are part of a patchy landscape. But the fragments are not islands and it is nonsense to consider them as such. What

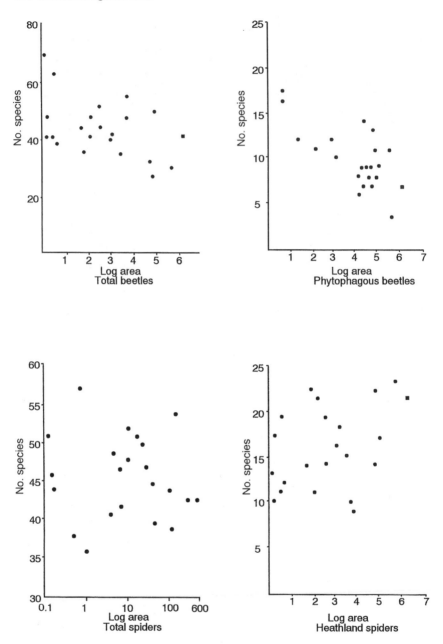

Fig. 7.4. Analysis of area of heathland fragments and the species richness of spiders and species richness of beetles. (Data from Hopkins, P. J., 1983, Invertebrate diversity and composition on fragmented heathland. Ph.D. thesis, University of Southampton. Reproduced with kind permission of Peter Hopkins.)

advice could be given to the conservation authorities who had asked for recommendations for the conservation of the remaining heathlands? This would depend on the conservation objective. What is the protected area of heathland for? If it is to conserve heathland plant communities or heathland species that are not very mobile, then it would be best to have as large an area as possible and possibly include a 'buffer zone' around the protected area. On the other hand, for invertebrates that are mobile and can exploit both the heathlands and habitats outside the heathlands it would be better to conserve a series of heathland fragments.

If the objective was to conserve populations of some of the endangered reptile species, then many of the heathland fragments that have been invaded by non-heathland plants and have been subjected to physical disturbance would be best in terms of providing the necessary ecological resources. Furthermore, the future of the reptiles would be more secure if conserved as a series of populations, to minimise the impacts of fires. If one piece of heathland was burnt and the reptile habitat and reptiles in it were lost (as does happen), other heathlands untouched by fire and with their own reptile populations would ensure the survival of the species.

7.4 What is the optimal area for a woodland nature reserve for birds?

The relationship between woodland area and the number of species of birds has been researched many times by biogeographers throughout the world. Much of that research has been led by an expectation that there will be clear species–area relationships. There are, in general, many good examples of log–log species–area curves in which it can be seen that larger areas support more species than do smaller areas.

In many countries such as Britain, where land is under great pressure from many demands, it might seem useful to look at woodland area and birds species richness as a basis for drawing up guidelines for nature reserves. Is there an optimum area of woodland for the conservation of birds and is there a minimum size below which the woodland is hardly worth conserving?

The British Trust for Ornithology (BTO) has for many years undertaken a census of birds in woodlands and other habitats. That organisation now has one of the most important biological databases which has important implications not only for conservation of birds but also for monitoring the state of the environment. As a basis for a class exercise and courtesy of the BTO, we have used an example of a small set of the information from the BTO records. For the purposes of this exercise, students are provided with a table with a list of woodlands, the area of those woodlands, the number of species of birds recorded in those woodlands (average figure for several years) and the number of species holding territories in the woodlands (Table 7.1). Against a background of information about species–area curves, the students are asked the question 'What is the optimum area for a woodland nature reserve for birds in England?'

When the data are plotted graphically, students are often disappointed with the result because there is no single, clear species area curve! But discussion soon turns to the question of what causes variation in species numbers in different-sized woodland fragments. There are, in general, many good examples of log–log species–area curves, but such observations almost certainly hide intricate interrelationships. Many other factors may play important roles.

7.5 What was the question again?

There has been much discussion about the desired area, shape and design of nature reserves. In particular much of the discussion has been about area size. It was probably the extensive research on the biogeography of birds and subsequent suggestions for reserve design which were the main incentives for the wide-ranging debate on the criteria for selecting large reserves. It is true that many (perhaps hundreds) of studies have shown logarithmic relationships between size of habitats and species richness. However, despite the common belief that reserves should be as large as possible, there were many biogeographers who were saying that, given a choice, a better alternative to a single large reserve would be several small reserves. Small reserves may act as 'stepping stones' and facilitate dispersion. One small reserve amongst many others might survive when disaster struck. Thus the acrimonious 'Sloss' debate (Single, Large or Several Small) was launched and it did little for the integrity of and respect for conservation biology.

Much depends on what question is asked. The most simple has been 'What is the relationship between areas and the number of species?', a question that assumes area will determine the number of species. It is difficult to show cause and effect between area and species richness and indeed the effects of habitat fragmentation are complex and variable. Earlier research on this topic tended to be directed towards analysis of apparent effects of area, isolation and vegetation structure. Later research has tended to be directed towards the

Table 7.1. *A list of woodland areas in England, the number of bird species in each and the number of birds with territories*

Entry No.	Area ha.	Spp.	Spp. T.	Entry No.	Area ha.	Spp.	Spp. T.	Entry No.	Area ha.	Spp.	Spp. T.
1	1.6	26	18	30	14.2	31	24	59	28.4	32	28
2	4.8	27	19	31	14.4	38	31	60	28.7	44	31
3	5.0	29	15	32	15.3	39	29	61	29.1	33	32
4	5.6	16	14	33	15.2	41	31	62	29.6	39	31
5	6.1	25	20	34	15.4	42	37	63	30.4	42	33
6	6.5	30	25	35	15.4	33	25	64	34.4	57	41
7	6.6	25	19	36	15.6	35	29	65	36.3	34	24
8	6.7	39	29	37	15.8	34	27	66	39.4	43	35
9	8.1	29	28	38	16.1	41	31	67	42.5	48	34
10	8.1	25	21	39	16.2	44	42	68	42.9	50	37
11	8.5	38	31	40	16.6	35	30	69	45	48	39
12	8.5	27	23	41	16.7	34	27	70	45	31	27
13	9.2	29	28	42	17.4	35	30	71	46.7	50	45
14	10	38	27	43	17.4	33	24	72	47	42	31
15	10.1	37	27	44	18	47	36	73	48.8	50	36
16	10	37	27	45	18.2	41	31	74	54	49	32
17	11.1	38	28	46	18.2	43	32	75	67.9	45	39
18	11.1	32	29	47	18.2	50	36	76	68	39	36
19	11.3	30	23	48	18.4	39	35	77	72.9	42	30
20	11.5	36	28	49	20.7	42	33	78	85.8	37	32
21	12.1	36	27	50	21.5	33	23	79	111.3	41	29
22	12.8	35	29	51	21.6	30	24	80	116.6	43	39
23	12.9	28	23	52	22	50	42	81	132	54	40
24	13.4	33	25	53	22	39	32	82	162	47	31
25	13.4	48	39	54	23.7	55	38	83	193	40	39
26	13.5	34	28	55	24	38	32	84	220	40	39
27	13.6	41	37	56	25.2	35	32	85	245	47	41
28	13.8	38	34	57	25.3	36	25				
29	13.8	46	40	58	26.6	38	31				

Data kindly provided by the British Trust for Ornithology and obtained from woodlands in the south of England. From Spellerberg, I. & Hardes, X., 1992, *Biological Conservation*, Cambridge University Press.
Spp, total number of species; Spp.T, number of species holding territories. (Mean values for various woodlands).

nature of population structure and movement of individuals in a matrix of habitats. The effects of habitat fragmentation are complex and it is unlikely that there will ever be any universal rules which can be learnt from this research and applied to conservation biology.

In the exercise using BTO bird data, we have encouraged students to think not only about these questions but also about the questions that might be asked by any conservation agency. The data we use do not name the species themselves, just the numbers of different species. There may be some particular species which, for whatever reason, still survive in a small woodland. Choosing a large woodland on the basis of the misapplication of species–area theory would indeed be a mistake. Why do birds use woodlands? Some use woodland as breeding area but others may use it as a place for feeding, roosting or even for overwintering. Different species may be using the woodland at different times of the year.

Large reserves may not always be appropriate for the particular conservation objective. We therefore believe that there has been no need to invoke the use of theories or observations from island biogeographical studies in conservation biology. Identifying what is a habitat fragment or patch is also questionable. Where does the patch start and where does it end? What we see as habitat fragments or patches in Fig. 7.1 is the result of our subjective assessment. The boundary between the woodland and agricultural land may indeed, for some species, be the spatial limits within which resources are suitable. That boundary or 'ecotone' may also be, for some species, a barrier preventing dispersal. For other species such as large mammals or birds, a patch for them may include woodland habitats in an agricultural setting and their perception of a patch may be quite different from what we see and have quite different boundaries.

7.6 Selecting areas for protection

There are hundreds of different named types of protected areas for the conservation of nature, many of which are designated and managed according to specific kinds of legislation. For example there are nature reserves, Sites of Special Scientific Interest (SSSIs), national parks, wildlife parks, wildlife sanctuaries and biosphere reserves. There are also many international and national agencies throughout the world involved in designating areas (land, fresh water and sea) for the conservation of nature, landscapes and culture. For example, UNESCO has established a series of Biosphere Reserves within the framework of the Man and the Biosphere Programme (MAB). Here is an attempt to address conservation issues alongside that of sustainable use of resources (Box 7.1).

One important question is 'Where should nature reserves be?' Equally important is 'What number and location of a matrix of reserves would conserve the maximum number of species?' These are all very important questions for conservation. If island biogeographical theories cannot help, how do you go about selecting areas of land, fresh water and sea which will make the most effective contribution to conservation? Very often there is no choice because most protected areas for nature are in locations that have no agricultural, urban, mineral or other immediate value.

Nevertheless there are occasions where choices have to be made about which areas to protect and where. There are opportunities to ensure that biogeographical research can be applied to ensure the most effective conservation of certain taxa. One of the earliest attempts to apply specific criteria to the selection of national nature reserves was that developed by Derek Ratcliffe in Britain in the 1970s. Ten criteria provided the basis for this method and since that time these criteria have commonly been used in different combinations for selecting areas for conservation. The first criterion was area size, not necessarily because it was thought more species would occur on larger areas but because it was recognised that there might be a minimum area necessary for the conservation of some species. Other criteria included diversity, naturalness, rarity, fragility and typicalness. Detailed explanations can be found in many texts including that of Spellerberg (1991).

An alternative approach is to identify where there are the greatest levels of species richness or endemism for any particular taxonomic group (see also Table 3.2 and Fig. 5.10). Having identified those localities, it seems sensible to locate nature reserves there so as to conserve as much diversity or as many levels of endemism as possible. Some international agencies have adopted this approach: for example, the International Council for Bird Preservation (ICBP) initiated a Biological Diversity Project in 1988 with the objective of providing information for identification of such key areas for conservation.

The use of protected areas has been the main method for the conservation of nature. But there are limitations and there may be gaps. For example, do the existing protected areas conserve as much nature as possible. Would a more systematic selection of reserve locations lead to a greater conservation effort? Different matrices and numbers of reserves might achieve different levels of conservation. One example of this is the iterative approach (meaning stated or checked repeatedly). This is based on the assumption that there have to be priorities for designating sites but the problem remains which proportion of potential protected areas (20 per cent, 40 per cent, 90 per cent) would

Box 7.1. Biosphere reserves. UNESCO, within the framework of the Man and the Biosphere Programme, has prompted the establishment of biosphere reserves around the world. (Reprinted with kind permission of UNESCO Publishing)

What is a Biosphere Reserve

Biosphere Reserves are areas of terrestrial and coastal ecosystems which are internationally recognized within the framework of UNESCO's Man and the Biosphere (MAB) Programme. Collectively, they constitute a World Network. They are nominated by national governments and must meet a minimal set of criteria and adhere to a minimal set of conditions before being admitted into the World Network. Each Biosphere Reserve is intended to fulfill three basic functions, which are complementary and mutually reinforcing:

- a conservation function – to ensure the conservation of landscapes, ecosystems, species and genetic variation;
- a development function – to promote, at the local level, economic development which is culturally, socially and ecologically sustainable;
- a logistic function – to provide support for research, monitoring, education and information exchange related to local, national and global issues of conservation and development.

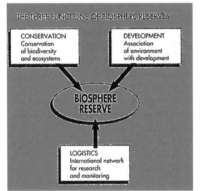

Each Biosphere Reserve is intended to fulfill three basic functions which are complementary and mutually reinforcing: conservation, development, and logistic support for research and education.

Individual Biosphere Reserves remain under the jurisdiction of the countries in which they are situated. Some countries have enacted legislation specifically to establish Biosphere Reserves. However, in many cases, advantage is taken of the existence of areas already protected under national law to establish Biosphere reserves. While their configuration depends on local situations, Biosphere Reserves include a core area, a buffer zone and a transition area. A number of Biosphere Reserves simultaneously encompass areas protected under other systems (such as national parks or nature reserves) and other internationally recognized sites (such as World Heritage or Ramsar wetland sites.)

© UNESCO 1996

Why World Network?

Although Biosphere Reserves have very different geographical, economic and cultural contexts, they do have a common interest to seek concrete solutions to reconcile the conservation of biodiversity with the sustainable use of natural resources, for the benefit of local people. The World Network fosters exchanges amongst Biosphere Reserves – for example, research results, management methods or experience in resolving specific issues. It facilitates co-operative activities and specialist training. Co-operation can take the form of exchanges of information material, articles in the *International Bulletin on Biosphere Reserves*, co-operative projects, twinning arrangements, swapping personnel, organizing visits, or correspondence by electronic mail. The World Network is supported by regional or sub-regional networks such as in East Asia, or thematic networks, for example for studying biodiversity. The creation of new sub-networks such as these is encouraged. Progressively, it is intended to link all Biosphere Reserves through modern communication channels.

The World Network of Biosphere Reserves facilitates sharing of information and the transfer of technology to tackle specific problems, for example, computerized Geographic Information Systems (GIS) to improve the management of Biosphere Reserves. Photo: UNESCO-ITC training courses on the use of GIS in Wuyishan Biosphere Reserve, China. © Han Qunli/UNESCO.

The World Network is governed by a Statutory Framework formally adopted by the General Conference of UNESCO at its 28th session. This Statutory Framework defines the functioning of the World Network and foresees a periodic review of Biosphere Reserves. Activities of the World Network are guided by the 'Seville Strategy for Biosphere Reserves' drawn up at the International Conference on Biosphere Reserves fully participate at the Network and these guiding documents will help to improve their functioning in the forthcoming years.

result in the best conservation effort? This iterative approach has been the basis of much research in Australia.

Protected areas do play an important role in conservation but are there gaps? How do you check to see whether protected areas have omitted something of importance? This is where GAP analysis has an important role to play (see Section 2.5).

7.7 Biogeographical analysis of habitat fragmentation

Our environment is continuously changing and humans are causing most of the degradation that is occurring. What is the rate of that degradation and how best can we monitor it? Measures of the state of various components of the environment are not new, for example descriptions of weather and climate, elements in the soil, pollution in air, and water and land use. Often, ecological indicators and indices are used to report the level and extent of these variables. Measuring the state of the environment has now started to include measures of amounts of different kinds of vegetation cover and also changes in habitat fragmentation. There has been a growing interest in ecological indices for use in monitoring forest fragmentation. In Argentina, for example, Diana De Pietri has developed an ecological indicator of landscape degradation (De Pietri, 1995). The index uses three attributes: the fraction (percentage) of area of forest and grassland, the area/perimeter of vegetation, and a measure of complexity of the edge of each fragment. This kind of index can be used as a quick way to identify the state of forest fragmentation but would require a more detailed analysis before any management recommendations could be made.

Sadly, fragmented habitats are all too common and they present many conservation challenges. Conservation of the species and communities in fragmented habitats and the restoration of fragmented habitats should be based on biogeographical and ecological research. There are many biogeographical questions to be addressed (and more than just those associated with species–area curves!). Imagine a landscape containing fragments of 'natural' vegetation (with different kinds of vegetation formation, different sizes of area, and different shapes and positions of surrounding areas) and imagine that there is a research programme on the biogeography and conservation of the flowering plants of those woodland fragments – the aim being to design conservation management strategies. Biogeographical questions could be directed towards the relative variety of vegetation formations, species composition (indigenous and introduced), species richness and species diversity of the flowering plants in the different woodlands. For example, are there any differences in these species characteristics between woodlands, or do woodlands below a certain area size have species compositions different from those of large woodlands? Does the surrounding environment of each habitat fragment prevent dispersal and does distance from larger woodlands seem to have any effect on species composition, etc.?

As a first step, there are a number of interesting ways of analysing the variety of vegetation patterns, the spatial distribution of habitat fragments and also the shapes and other characteristics of individual habitat fragments. The contribution that any one of the many variables makes to species richness and species composition could usefully be explored as part of the research underlying the development of conservation strategies to help to minimize or overcome the effects of habitat fragmentation.

For some groups of organisms, more species will be supported where there is a greater variety of structure and vegetation formations. The variety in the latter (or variety of any biogeographical variable) can be analysed using one of many of the indices of diversity. These indices are often used to analyse species diversity in terms of the equitability or evenness of the abundance of the species. High diversity is where the abundance of different species is the same. A low diversity index would occur when one species is very abundant and others are represented by only a few individuals (Spellerberg, 1991). One index of diversity is the Simpson Index:

$$D = \sum P_i^2$$

where P_i is the relative abundance of the ith species or, in this case, the vegetation formation.

Imagine three kinds of vegetation formation, A, B and C where A is represented by 47 units, B is represented by 4 units and C is represented by 22 units.

$$\text{Diversity} = \sum (47/73)^2 + (4/73)^2 + (22/73)^2$$
$$= 0.51$$

As D increases, diversity decreases and so the Simpson Index is usually written as $1 - D$. Furthermore, for a finite community the Index as shown above is biased (it is sample-size dependent) and may have to be corrected:

$$D_{corrected} = \frac{[(ND) - 1]}{N - 1}$$

where N is the number of individuals or samples, etc.

Box 7.2. **Examples of analysis of habitat fragments and habitat fragmentation**

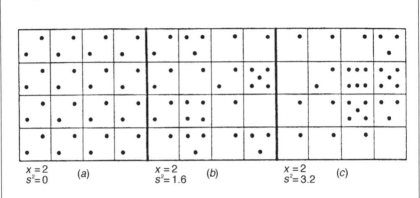

| $x = 2$ $s^2 = 0$ | (a) | $x = 2$ $s^2 = 1.6$ | (b) | $x = 2$ $s^2 = 3.2$ | (c) |

1. Spatial distribution (regular, random or clumped)

Spatial positions of fragmented habitats (each dot represents a fragment). (*a*) Regular pattern where there is no variance. (*b*) Approaching a random distribution and the variance would equal the mean if it was a perfectly random distribution. (*c*) Here there is clumping or aggregation and the variance is much greater than the mean.

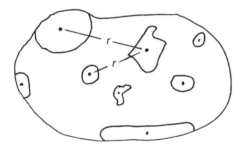

2. Spatial distribution (nearest-neighbour analysis)

For each point in the centre of a habitat fragment, calculate the distance to the fragment central point (*r*).

Calculate the mean $\bar{r}_A$

$$\bar{r}_A = \sum r/N$$

where *N* is the total number of fragments.

Calculate the number of fragments per geographical area (density, $D = N/A$).

Calculate the expected mean distance between the points for randomly distributed habitat central points.

Box 7.2 (*cont.*)

$$\bar{r}_E = \frac{1}{2\sqrt{D}}$$

Calculate the ratio R which is a measure of the degree to which $\bar{r}_A$ departs from $\bar{r}_E$

$R = \bar{r}_A/\bar{r}_E$
$R = 1$ for randomness
$R = 0$ for maximum aggregation

3. Edge diversity,

The characteristics of the edge or perimeter of a habitat fragment could range from a simple circular boundary to a very irregular edge. How do you measure the diversity of an edge? A perfectly circular habitat has the smallest edge. Change the circle into a square or rectangle and the edge increases while the area of habitat remains almost the same. Add variation to the edge and the extent of edges increases even further. Being able to quantify and compare the extent of edges has become important in conservation and there is a simple equation which gives an index of edge diversity.

A circle is a geometric figure with the combined greatest area and least edge. There is a simple equation incorporating the area of a circle, the circumference and π that has a value of 1. A square will have a slightly larger value and a rectangle an even larger one. Therefore any value larger than 1 is a measure of the irregularity (3 to 4 for high levels). The following from Patton (1975) is the equation which can be used to give an index of the diversity of an edge.

$$D_i = P/2(A\pi)^{0.5}$$

where D_i is the edge diversity; P is the perimeter of the fragment, patch, lake etc.; A is the area of the habitat.

For example, a circle of habitat with an area of 1256.64 square metres has a circumference of 125.6 metres. The edge diversity 1. A square of woodland of the same area has an edge diversity of 1.12; that is, the edge diversity of the square is 0.12 times greater than the edge diversity of the circle.

For some species, it may be useful to designate groups of fragments as conservation areas, but how do you identify fragments that are grouped or clumped together as opposed to being randomly or evenly distributed? The extent to which habitats are distributed randomly, clumped or aggregated, or distributed in a regular fashion is easily analysed. Landscape ecologists refer to clumping into patches as 'contagion'. By overlaying a map or aerial photograph of the fragments with squares, it is possible to analyse the pattern of distribution (Box 7.2). The mean number of fragments in each square and variance (square of the standard deviation) is calculated. If the fragments are distributed uniformly then the variance is zero. As the pattern becomes more random then the variance approaches the mean. The variance is greater than the mean when there is clumping or aggregation of the fragments.

The spatial configuration could also be analysed using a modification of any of the nearest-neighbour techniques first described in the 1950s (see King, 1969; Wratten & Fry, 1980). The methods for nearest-neighbour analysis were designed for the analysis of patterns of points. Here we are dealing with geometric figures but the 'central' point could be used for the analysis. In the example shown in Box 7.2, the mean distance between the central points of the fragments is compared to the mean distance between randomly distributed points. It should be recognised that a limitation of this approach is that it is difficult to be precise about the 'central' point of each patch.

Some conservation objectives could include as many edge habitats as possible. The extent of edge is related to the shape of a fragment; the shape could range from a perfect circle (completely compact) to that of a shape with a highly variable edge. There are two characteristics here: the diversity of the edge and the degree of compactness. How do you measure the diversity of an edge? A perfectly circular habitat has the smallest edge. Change the circle into a square or rectangle and the edge increases while the area of habitat remains the same. Add variation to the edge and the extent of edges increases even further. Being able to quantify and compare the extent of edges has become important in conservation and there is a simple equation which gives an index of edge diversity (see Box 7.2).

The edge of a habitat may not be clearly identifiable (after all the edge is something which human beings see and may not be seen as an edge by other species). There may be 'hard' edges and 'soft' edges. Stamps *et al.* (1987) have proposed methods for analysis of 'softness' or permeability of an edge for dispersing individuals on the basis of the proportion of potential emigrants that reach a habitat fragment and then cross over it. The proportion could vary among habitat patches and from species to species.

These methods of analysis and many others using GIS are being used more and more often on research projects ranging from student investigations to international research programmes. They are only a small way of showing that biogeography is certainly not confined to being a descriptive subject. The application of GIS is just one of the many areas of biogeography which has important implications for conservation. For example, in Australia, Leadbeater's possum (*Gymnobelideus leadbeateri*) generally occurs in small forest fragments as disjunct populations. These populations are at particular risk where forests are being logged and where there is a risk of fire. The development of a conservation strategy for the species requires analysis of the probability of extinction for different populations. That analysis can be complex because of the many variables, which include dispersal behaviour, occurrence and extent of forest fires, logging prescriptions and quality of the habitat. Two researchers, David Lindenmayer and Hugh Possingham (1996) have developed a computer simulation model which derives estimates of the probability of extinction of populations of this possum in different forest blocks. The data on habitat patches within various forest blocks were captured in the database of a GIS. Their analysis highlighted large differences in the likelihood of persistence of the populations and these were attributed to differences in spatial distribution and size of the habitat patches in a forest block. This research demonstrated the importance of biogeographical analysis and its application in conservation (see also Sections 9.8 and 9.9).

References

De Pietri, D. E. (1995). The spatial configuration of vegetation as an indicator of landscape degradation due to livestock enterprises in Argentina. *Journal of Applied Ecology*, **32**, 857–865.

Diamond, J. M. (1975). The island dilemma: lessons of modern biogeographical studies for the design of natural reserves. *Biological Conservation*, 7, 129–146.

Harrison, S. (1994). Metapopulations and conservation. In Edwards, P. J., May, R. M. & Webb, N. R. (eds), *Large-scale Ecology and Conservation Biology*, BES 35th Symposium, pp. 111–128. Oxford, Blackwell Scientific Publications.

Hopkins, P. J. (1983). Invertebrate diversity and composition of fragmented heathland. Ph.D. thesis, University of Southampton.

Lindenmayer, D. B. & Possingham, H. P. (1996). Modelling the inter-relationships between habitat patchiness, dispersal capability and metapopulation persistence of the endangered species Leadbeater's possum, in south-eastern Australia. *Landscape Ecology*, **11**, 79–105.

Neve, G., Barascud, B., Hughes, R., Aubert, J., Descimon, H., Lebrun, P. & Baguette, M. (1996). Dispersal, colonization power and metapopulation structure in the vulnerable butterfly *Proclassiana eunomia* (Lepidoptera: Nymphalidae). *Journal of Applied Ecology*, **33**, 14–22.

Patton, D. R. (1975). A diversity index for quantifying habitat edge. *Wildlife Society Bulletin*, **294**, 171–173.

Spellerberg, I. F. (1991). *Monitoring Ecological Change*. Cambridge, Cambridge University Press.

Stamps, J. A., Buechner, M. & Krishnan, V. V. (1987). The effects of edge permeability and habitat geometry on emigration from patches of habitat. *American Naturalist*, **129**, 533–552.

Webb, N. R., Clarke, R. T. & Nicholas, J. T. (1984). Invertebrate diversity on fragmented *Calluna*-heathland: effects of surrounding vegetation. *Journal of Biogeography*, **11**, 41–46.

8

Biogeography of linear landscape features

8.1 Introduction

During the late 1980s and in the early 1990s, much was being written about 'wildlife corridors' and 'greenways'. For example, the 1990 June issue of *National Geographic* had an article entitled 'Greenways: paths to the future'. Some of the text included the following:

> Verdant corridors are snaking across America, connecting parklands and inviting our urban population outdoors. Called greenways, they aim at improving recreation, aiding wildlife migration, and protecting scenic regions (Grove, 1990).

In other biogeographical regions, wildlife corridors were being established. One example was the purchase of land in eastern Brazil to serve as a corridor for the golden-headed lion tamarin (*Leontopithecus chrystomelas*). This news was reported in 1990 by the Jersey Zoo Wildlife Preservation Trust. Jersey Zoo is on one of the small group of Channel Islands in the English Channel. Long known for the work of Gerald Durrell, the Trust reported in its journal *On the Edge* about a commemorative plaque at the forest reserve in southeastern Bahia which reads,

> To commemorate a visit by H.R.H. The Duke of Edinburgh, the Prince Philip, President of WWF, to the Una Biological Reserve, to register the gift of a forest corridor to IBAMA presented by Fundaco Biodiversita with funds donated by WWF and the Jersey Wildlife Preservation Trust. Una, 14th March 1991.

The possibility that wildlife may disperse along linear landscape features such as road edges and field boundaries has given rise to the concept of wildlife corridors. If dispersion did take place along these linear features then this could be a way of reducing the effects of fragmentation of wildlife habitats. Not only has there been a growing interest in the conservation aspects of linear landscape features but there has also been a growing interest in the role of linear landscape features for recreation. Features about wildlife corridors of all kinds have been newsworthy (Fig. 8.1).

Biogeographers have an interest in linear landscape features because such features may contribute to the distribution patterns of biota: linear features may be habitats, they may act as barriers acting against dispersion and they may facilitate links between populations in subdivided habitats.

In this chapter we discuss several aspects of the biogeography of linear landscape features, including (1) corridors and barriers for wildlife, (2) habitats for wildlife and (3) applied aspects of linear wildlife habitats and wildlife corridors.

8.2 Linear features as wildlife corridors

All landscapes contain linear features; some are natural and some are the product of human activities. There are linear boundaries between land and water, rivers and river banks, mountain ranges, canals, roads, pylon swathes, hedgerows, windbreaks, etc. (Table 8.1). Names for these features are many and the term 'linear landscape feature' is used here in a generic sense. There is also another important reason for using this term as will become clear later.

There are many examples of so-called wildlife corridors and, for some forms of wildlife, these linear landscape features may indeed be corridors which facilitate movement between populations. These linear landscape features vary greatly in size. Some span continents, while others are edges of tracks through forests. There are also marine wildlife corridors. For example, leatherback turtles migrate along underwater mountain ranges. Some of these marine corridors may justify protection as part of the conservation of the leatherback turtle. Some wildlife corridors may facilitate movement for certain species, yet not be a continuous linear feature. A series of grassland habitats, a series of islands or a series of fragmented hedges in a city while not continuous could be like stepping stones across a river and so be used by some species for dispersion. On the other hand, too many breaks or too large a break in the corridor could prevent some organisms from using the linear feature as a means of dispersal.

A Toad
Love-tunnel

CITIES
NEED HEDGES

These vital wildlife corridors
that connect town and country
are too frequently taken for
granted, writes Jeremy Herbert

Seeing the wood for the trees in Knowsley

Fig. 8.1. The concept of 'wildlife corridors' has been very popular, according to these reports in the press.

Table 8.1 *Examples of linear landscape features*

A. Terrestrial
Mountain ranges
Fences
Hedgerows
Dry stone walls
Walls of defence
Shelter breaks and windbreaks
Railway line embankments
Road edges
Strips of urban gardens
Avenues of trees
Urban paths and cycleways
Pylon swathes
Forest plantation rides
Firebreaks in plantations

B. Aquatic
Ditches
Irrigation channels
Canals
Streams and rivers
Lake shores
Coastlines

After Spellerberg & Gaywood, 1993.

In many instances linear landscape features are not wildlife corridors but are linear habitats. The term wildlife corridor infers movement of wildlife along some linear landscape feature (the corridor). However, the term is commonly used when there may be no evidence to support the concept of a corridor along which wildlife moves. What in fact is called a wildlife corridor may be a wildlife habitat but no more. So, what evidence is there to show that wildlife moves along linear features? Can linear features help to overcome problems of habitat fragmentation (Section 7.2)? What makes a 'good' wildlife corridor and how can they best be established and managed?

Despite the wide misuse of the term wildlife corridor (used when the strict sense of the term is neither proved nor justified) there is an increasing body of evidence and growing amount of research to support the concept that linear features can be wildlife corridors. Evidence has come either in the form of direct observations of animals moving along a linear feature such as a road verge or from the results of radio-tracking or mark-recapture techniques. The movement of organisms along linear landscape features can result from the following:

1. The linear feature is part of the organisms' home range or territory.
2. Linear features are used as a shelter or refuge when moving across the landscape.
3. Linear features are used as migratory routes.
4. Linear features are used as a means of dispersing between habitat fragments.

Some groups of wildlife do indeed use linear landscape features as corridors for movement. These groups included beetles, butterflies, reptiles, amphibians, birds and mammals. For example, in Australia, individual long-nosed potoroos (*Potorus tridactylus*) and bush rats (*Rattus fuscipes*) were recorded in one study to move 1.1 kilometres between two forest patches along a road verge (Bennett, 1990). In North America, 'travel corridors' were established to provide wild turkeys easy access to habitats in pine plantations. The population of birds increased from 276 in 1959 to 410 in 1973 (Gehrken, 1975). The research on wildlife corridors continues and is very topical. For example, in the October 1996 issue of the journal *Conservation Biology* there are two reports about wildlife corridors: one concerned a study of ringlet butterflies (*Aphantopus hyperantus*) moving between woodland clearings, possibly along woodland rides in England (Sutcliffe & Thomas, 1996); the other concerned the use of riparian strips in mixed-wood forests in Alberta by birds, particularly juveniles (Machtans *et al.*, 1996).

Dispersal of plants along linear features may be facilitated by animal carriers and, indeed, the establishment of plants along fences can be attributed largely to birds dispersing seeds via their droppings. It seems that it has been very difficult to show whether or not plants move along linear landscape features. For both animals and plants, much research has yet to be done to show whether or not so-called wildlife corridors help to reduce the effects of habitat fragmentation. The role of linear features in the distribution of genetic diversity within species is poorly researched. We do not know whether, if linear features facilitate movement between populations, there is interbreeding between populations.

8.3 Linear features as barriers

For some wildlife, linear features can act as barriers and prevent dispersal or at least increase risks during dispersal. Roads, railways, powerline swathes and canals can all be barriers for some forms of wildlife. Roads in particular present obstacles for small vertebrates, including amphibians, reptiles and some mammals. The road edge can be a barrier simply by virtue of the change in microclimate and because of the impact of pollutants and noise from traffic.

In many parts of the world, tunnels for wildlife have been built under roads to help to reduce the effects of roads as barriers. For example, in Australia, an interesting example of the effects of road barriers was found to be affecting one of the most threatened marsupials, the pigmy possum (*Burramys parvus*), within some ski resorts. At one site the breeding area had become bisected by a road. A 60 metre corridor was constructed leading to two tunnels beneath the road, thus restoring the habitat continuity. This allowed males to disperse from the females' breeding areas, an essential element in the social organisation of the pygmy possum. After construction of the corridor and tunnel, the population structure and survival rates in the disturbed area changed to those observed in the undisturbed and unfragmented areas.

8.4 Linear habitats for wildlife

In many regions of the world, the landscape is a cultural landscape dominated by agriculture, forestry, urbanisation and infrastructure such as roads and railways. The biological communities have long gone or have been greatly modified. In some of these landscapes, linear landscape features may provide the only habitats for a variety of taxonomic groups. Other linear features provide unusual habitats. For example, the strips of land created either side of the Berlin Wall now provide habitats for hundreds of species of plant life, some usually found much further south. Has anyone researched the biogeography of country wide walls such as the Berlin Wall and far more ancient walls such as the Great Wall of China?

Linear landscape features which have been the subject of much biogeographical and ecological research are hedgerows. These are narrow bands of trees, shrubs and other plants that separate fields. Field boundaries such as dry stone walls (Fig. 8.2) and networks of hedges or hedgerows (or a 'bocage') are characteristic of the western European landscape. The hedgerows of the

Fig. 8.2. Examples of field boundaries including hedgerows.

Great Plains of North America are almost all planted but, in the eastern side of the USA and southern Canada, most of the hedgerows have regenerated naturally and are called fencerows. Fencerows are therefore hedgerows that have formed where a fence is or was present. Similarly in Europe, some hedgerows have become established naturally along fences and other types of boundary, but some are linear remnants of woods. Most are the result of deliberate planting. Documentary evidence shows that some hedges in the UK were planted over 1000 years ago.

In Britain, hedgerows can be very rich in wildlife and as many as 500 to 600 plant species have been recorded in some English hedgerows. It has been estimated that as many as 21 out of 28 lowland terrestrial mammals species (excluding bats), breed in hedges in Britain. Of 91 British bird species and 54 butterfly species from lowland terrestrial habitats, about 65 and 23, respectively, breed in hedges.

Field boundaries have many benefits: they may be linear habitats for predators of insect pests, they moderate the microclimate and provide shelter for stock, and they are considered by some to have an aesthetic value. Despite the many benefits of hedgerows, agricultural expansion and intensification has meant that many kilometres of hedgerows have been removed. There is now much written about the extent and rate of removal of hedgerows from the English countryside, especially the removal which took place in the few decades following the Second World War. The loss of hedgerows was a serious blow to conservation but it was justified at the time on the grounds of the need to increase agricultural efficiency; removal of hedges provided greater manoeuvrability for large machinery and provided more land for crops.

The controversy surrounding hedgerow removal continues to this day, with some people strongly advocating hedgerow protection and others pointing out that hedgerows may harbour pests and divide the land into unmanageable small units. That controversy has spilled over into many bitter debates about the figures produced for hedgerow loss and that in turn has prompted much thought about methods used to calculate that loss and about the definition of a hedge.

Calculating the rate of loss of hedgerows across a whole country is difficult because of the spatial scale of data collection and unfortunately the often quoted figures of rates of hedgerow loss are rarely accompanied by a description of the methods of data collection. How often and over what parts of the country was hedgerow loss recorded? Were the data representative of the whole country? It may seem strange that the definition of a hedgerow could have implications for quantifying rate of hedgerow loss. Could the definition of a hedgerow include a few trees in a line or a fence with some occasional shrubs? A change in the definition of a hedgerow can and did have implications for the published figures of hedgerow loss. In some parts of the country hedgerows have been planted. But overall there has been a net loss of hedgerows in Britain and the rate of that loss increased during the past few decades. The difficulties of quantifying that loss must not hide the fact that hedgerow loss meant the loss of wildlife habitats in a landscape where there were few or no other kinds of habitat for vertebrate wildlife. Whereas once photographic records and periodic site visits to selected areas of the countryside provided a basis for recording hedgerow loss there are now methods of data collection that can deal with large-scale, countrywide data collection. With the advances in computer technology, Geographical Information Systems (GIS) have facilitated collection and analysis of large amounts of spatially orientated data.

Hedgerows have many functions and today there is an increasing awareness of the many benefits of hedgerows, so much so that the UK government has introduced incentives to plant and conserve hedgerows. In 1996 it was announced that landowners could face fines of up to £5000 for removing hedgerows that supported rare species. Protection will also be given to old hedges; those containing seven or more native woody plant species in a 30 metre length. Such incentives are to be encouraged but from a biogeographical point of view, where should hedges be planted? Which hedgerows (in addition to old ones) should be conserved? Perhaps it would have been better to have a countrywide policy for the hedgerow scheme, based on a biogeographical approach. A strategy could have been developed to address the questions 'Where are the hedges most needed and which are most worthy of protection?'

What makes a good hedgerow for wildlife? A scheme for calculating the conservation value of a hedgerow could be based on the physical dimensions of the hedge, its position in relation to other natural landscape features and the species richness of the plants.

8.5 Establishment of linear wildlife habitats in agricultural ecosystems

Intensive agriculture with accompanying use of chemicals may have contributed to increases in crop yields but at the expense of many losses in wildlife in agricultural ecosystems. The use of herbicides has greatly affected the numbers of many plant species. In Europe, for example, 80 of about 800 so-called arable weeds are now classed as rare species. Insecticides have similarly had considerable effects on non-target insect species. Indicators of change in insect abundance can be found in studies of some game birds such as the partridge (*Perdix perdix*). Insects are a staple part of the diet of partridge chicks and research by the Game Conservancy in the south of England has shown that this bird has declined by as much as 80 per cent since 1945. This decline has been attributed to chick mortality resulting from a decrease in food abundance.

Restoration and enlargement of field boundaries (linear wildlife habitats) has been undertaken as part of some programmes of research to investigate what can be done to help to reverse the trends in losses of wildlife. For example, the Game Conservancy introduced a conservation strategy for field margins (Fig. 8.3). In the outer 6 metres of arable fields the use of pesticides is restricted to selected herbicides only and in the uncropped headlands no crop is sown, there are no fertilisers and pesticides are restricted. Within a short time of the 'conservation headlands' being established, many species of wildlife, including species of butterflies, hover flies, some carabid beetles, wild game birds, small mammals and rare arable weeds had increased in abundance. Clearly, the establishment and management of these linear habitats have implications for the biogeography of farmland.

Field margins or field boundaries are examples of linear habitats that have attracted considerable interest from ecologists working on agricultural ecosystems because of the potential for habitats to support natural predators of crop pests. Predatory arthropods have a role in the suppression of insect pests and it would appear that field boundaries not only provide a habitat but also a wintering site for the beneficial arthropods (that is, the boundary has implications for movements of the organisms). The problem is that any benefits are limited to the area of crop in which the beneficial arthropods can disperse: that may be only a few metres from the field boundary. Research at Southampton University in England led to trials and eventually the establishment of raised earth banks extending into the fields, popularly called 'beetle banks' (Thomas *et al.*, 1991). These banks were sown with tussock-forming grass and within two years of establishment it was found that high population densities of predatory arthropods were overwintering on these linear habitats. The populations provided a nucleus population from which dispersal into the crop could take place. The space taken up by the earth banks and subsequent loss of crops could be balanced by the need to use fewer chemicals, and smaller amounts, to control pests. Here was a case of creating linear wildlife habitats to facilitate dispersal of wildlife.

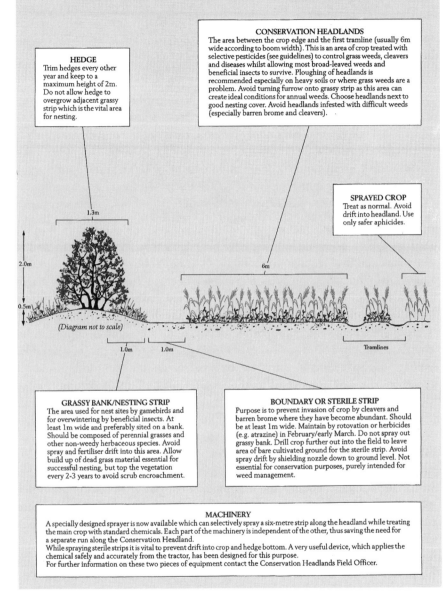

THE GAME CONSERVANCY'S FIELD MARGIN

HEDGE
Trim hedges every other year and keep to a maximum height of 2m. Do not allow hedge to overgrow adjacent grassy strip which is the vital area for nesting.

CONSERVATION HEADLANDS
The area between the crop edge and the first tramline (usually 6m wide according to boom width). This is an area of crop treated with selective pesticides (see guidelines) to control grass weeds, cleavers and diseases whilst allowing most broad-leaved weeds and beneficial insects to survive. Ploughing of headlands is recommended especially on heavy soils or where grass weeds are a problem. Avoid turning furrow onto grassy strip as this area can create ideal conditions for annual weeds. Choose headlands next to good nesting cover. Avoid headlands infested with difficult weeds (especially barren brome and cleavers).

SPRAYED CROP
Treat as normal. Avoid drift into headland. Use only safer aphicides.

2.0m

1.3m

6m

0.5m

(Diagram not to scale)

1.0m 1.0m

Tramlines

GRASSY BANK/NESTING STRIP
The area used for nest sites by gamebirds and for overwintering by beneficial insects. At least 1m wide and preferably sited on a bank. Should be composed of perennial grasses and other non-weedy herbaceous species. Avoid spray and fertiliser drift into this area. Allow build up of dead grass material essential for successful nesting, but top the vegetation every 2-3 years to avoid scrub encroachment.

BOUNDARY OR STERILE STRIP
Purpose is to prevent invasion of crop by cleavers and barren brome where they have become abundant. Should be at least 1m wide. Maintain by rotovation or herbicides (e.g. atrazine) in February/early March. Do not spray out grassy bank. Drill crop further out into the field to leave area of bare cultivated ground for the sterile strip. Avoid spray drift by shielding nozzle down to ground level. Not essential for conservation purposes, purely intended for weed management.

MACHINERY
A specially designed sprayer is now available which can selectively spray a six-metre strip along the headland while treating the main crop with standard chemicals. Each part of the machinery is independent of the other, thus saving the need for a separate run along the Conservation Headland.
While spraying sterile strips it is vital to prevent drift into crop and hedge bottom. A very useful device, which applies the chemical safely and accurately from the tractor, has been designed for this purpose.
For further information on these two pieces of equipment contact the Conservation Headlands Field Officer.

Fig. 8.3. A design of field margins including hedge design and conservation headlands. (Reproduced from the 1989 *Game Conservancy Review* with kind permission Nigel Boatman, Allerton Research and Educational Trust.)

8.6 Ecotones

The concept of the ecotone was introduced early this century when it was used to imply a junction zone between two communities. In 1971 Odum defined it as:

> a transition zone between two or more diverse communities. It is a function zone or tension belt which may have considerable linear extent, but it is narrower than the adjoining community areas themselves. The ecotonal community commonly contains many of the organisms which are characteristics of, and often restricted to, the ecotone. Often, both the number of species and the population density of some of the species are greater in the ecotone than in the communities flanking it. The tendency for increased variety and density of community functions is known as the 'edge effect'.

Examples of ecotones include the edge between a woodland and grassland, a river bank and the intertidal zone (Fig. 8.4). It might be thought that edges do not really have any significance because they are based on a subjective classification of the landscape. The question we should be asking is 'Do these landscape boundaries have any part to play in the distribution of organisms?' The answer is certainly 'yes'. Ecotones do have important implications for the distribution, dispersion and dispersal of wildlife across the countryside. Perhaps not surprisingly, therefore, much research has been undertaken on ecotones, they are important in the management of the environment for wildlife and there have been several international meetings on ecotones since 1987. In brief, an increasing number of biogeographers support the view that ecotones have a practical value and that some can support rich assemblages of plants and animals.

It is amongst monocultures such as plantation forests that edges (along with glades, streams and ponds) may provide habitats in biotic communities otherwise lacking in structural variety. In most well-established or mature plantation forests, the trees grow so close together that light is prevented from reaching the ground. Consequently few forms of life can exist below the dense and uniform canopy of trees. However, the edges of blocks of trees within the plantations and edges of roads or rides throughout the plantations can provide habitats for some forms of wildlife, including butterflies and other insects, reptiles and small mammals.

With different forms of management, these edges can be improved to enhance the provision of habitats. The opportunities to do this have increased

Fig. 8.4. Examples of ecotones.

with the growing acceptance of multi-use plantation forests. These are forests which are grown primarily for timber but are nevertheless also managed for other purposes, which may include environmental education, recreation and wildlife. In some countries it is now mandatory for forest managers to provide for forest uses other than merely timber production.

Management in forest plantations for wildlife habitats has been directed largely at edges: the edges of forest blocks or stands, and edges along the rides. A forest block with mature uniform trees or all the same species planted right up to the ride provides little in the way of useful habitat. Obvious ways of increasing edge habitats include not planting to the edge, not planting in straight lines, and planting different tree species. A combination of anything but straight lines such as 'scalloped edges' and mixed species of tree has been found to improve forest plantation edges for many species of butterfly.

While changes in the simple design of edges in forest plantations can provide habitats for wildlife, there is an interesting temporal problem that occurs, particularly from the time of first planting to the time of mature stands in the forest. Over time, the trees reach heights and densities which may eventually alter the local microclimate, slowing changing the edge habitat or even destroying it. Forests are forever changing and ride edges can, within a few years, become unsuitable as habitats for some forms of wildlife (Box 8.1).

Some forest plantations are made up of a mixture of blocks or stands of trees of different ages and sometimes even different species. There can be an ongoing process of harvesting and planting which results in a plantation which is far from homogeneous. Habitats for some forms of forest wildlife will occur in different places at different times. With some planning and management, it is possible to ensure continuity of edge habitats. That is to say, modelling can be used to predict when some edges in forests such as roadside or ride edges may become unsuitable for certain forms of wildlife. Such models take into consideration the growth of the planted trees and the effect of that growth on the microclimate of edges. One example was the analysis undertaken of the changing habitats of a lizard in forest plantations in the south of England (Fig. 8.5) and the subsequent development of a model. The application of this model ensures that there is a continuity of suitable ride edge habitats available for this lizard species and other species of wildlife while the forest is managed as a timber resource. The forests are a matrix of different ages of forest stands and these are continuously changing as the trees grow, as the trees are removed and as replanting takes place. Within the context of the forest matrix, the model can help to predict where habitats will eventually be lost. Knowing that, it is possible to plan forest management practice to ensure a continuity of the habitats.

Box 8.1. Edges of forest rides ranging from those which support little wildlife to those which have been managed for wildlife

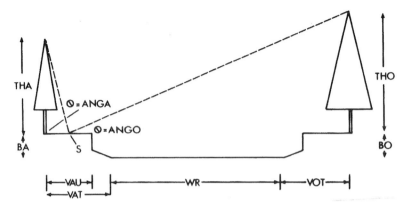

Fig. 8.5. A model for management of linear habitats for an endangered lizard. Environmental variables were used to determine insolation characteristics and suitability of a habitat for a small lizard (the sand lizard, *Lacerta agilis*) inhabiting edges of forest plantation rides in southern England. S, position of lizard; THA/THO, mean height of trees on either side of the ride; VAT/VOT, verge width; BA/BO, height of bank; WR, ride width; ANGA/ANGO, angles used to derive an index of sunshine availability; VAU, distance between trees and edge of the ride. These variables could be incorporated into a model for predicting when the habitat would no longer be suitable for the lizards as a result of the growth of the trees and shading of the ground. (From *Biological Conservation*, **42**. S. Dent & I. F. Spellerberg, Habitats of the lizards *Lacerta agilis* and *Lacerta vivipara* on forest ride verges in Britain, pp. 273–286, 1987. Reproduced with kind permission from Elsevier Science Ltd, UK.)

8.7 Wildlife as incidental to the management and construction of linear landscape features

It is only recently that linear landscape features have been managed or established especially for wildlife. However, the distribution and movement of wildlife may long have been a by-product of linear features which were originally valued not for wildlife but for landscape or 'environmental' reasons. For example, some linear landscape features may have aesthetic values, amenity values, recreational function and environmental benefits. Field boundaries such as hedgerows are an integral part of some landscapes; they may be perceived by some to add to the value of the landscapes and to contribute to their attractiveness. Linear landscape features can provide shelter for stock and help to stabilise loss due to erosion. In urban areas, linear landscape features such as avenues of trees may help to ameliorate the environment.

In many urban environments, open spaces such as parks and public gardens may be scarce; any linear features may therefore have an important amenity and recreational role to play. Natural linear features such as rivers and many artificial linear features such as park boundaries, hedgerows and canals provide a basis for planners to enhance landscaping within urban environments. Cities around the world have included 'greenways' into their city plans (Fig. 8.6) and in some cities there are considered to be many benefits to be derived from such planning (Box 8.2).

It has been suggested that green areas should be located in the form of wedges, with the point near the city centre so as to accelerate horizontal airflow, help to moderate temperatures and act as a sink for pollutants. Strips of vegetation may act as a buffer against noise pollution, especially that resulting from traffic. In Rome, which has one of the highest levels of noise recorded in European cities, plans have been drawn up to develop suitable acoustic barriers of trees and other vegetation along busy roads. But it is not only noise which can be a nuisance in cities. The bright lights of traffic can be avoided by appropriate use of linear features. For example, trees can shield houses from the glare of street lights and can also be used to separate lanes of traffic. Trees may be an important biological sink for heavy metal pollutants and may help to filter particulates and dust from air.

Early in the 1980s, one of the UNESCO Man and the Biosphere projects called the Dayton Climate Project was initiated to study how in Ohio, USA, the City of Dayton's trees and other vegetation functioned as part of the urban ecosystem. The Dayton Climate Project has identified the importance of vegetation in reducing water run-off. It was calculated that after a severe storm, tree crowns in the city lowered run-off volumes by at least 7 per cent from what it could have been if the trees had not been present. Storage of precipitation in the tree canopies results in increased ground water recharge potential and reduced overland flow. Soil erosion is just as much a problem in urban environments as in the countryside. The Dayton Climate Project has calculated that almost 12 000 tons of soil is removed from just under 500 acres (200 hectares) of exposed soil in the city each year. Vegetation could be used to reduce such erosion.

Linear landscape features have many applications, environmental, educational and ecological (Box 8.3). Perhaps the ultimate in linear landscape features in cities has been the suggestion that there be actual linear cities (Fig. 8.7), as described by the architect Gilles Gauthier in Canada in 1995. He strongly believed that the linear city could bring interesting and realistic solutions to energy, transport, social and ecological problems. There may also be biogeographical considerations: what would the implications be for wildlife if such linear cities were built?

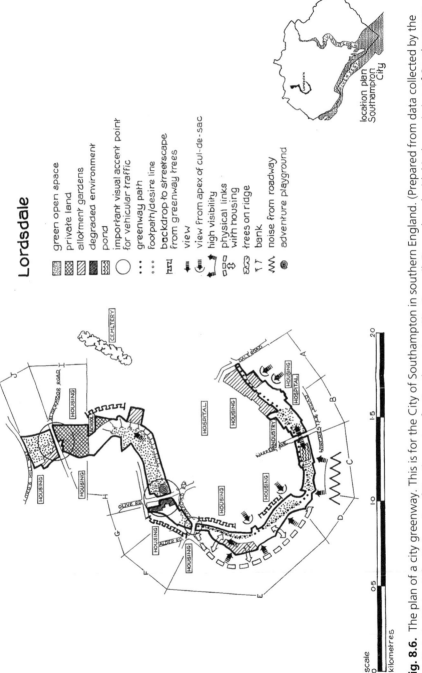

Lordsdale

green open space
private land
allotment gardens
degraded environment
pond
important visual accent point
for vehicular traffic
greenway path
footpath/desire line
backdrop to streetscape
from greenway trees
view
view from apex of cul-de-sac
high visibility
physical links
with housing
trees on ridge
bank
noise from roadway
adventure playground

location plan
Southampton
City

Fig. 8.6. The plan of a city greenway. This is for the City of Southampton in southern England. (Prepared from data collected by the GeoData Institute at the University of Southampton for Southampton City Council. Reproduced with kind permission of Southampton City Council.)

Box 8.2. Benefits of urban greenways. (From an American study adapted from the National Park Service 1990, *Economic Aspects of Protecting Rivers, Trails and Greenway Corridors*, National Park service, USA)

Summary of findings

Real property values	Many studies demonstrate that parks, greenways and trails increase nearby property values. In turn, increased property values can increase local tax revenues and help to offset greenway acquisition costs
Expenditures by residents	Spending by local residents on greenway-related activities helps to support recreation-oriented businesses and employment, as well as other businesses which are patronised by greenway and trail users
Commercial uses	Greenways often provide business opportunities, locations and resources for commercial activities such as recreation equipment rentals and sales, lessons, and other related businesses
Tourism	Greenways are often major tourist attractions which generate expenditures on lodging, food, and recreation-oriented services. Greenways also help to improve the overall appeal of a community to prospective tourists and new residents
Agency expenditures	The agency responsible for managing a river, trail or greenway can help to support local businesses by purchasing supplies and service. Jobs created by the managing agency may also help to increase local employment opportunities
Corporate relocation	Evidence shows that the quality of life in a community is an increasingly important factor in corporate relocation decisions. Greenways are often cited as important contributors to the quality of life

Box 8.2. (*cont.*)

	Summary of findings
Public cost reduction	The conservation of rivers, trails, and greenways can help local governments and other public agencies to reduce costs resulting from flooding and other natural hazards
Intrinsic value	While greenways have many economic benefits, it is important to remember the intrinsic environmental and recreation value of preserving rivers, trails and other open space corridors

For centuries, various forms of linear landscape feature have been built to enclose livestock and also to protect livestock and crops from harsh weather conditions. For example, dry stone walls, hedges and lines of trees such as poplars (*Populus* spp.) have been established in many countries as windbreaks and shelterbelts. These linear landscape features may also have other benefits. For example, on hilly terrain, such features can moderate soil erosion.

8.8 Applications of the biogeography of wildlife habitats and wildlife corridors

The role of linear landscape features as habitats or as wildlife corridors has biogeographical applications for designing species recovery plans (see Section 6.3.7). Recognising that linear landscape features may benefit wildlife and humans, local authorities in some countries have established strategic plans for conservation of potential urban wildlife corridors and greenways. Barker (1984), for example, has suggested the following as a basis for planning such features:

1. Surveys to identify the main reservoirs of wildlife.
2. Identification of the main potential linear habitats permeating the built up area.
3. Identification of the key linear habitats between reservoirs.
4. Protection and management of the reservoirs and linear habitats.

Box 8.3. Functions of linear landscape features. (From Spellerberg & Gaywood, 1993)

Environmental benefits provided by the presence of linear habitats and corridors
(1) Microclimate
    Hedges act as windbreaks and affect crop yields
    Temperatures in urban environments may be moderated by the presence of wooded areas
(2) Reduction in soil erosion
    Windbreaks
    Water run-off moderated (e.g. wide riparian corridors)
(3) Reduction in pollution, especially in urban environments. Examples include:
    Noise pollution
    Light pollution (car headlamp glare, etc.)
    Dust
    Heavy metals

Ecological benefits provided by the presence of linear habitats and corridors
(1) Increase in the rate of immigration into habitat patch
    Increase and/or maintenance of species diversity
    Increase of population size for certain species and reduced risk of extinction within a habitat patch. If a local extinction occurs within a habitat patch, then it may be more readily colonised
    Maintenance of genetic variation within populations and the prevention of inbreeding depression
(2) Provision of escape routes from habitat patch after large-scale disturbance such as fire
(3) Provide habitat for many species
    'Margins' may be sources of beneficial species such as insect pollinators and polyphagous predators of agricultural pests
    Can provide networks of habitat for animals with large home ranges or territories in an otherwise degraded environment
    Provision of cover from predators between patches

Educational and recreational benefits of linear features
(1) Recreation
(2) Education
(3) Aesthetic appearance
(4) Limit to urban sprawl ('green belt')

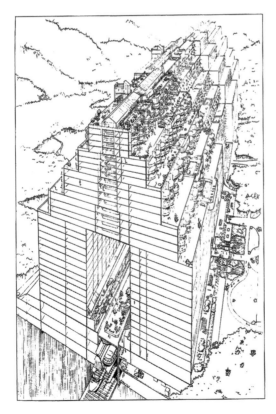

Fig. 8.7. Sketches of a linear city as proposed by Gilles Gauthier. (See *Environmental Conservation*, 1995, **22**, 273–275. From original material kindly provided by Gilles Gauthier.)

5. Identification of the main areas where semi-natural habitats are not open for access.
6. Development of policies to improve areas.
7. Development of policies to ensure that the public can enjoy wildlife areas.
8. Insistence on design standards for building developments which make the most of the opportunities to add wildlife habitats and which cause the least possible damage to existing wildlife habitats.
9. Development of initiatives to encourage all of the above.

Not all the effects of linear landscape features on wildlife are welcome. Some have assisted pest species to disperse and the role of roads and traffic in the dispersal of weed seeds has been well documented. New roads in relatively undisturbed areas contribute not only to the fragmentation of habitats but also to pest invasions. In Indiana in the USA, Brothers & Spingarn (1992) have drawn attention to the possibility of forest fragmentation encouraging invasions of alien species for at least two reasons. First, fragmentation increases the ratio of non-forest species to forest species and also of forest edge species to interior species. Secondly, changes in microclimate and other parameters at forest edges provide points of entry for alien species. In New Zealand it has been found that the most important factors influencing the number of problem weeds in nature reserves are, amongst other things, distance from roads and railway lines.

As the interest in wildlife corridors increases, so also does the research on what makes a suitable wildlife corridor. How wide, how narrow, what is the best kind of vegetation and how should it be managed? The structure, width and species composition of the trees, shrubs and ground cover seem to be important attributes of linear features if they are to act as corridors. In terms of corridor width, the wider the better seems to make sense. This may not be the case for some species, as has been found from recent research on corridors for root voles (*Microtus oeconomus*) in Norway (Andreassen *et al.*, 1996). Furthermore, an understanding of the organism's behaviour is also important. For example, the voles studied were found to have zig-zag movements. These movements and also the detection of habitat edges influence the animals' movements.

There has been much work on restoration of riparian habitats for wildlife, particularly such habitats in urban areas. Generally speaking, riparian habitats can be improved by ensuring that there is a succession of plants from the water to the level of the flood plain (the width of the riparian zone). These efforts to restore riparian habitats in urban areas also offer opportunities to

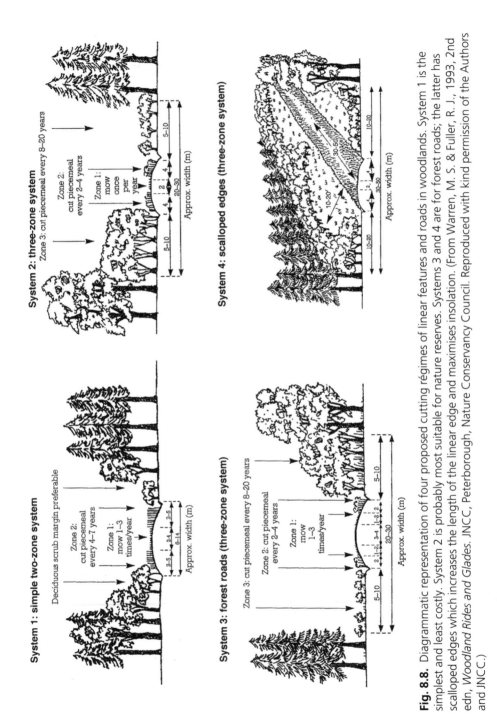

Fig. 8.8. Diagrammatic representation of four proposed cutting régimes of linear features and roads in woodlands. System 1 is the simplest and least costly. System 2 is probably most suitable for nature reserves. Systems 3 and 4 are for forest roads; the latter has scalloped edges which increases the length of the linear edge and maximises insolation. (From Warren, M. S. & Fuller, R. J., 1993, 2nd edn, *Woodland Rides and Glades*. JNCC, Peterborough, Nature Conservancy Council. Reproduced with kind permission of the Authors and JNCC.)

change the criteria for selection of plant species, from purely aesthetic (and often exotic) to native species which can also be aesthetic.

Forest plantations present challenging opportunities for the creation of linear habitats and potential wildlife corridors, as well as features of amenity and educational interest. The simple schematic diagram in Fig. 8.8 arose out of intensive research on the needs of butterflies and other invertebrates in forest plantations.

References

Andreassen, H. P. Halle, S. & Ims, R. A. (1996). Optimal width of movement corridors for root voles: not too narrow and not too wide. *Journal of Applied Ecology*, **33**, 63–70.

Barker, G. (1984). Urban nature conservation abroad. *The Planner*, **70**, 21.

Bennett, A. F. (1990). Land use, forest fragmentation and the mammalian fauna at Naringal, south-west Victoria. *Australian Wildlife Research*, **17**, 325–347.

Brothers, T. S. & Spingarn, A. (1992). Forest fragmentation and alien plant invasion of central Indiana old-growth forests. *Conservation Biology*, **6**, 91–100.

Gehrken, G. A. (1975). Travel corridor technique of wild turkey management. In Halls, L. K. (ed.), *National Wild Turkey Symposium*, pp. 113–117. Austin, TX, The Wildlife Society.

Grove, N. (1990). Greenways: paths to the future. *National Geographic*, **177**, 77–99.

Machtans, C. S., Villard, M.-A. & Hannon, S. J. (1996). Use of riparian buffer strips as movement corridors by forest birds. *Conservation Biology*, **10**, 1366–1379.

Odum, E. P. (1971). *Fundamentals of Ecology*, 3rd edn. Philadelphia, Saunders.

Spellerberg, I. F. & Gaywood, M. J. (1993). Linear features: linear habitats and wildlife corridors. *English Nature Research Reports*, **60**. Peterborough, Cambs, English Nature.

Sutcliffe, O. L. & Thomas, C. D. (1996). Open corridors appear to facilitate dispersal by ringlet butterflies (*Aphantopus hyperantus*) between woodland clearings. *Conservation Biology*, **10**, 1359–1365.

Thomas, M. B., Wratten, S. D. & Sotherton, N. W. (1991). Creation of 'island' habitats in farmland to manipulate populations of beneficial arthropods: predator densities and emigration. *Journal of Applied Ecology*, **28**, 906–917.

9

Future developments

9.1 Introduction

In 1995, Jeffrey McNeely (Chief Scientist for the IUCN, the World Conservation Union) was asked by the Director General to prepare a discussion document on IUCN in the year 2025. The purpose was to prompt discussion about how to respond to change. Change in populations, cultures, climate, economics, technology, information and biological diversity. We will see much environmental change in the future. Partly as a result of that change, the world will see more discussion and possibly conflicts about the pricing of biological resources as services, about the ownership of nature, and about concessions for biological prospecting. Biogeographical knowledge is fundamental to all of the above in a world of change.

In this chapter we use climate change as one example of global environmental change and look at some of its biological consequences. In particular we examine the potential impact that climate changes can have on species distributions. We discuss the importance of studies of biogeography in the detection and explanation of environmental change and for monitoring its effects. We describe how biogeography can be applied to mitigate some of the potentially adverse effects of environmental change on humans and the biosphere. We outline some of the most recent developments in studies of biogeography, such as the development and application of ecological models. We then gaze into the crystal ball and predict what could be roles for biogeography in the next century and what alternative perspectives might be used.

Table 9.1. *Factors that can change climate*

Variation in output of energy from the sun
Variations in the Earth's orbit
Changes in the concentration of greenhouse gases in the Earth's atmosphere
Changes in concentration of aerosols (small particles) in the Earth's atmosphere

9.2 What is climate change and what are the implications?

The Earth's climate (the prevailing characteristics of the weather at any particular time and place) is changing. Climate change can manifest itself in various ways but is generally an increase or decrease in warmth, precipitation or climatic variability. The rate at which climate change occurs may also be subject to change. Climate has always been changing and the degree to which it has changed depends on the time scale. The latter is important because a description of climate based on observations of weather taken over only a few months can be quite different from a summary based on many years of observations.

9.3 What causes climate change?

Climate change is caused partly by human activities. Factors that can change climate are shown in Table 9.1. Climate may be affected by any alteration in the radiation received by the Earth from the sun, the radiation lost to space from the Earth, and the redistribution of energy within the atmosphere (and among the atmosphere, land and ocean).

Factors that contribute to a changing climate may include alterations in the atmospheric concentration of 'greenhouse gases' such as carbon dioxide (CO_2), methane (CH_4), chlorofluorocarbons (CFCs), and nitrous oxide (N_2O). Humans have contributed to changes in atmospheric concentrations of those gases by the combustion of fossil fuels. Humans may also have caused changes to the atmosphere through other forms of air pollution and through ozone depletion. Other factors such as emissions from volcanic eruptions can also affect the atmospheric concentrations of CO_2.

9.4 Evidence for climate change

An Intergovernmental Panel on Climate Change (IPCC) was established in 1988 by the World Meteorological Organisation and the United Nations Environment Programme. The Panel, comprising scientists from around the world, was asked to assess the available scientific information on climate change, to assess its environmental and socioeconomic impacts, and to formulate response strategies. The IPCC First Assessment report provided the basis for negotiating the United Nations Framework Convention on Climate Change. The Panel stated that global mean surface air temperature increased by between 0.3 and 0.6 deg. C during the last 100 years but that warming was of the same magnitude as natural climatic variability. The Panel concluded that the atmospheric concentrations of greenhouse gases had increased substantially as a result of human activities but they were not able to say whether an enhanced greenhouse effect due to those activities had been observed (IPCC, 1990).

The Working Group II of the IPCC was asked more recently to review the state of knowledge concerning impacts of climate change on physical and ecological systems, human health and socioeconomic sectors. The Group also reviewed information on the technical and economic feasibility of a range of potential adaptation and mitigation strategies. They focused on assessing the sensitivity and vulnerability of systems to a range of climate change scenarios and concluded that 'human activities are increasing the atmospheric concentrations of greenhouse gases – which tend to warm the atmosphere – and, in some regions, aerosols – which tend to cool the atmosphere... '. Using climate models the group projected an increase in global mean surface temperature of about 1–3.5 deg.C by 2100 and an associated increase in sea level of about 15–95 centimetres. The results of that assessment have implications for the biosphere because of the sensitivity of most ecological systems to climate and the degree to which climate influences the distribution of species.

9.5 The effect of climate change on species

Not all species will respond to climate change in the same way and their response will depend partly upon their life history and adaptation strategies. Other factors including weather events (such as floods, droughts or prolonged cold periods) can also have a much greater impact on species distributions than changes to climate.

Table 9.2. *Some responses of species to climate change*

Physiology
Photosynthesis
Respiration
Stress
Dormancy

Phenology
Budburst
Onset of flowering
Growth pattern
Seed setting/ripening
Breeding pattern
Reproduction success
Migration pattern

Interactions between species
Pollination
Symbiosis
Pests and pathogens
Predation
Competition

From De Groot *et al.*, 1995, selection and use of bio-indicators to assess the possible effects of climate change in Europe. *Journal of Biogeography*, **22**, 935–943. Published with kind permission of Blackwell Science Ltd.

In some instances climate change may affect the physiology and phenology of a species and also the interactions between species. The geographical distribution of species could be affected by a latitudinal shift; as the climate warms, the species range migrates poleward. Species may also respond by way of an altitudinal shift in their range so that in general, when climate warms, terrestrial species tend to move upwards. Some responses are shown in Table 9.2 and each may directly influence abundance and distribution.

The photosynthetic activity of plants and respiration by plants and animals is determined to a large extent by the atmospheric concentration of CO_2 and temperature. Higher atmospheric CO_2 concentrations may increase the net primary productivity of some plants. Climate change may therefore affect the physiology of plants and animals by altering their rate of growth, mobility and development (Table 9.2). Physiological changes could affect the continued survival and competitiveness of species and so determine their potential distribution. Temperature changes can influence the growth dynamics of invertebrates such as aquatic insects by affecting their activity, metabolism and rate of ingestion. Higher temperatures may also reduce water availability to some plants, thereby limiting their development. For example, yields of wheat and rice are expected to decrease owing to reduced water availability as a result of climate change in China (Wang & Zhao, 1995).

The phenology of a species is determined by climate and therefore climate change will affect the timing of phenological events of plants such as budburst, the ripening of seed or the reproductive success of the species. Phenological changes can also affect animals whose survival is dependent on pollen or fruit availability at specific times of the year. For example, climate change may affect the timing of leaf abscission and so influence when leaf material becomes available as food for aquatic insects.

Climate change can also affect species' responses by changing the nature of their interactions with each other (Table 9.2). Species interactions such as predation, parasitism and competition may all be affected if the species composition in any given area, or the abundance of a species, changes. The competitive balance among different species and the competition between individuals of a species may both be affected by climate change as individual organisms establish themselves in new climatically favourable areas. Species may have to compete with 'exotic' predators, pathogens or other species whose distributions have changed. For example, Tasmania's temperate rain forest is a forest community in which structure and functioning may be changed because of a rise in winter temperatures and this may cause an invasion of less 'frost-tolerant' species (IPCC, 1990). Some species rely on birds or other animals for their dispersal or pollination and if the geographical distribution of the dispersal agent shifts because of climate change then that may have an effect on the dispersal capabilities or reproduction of the dependent species. Climate changes affecting the species composition of a local flora could potentially have implications for animal communities (such as invertebrate assemblages) whose survival is dependent on the suitability of the replacement plant species as food sources.

There are certain factors that influence whether a species will respond to climate change by moving into climatically favourable areas. Those factors include the availability of suitable habitat, the existence of physical or biological barriers to the dispersal of the species, the reproductive success of the species, the time taken for an individual of that species to reach reproductive maturity, and the mobility of the species (Hughes et al., 1996). The ability of species to respond to climate change and shift habitat will also vary depending on the rate and nature of climate change. Some organisms may be unaffected

Table 9.3. *Some groups of species that may be particularly sensitive to climatic change*

Species at the edge of (or beyond) their known range or at their biological limits in terms of temperature and moisture
Geographically isolated species (such as those found on islands, on mountain peaks, in patches of remnant vegetation, in parks and reserves)
Genetically impoverished species
Specialised organisms that occupy specific niches (e.g. ice-dependent sea mammals and birds)
Species with poor dispersal ability
Species that reproduce slowly
Localised populations of annual species

Adapted from the Policy Makers' summary of the *Report of the Working Group II to the Intergovernmental Panel on Climate Change*, 1990. Published with kind permission of Australian Government Publishing.

by climate change if they can move to more climatically favourable conditions. It has been projected that coniferous and broad-leaved thermophilic tree species will migrate and find favourable environments further poleward than their current limits, despite their sensitivity to climate change (IPCC, 1990). Other groups of species such as birds, marine fish, bacteria and some land mammals also may be able to shift habitat relatively easily in response to climate change. There are, however, some groups of species that may be particularly sensitive to climate change and these are shown in Table 9.3. They include species that have limited adaptive options available to them.

9.6 The effect of climate change on various levels of biological diversity

The many responses of species to climate change may affect the geographical distribution of all levels of biological diversity (Fig. 9.1). For example, the potential distribution of the world's biomes is projected to change during the next 50 years as the world's climate zones move poleward and to higher elevations. The potential boundaries of vegetation zones, such as temperate

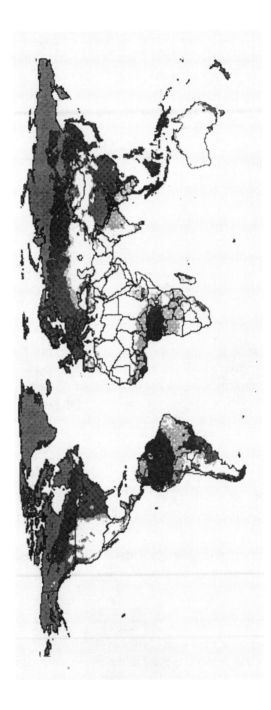

Fig. 9.1. Potential distribution of the world's major biomes under current climate conditions (*above*) and as a result of simulating the effects of a doubling in atmospheric concentration of CO_2 (*below*). (From Watson et al., 1996, *Climate Change 1995: Impacts, Adaptations and Mitigation of Climate Change: Scientific–Technical Analyses*, Cambridge University Press. Adapted from Neilson, R. P. and Marks, D., 1994, A global perspective of regional vegetation and hydrologic sensitivities from climatic change. *Journal of Vegetation Science*, **5**, 715–30. Published with kind permission of the Intergovernmental Panel on Climate Change.)

Tundra. Taiga-Tundra, Ice

Boreal Forests

Temperate Forests

Tropical Forests

Savannas, Dry Forests, Woodlands

Grasslands, Shrublands, Deserts

forest and grasslands, are expected to shift several hundreds of kilometres during that time and this will affect the floristic composition of those zones and their associated fauna. Figure 9.1 shows how a doubling of equivalent atmospheric CO_2 concentrations may affect the potential distribution of the world's major biomes.

The effect of climate change on the biogeography of plants and animals also has implications for the composition of communities and for the composition, structure and functioning of their ecosystems (Box 9.1). Scientists have investigated the effects of climate change on five steppe grassland communities in Inner Mongolia comprising species such as *Stipa grandis* and *Leymus chinense* (Xiao *et al.*, 1995). They demonstrated how each plant community was sensitive to climate change and how its primary productivity (and therefore its survival and distribution) would be affected.

Some types of biological community that may be particularly sensitive to climate change include coral reef, coastal, montane, alpine, island and remnant communities (IPCC, 1990). Climate change can, in theory, cause a reduction in the spatial extent of an alpine community (Fig. 9.2). The alpine vegetation of Tibet is one example of a community which will probably reduce in extent as a direct result of climate change (Wang & Zhao, 1995).

The biological effect of climate change also extends to populations of species and individual organisms (Box 9.1). Species populations are most sensitive to climate change when they are close to their biological limits in terms of temperature and availability of moisture; such populations can often be found at the geographical limits or altitudinal limits of the species range. Those populations may enable a species to migrate in the wake of projected climate change and their movements could be used as indicators of environmental change.

The full ecological effects of climate change on natural ecosystems are not well understood because of several uncertainties including the nature of current and future climate changes, the accuracy of human estimation of climate change, and the effects of human activities on climate in the future. The impact of future natural climate changes is also unknown and largely unpredictable. It is unlikely that climate change will manifest itself in the same way across the whole of the Earth's surface. Regional variations in climate change are expected and these will influence how the regional components of the Earth's biota will be affected. Working Group II of the IPCC observed that 'the reliability of regional-scale predictions of climate change is low...' (Houghton *et al.*, 1996), so conclusions are limited about how climate change will affect the distribution of plants and animals and other organisms at a regional level.

Box 9.1. Climate change will affect the geographical distribution of various levels of biological diversity including biomes, communities of species and individuals and populations of species

Level of biodiversity	Example of effect	Reference
Biome	The potential distribution of the world's major biomes is projected to change	Neilson & Mark, 1994
Community	Some plant communities such as the alpine vegetation of Tibet will probably reduce in spatial extent	Wang & Zhao, 1995
Population	The potential distribution of some populations of some species such as those of the Lizard orchid (*Himantoglossum hircinum*) is projected to change	Carey & Brown, 1994

9.7 What is the role of biogeography?

There are several applications of biogeography to the study and management of environmental change (Box 9.2). Changes to species distributions resulting from environmental change often cannot be prevented and therefore some people may question whether concern about those changes is justified. However, predicting potential outcomes of environmental change for species can be valuable, particularly if it allows mitigation of the potentially adverse effects of that change.

Biogeography could be used to increase the reliability of regional-scale predictions of the likely effects on the biosphere of climate change through the monitoring of the geographical distribution of species (as indicators of environmental change). Baseline information about the distribution of plant and animal taxa can be used in future comparative analyses of the distribution of those taxa to determine whether species are changing their distributions. For example, information about the expected changes to species ranges in response to climate change has been used to identify bio-indicators in the Netherlands (De Groot *et al.*, 1995). In that case, possible indicator species for climate change were identified, including herbaceous plants such as

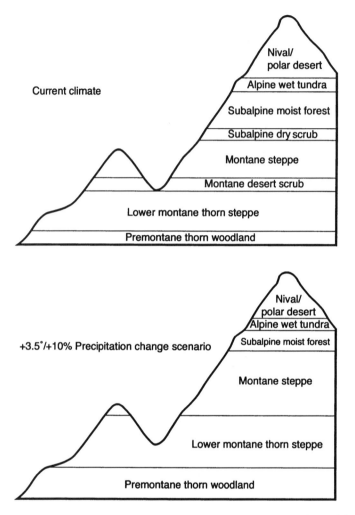

Fig. 9.2 Comparison of current vegetation zones at a hypothetical dry temperate site with simulated vegetation zones under a climate warming scenario. Note how the nival/polar desert zone shrinks and the montane steppe zone expands. (From Beniston, M., 1994, *Mountain Environments in Changing Climates*, Routledge Publishing Company. Published with kind permission of Routledge Publishing Company.)

Box 9.2. Future roles of biogeography

1. Environmental monitoring
   To determine the effects on the biosphere of environmental changes and to determine the rates at which those changes are occurring.

2. Public health
   To design strategies to control vectors of human diseases.
   To manage the potential impacts of environmental change on human health.

3. Management of commercially valuable species
   Identification of species most suitable for commercial enterprise in any particular location now and in the future.

4. Nature conservation
   To evaluate the conservation status of species, communities and ecosystems.
   To design control strategies for pest species.
   To set priorities for the conservation of biological diversity.

5. Ecological studies and restoration
   To help to develop models to explain and predict the distribution of plants, animals and other organisms.
   To provide information about the former distribution of species and their respective communities and to guide development of ecological restoration initiatives.

Eragrostis pilosa (Indian lovegrass), butterflies such as *Nymphalis antiopa* (morning cloak) and breeding birds such as *Asio otus* (long-eared owl). Distribution information about those species will provide a basis for future modelling of climate change.

There are potential epidemiological applications of studying the effects of a changing climate on the geographical distribution of some organisms (Box 9.2). One example is the effect of climate change on the distribution of vectors of diseases. Studies of the factors that determine the distribution of disease vectors have demonstrated that a changing climate and associated regional temperature changes could alter the distribution of those vectors (although several other factors may also control the spread of those diseases). Biogeographical models may be applied to project how the distribution of disease vectors will respond as climate changes. Modelling future changes in the distribution of those organisms could be part of a strategic approach to prevent the spread of diseases.

Some diseases (and their associated vectors) whose distribution is determined to a large extent by climate (and in particular temperature) is shown in Table 9.4 Arthropod-borne viruses (arboviruses) are those carried and transmitted mainly by mosquitoes. Changes to the distribution of mosquitoes that carry arboviruses could have implications for the geographical distribution of diseases such as Japanese encephalitis virus, which is now invading India and parts of Asia where it has previously not been recorded.

Climate change has implications for species used in agriculture, horticulture and forestry because regional climates may become unsuitable for those commercial species (Fig. 9.3). A country's agricultural production may have to be changed if it is to remain economically viable, given predicted climate changes. Comparative analyses of where commercial species are currently grown and the distribution of where those species will be most effective in the future can be used to develop land use plans to ensure global food security. Biogeographers have modelled how climatically favourable regions for some species will shift as climate changes. For example, the optimum growth areas of commercial tree species *Eucalyptus grandis* and *Pinus patula* in southern Africa may alter because of climate changes (Schulze & Kunz, 1995). That information may help to identify where paper mills and fruit-processing plants should be sited in future to take account of effects of altered climate.

Biogeography also has a role in describing how climate change can influence the distribution of pest plants and animals and in projecting how the potential impacts of those pest species will develop. For example, Williams & Liebhold (1995) investigated potential changes in the spatial distributions of outbreaks of two species of herbivorous insect that are known forest defoliators in the USA: the western spruce budworm (*Choristoneura occidentalis*) and the gypsy moth (*Lymantria dispar*). They used information about the geographical distribution of the impacts of the two species on forest foliage and correlated that with environmental variables to generate a model that explained the correlation. They then used the model to project how the defoliation impacts of the two species altered with various climate change scenarios.

Biogeography can also be used to determine whether existing protective networks for biodiversity will provide for the needs of species whose distributions are changing in response to the environment. Existing models of climate change indicate that the protected natural areas of the world will be inadequate to cope with altitudinal or latitudinal shifts in species distributions that

Table 9.4. *Diseases and their vectors whose distributions may be affected by climate change*

Disease		Disease vector whose distribution may be affected by climate change
Name	Organism	
Malaria	*Plasmodium falciparum*, *P. vivax*, *P. ovale*, *P. malariae*	*Anopheles* (female) (mosquito)
Yellow fever	*Flavivirus* sp.	*Aedes aegypti* (mosquito)
Sleeping sickness, trypanosomiasis	*Trypanosoma brucei gambiense*	*Glossina palpalis* (tsetse fly)
Leishmaniasis	*Leishmania* sp.	*Plebotomines* sp. (sand flies)
Bancroftian and brugian filariasis		*Culex quinquefasciatus*
River blindness (onchocerciasis)	*Onchocerca volvulus*	*Simulian* sp. (female) (blackflies)
Rocky mountain spotted fever	*Rickettsia rickettsi*	*Dermacentor variabilis* (tick, usual vector)
Lyme disease	Spirochete *Borrelia burgdorferi*	Ticks of various species including *Ixodes scapularis* (dog tick)
Chagas disease (American trypanosomiasis)	*Trypanosoma cruzi*	Blood-sucking species of Reduviidae (kissing bugs)

From *Control of Communicable Diseases Manual*, 16th edn. Copyright 1995 by the American Public Health Association, Washington, DC, USA. Adapted with permission.

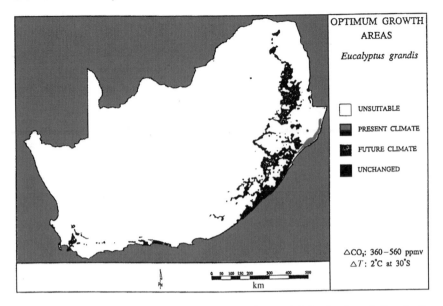

Fig. 9.3. Potential impact of climate change on the spatial distribution of climatically optimum growth areas of *Eucalyptus grandis* in southern Africa. From Schulze, R. E. & Kunz, R. P., 1995, Potential shifts in optimum growth areas of selected commercial tree species and subtropical crops in southern Africa due to global warming. Journal of Biogeography, 22: 679–688. Published with kind permission of Blackwell Science Ltd. ppmv, parts per million by volume.

will occur as climate changes (Peters & Darling, 1985). In theory, protected natural areas can become ineffective for conserving the species which they were originally established to protect (Fig. 9.4). Biogeography can therefore be used to evaluate how a protective network for biodiversity conservation will cope as climate changes. Biogeography could then be applied in the location of new protected area networks to conserve a region's biological diversity, taking into account the effects of climate change on species distributions.

Biogeography can be used to identify species populations at risk of extinction because of environmental changes (Box 9.2). For example, it has been demonstrated how substantial changes to the tree flora of Australia may be expected as a result of climate change (Hughes *et al.*, 1996). Information about the current geographical distribution of species of *Eucalyptus* and their current climate ranges was used to show how many species will have their entire present-day populations exposed to temperatures and rainfalls under which no individuals currently exist.

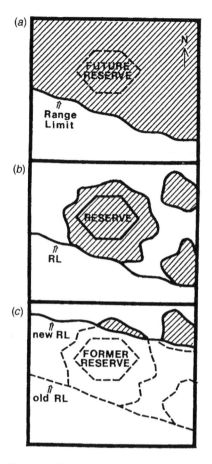

Fig. 9.4. Illustration showing how a protected natural area may be affected by climate change. The hatching indicates (a) range limit of species before human habitation or climate change, (b) fragmented species distribution after human habitation but before climate change, (c) species distribution after human habitation and climate change. (Taken from Peters, R. L., 1996, Conserving biological diversity in the face of climate change. (*Biodiversity and Landscapes: A paradox of humanity*, ed. Ke Chung Kim & R. D. Weaver, Cambridge University Press. Published with kind permission of Cambridge University Press.)
RL, range limit.

9.8 Models in biogeography and their uses

A model is a simplified representation of reality that can be used to extrapolate over a long time frame what might be the environmental consequence of a particular management strategy. There are several types of model used by ecologists, including physical models and mathematical models. Mathematical models were used by MacArthur & Wilson (1967) in the development of their theory of island biogeography (see Box 3.2). More recently there has been growing interest in ecological modelling and its use in the study of the geographical distribution of species and to that end it has a valuable contribution to make to studies of biogeography.

Ecological modelling involves the simulation of an ecological process or phenomenon with the aim of predicting a likely outcome or range of outcomes. Models are useful for conceptualising the real world and their use can be seen as complementary to other forms of ecological studies. Models may be used to explain the distribution of species or communities, to predict the effects of environmental change, to predict where a species should occur in the wild, and can be applied in the selection of survey sites for those species. Models can also be used to identify areas that are within the biogeographical range of a species and are suitable for species recovery work involving introduction of that species to new sites.

One example is the group of bioclimatic models developed in Australia for explaining the geographical distribution of some species. That work is based on the premise that climate sets broad limits to the distribution of most species. Analysis of climatic variables that may influence the distribution of a species allows the prediction and definition of the potential distributional limits of species (Lindenmayer et al., 1991). In Australia, the entire known range of Leadbeater's possum was found to be restricted to a narrow set of climatic conditions (see also Section 7.7). Through the development of a bioclimatic profile for Leadbeater's possum (Fig. 9.5) and using a modelling programme called BIOCLIM Lindenmayer et al. predicted and defined the potential limits of its distribution and that hypothesis was used to select survey sites for the species outside of its current known range. Lindenmayer and his colleagues were then able to use the bioclimatic model to predict the effect that climate change will have on the species distribution.

Studies have also been undertaken in England to determine how some species will respond to environmental change and in particular how species will respond to climate change. Carey & Brown (1994) used a climate suitability model for *Himantoglossum hircinum* (lizard orchid) an uncommon species of orchid. They used that model in combination with a soil suitability map to determine the 'environmental signature' of the site that currently supports the largest population of the species. They assumed that the relationship between species distribution and climate will remain the

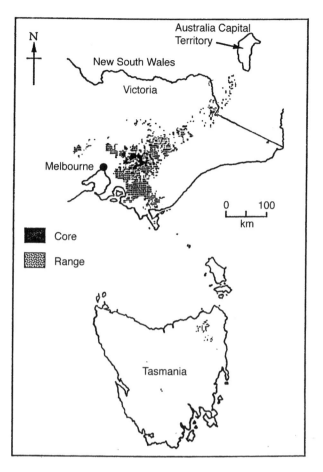

Fig. 9.5. The predicted 'core' and 'range' distribution of *Gymnobelideus leadbeateri* (Leadbeater's possum) derived from the species bioclimatic profile. (From Lindenmayer *et al.*, 1991, The conservation of Leadbeater's possum, *Gymnobelideus leadbeateri* (McCoy): a case study of the use of bioclimatic modelling. *Journal of Biogeography*, **18**, 371–383. Published with kind permission of Blackwell Science Ltd.)

same over the course of time and that a species will respond to fill its new climatic envelope as climate changes. There is no certainty that these assumptions are true but nevertheless this kind of approach has applications to recovery work for species because it identifies sites to which they may be translocated.

9.9 GIS modelling of species distributions

Geographic Information Systems (GIS) are usually computerised and can capture and store data that describe places on the Earth's surface; they are one of many types of tool used in environmental management, ecological modelling and data storage and dissemination. GIS can be of great value in biogeographical studies for several reasons: they can store large amounts of spatial information, they can be used to map data layers when performing gap analysis (see Section 2.5), and they can be used in ecology to model and thereby explain and predict patterns in the distribution of species and communities. GIS can also be used to store baseline information about the geographical distribution of species, communities or ecosystems for comparative analysis of future changes in their distribution and can therefore be used in ecological monitoring. Until recently, GIS were used primarily as descriptive tools for mapping and their value to biogeography has been widely recognised, but increasingly they are being applied in other ways such as GIS modelling.

GIS modelling is a research technique used in studies of biogeography to predict the distribution of a species. Information required to perform GIS modelling includes the current geographical limits of a species distribution, the factors that limit the species distribution, and the species habitat preferences. This information is not always available for all species. However, models to predict species distributions developed using GIS can sometimes be more accurate than empirical data, particularly in poorly surveyed areas.

GIS models have been developed by Scott and his colleagues in Idaho, USA, to predict species distributions (Scott *et al.*, 1993). They used a digital map of the vegetation cover types or animal habitat types, a digital map of the study area divided into geographical units or a grid system, a database predicting the presence or absence of a species in each of the geographical units, and a database predicting the presence or absence of each species in each vegetation or habitat type. GIS models of species distributions were used to show where species should occur based on the distribution of their preferred vegetation. For species such as the sharp-tailed grouse (*Tympanuchus phasianellus*), they predicted a distribution well beyond its known range and subsequently the grouse was indeed reported to occur at some of those predicted sites.

The predictive capability of some models for the distribution of taxonomic groups may not be accurate. For example, Scott and his colleagues found that reptile distributions were poorly predicted by vegetation models.

This is probably because reptiles respond strongly to climate rather than the vegetation cover types used in the models. A second limitation, which applies to all ecological modelling techniques, is that accurate descriptive information about species distributions may not be adequate for a model to be developed and for some species no distribution information may exist. Despite those limitations, GIS modelling has an important role to play in future biogeographical studies for explaining and predicting species distributions.

9.10 Where will biogeography be in 2020?

Biogeography holds the key to the survival of life (see Section 1.1). It will continue to be applied in many different ways, despite the fact that humans have altered the distributions of many species throughout the world. Information about the distribution of plants, animals and other organisms will be needed in environmental monitoring, in public health, in management of commercially valuable species, in nature conservation, and in studies of ecology and ecological restoration (Box 9.2).

Biogeography is currently limited in its applications due to the large number of undescribed species and the fact that ecologists are not agreed on a uniform scheme for classification of the world's plant and animal communities and ecosystems (a problem known as 'the taxonomic impediment'). Classification of all elements of biological diversity (species, communities, ecosystems and biomes) is fundamental to biogeography otherwise the distribution of those elements of biological diversity cannot be described (see Chapter 2). In future, as in the past, systematics and taxonomy will continue to provide the building blocks for biogeographical studies.

Another future problem for biogeography, related to taxonomy, is that only about 6 per cent of practising taxonomists are based in the developing countries in Africa, Asia and Latin America, where the greatest proportion of the planet's terrestrial diversity is believed to occur. In the future a redistribution of the world's taxonomists to reflect global patterns in species richness of undescribed species may be necessary to solve that problem.

Computer databases are being used more and more for storing, analysing and disseminating biogeographical information. It is hard to imagine what format biogeographical information will take in the year 2020, given the progress that has been made in the last 20 years in storage, access and dissemination of that information. In the past, biogeographical information has been available from herbaria, museum collections, scientific publications and other sources (see Table 6.1). In the future, it may be possible to access large amounts of biogeographical information through computer links with the World Wide Web. The Environmental Resources Information Network (ERIN) in Australia (see Chapter 6) is one example of what the future holds for storage and worldwide dissemination of biogeographical information (see Appendix II). Information about the geographical distribution of species, communities and ecosystems may be brought together most effectively through international computer linkages. However, some countries may not have the resources to develop computer systems to store biogeographical data sets. In those cases the existing methods of information storage (at herbaria) and dissemination (through published reports) will have to be used.

We envisage that by the year 2020 many countries will have national clearing houses for all biogeographical data sets. The work of the World Conservation Monitoring Centre will have been extended and have a status similar to that of the World Health Organization, the World Meteorological Organization and also the United Nations Environment Programme. By the year 2020 a World Biogeography Agency could provide the lead role in acquiring, storing and disseminating biogeographical information. Such an agency could provide information to resource managers and land use planners throughout the world. The agency could use biogeographical data to assist in the development of world strategies for resource management (to ensure global food security), nature conservation (in the development of protective networks for biological diversity), public health (in preventing the spread of arboviruses and other disease vectors) and ecological restoration (to show where restoration of species or communities should occur).

Biogeography will continue to be a critical tool for land use planning for the conservation of biological diversity and has a role to play in the identification of sites worthy of protection for the conservation of species whose existence is threatened. It will continue to be applied in setting priorities for conservation (see Chapter 2) and in the assessment of the conservation status of species, communities and ecosystems. Biogeography will also be applied in the identification of species whose distributions are severely restricted and potentially at risk of extinction due to catastrophic events. Biogeographical studies will be particularly important for species and communities that are not yet described or about which little is known concerning their current geographical distribution (such as cryptic species). Studies of the distribution of commercial species will continue to be used to benefit land uses by identifying commercial species best suited to certain local climatic and abiotic conditions.

Biogeography will continue to be used in ecological monitoring to understand the response of the biota of the Earth to a variety of influences, including climate and land use changes. The biogeography of some organisms, particularly those that may directly influence human societies and human health (for example, agricultural and forestry pests or vectors of human diseases) will continue to be studied so that strategies to control those species may be developed – so too will the distributions of organisms that are indicators of certain environmental conditions.

9.11 Other perspectives

Much of this book has concentrated on a scientific approach to the study of the geographical distribution of plants, animals and other organisms. That is biogeography from one narrow perspective and it is understandable given the background of the authors. A scientific approach to biogeography provides one way of looking at the world but it is certainly not the only way.

Different cultural groups, for example, have different perspectives on biogeography and view the distribution of plant and animal species in their environment in different ways. Culture can play a role in determining species distributions and those distributions can in turn affect culture (see Chapter 4). Culture is a property of a society or social grouping and is a consequence of the combined values of each of the members of that social grouping. One cultural group may place importance on the distribution of species that are used as food or clothing and may disregard species that have no known utilitarian value. Cultural perspectives of biogeography may reveal different interpretations about the distributions of plants and animals.

The Aborigines travelled widely across the Australian continent, hunting and gathering at each place they visited. The movements of those people reflected in part their need to harvest particular species at a particular time and place. They visited locations where they could harvest fruit (of a particular species of pine) and also coastal areas where certain species of shellfish could be found. The Aboriginal culture was driven in part by the availability of natural resources upon which its people were dependent. Understanding the perspective of the Aborigines towards their natural world could be applied in ensuring that the valued components of the distribution of species used by their cultural group were protected.

Perspectives of biogeography through cultural filters provides an alternative way to study the distribution of plants and animals and other organisms. Understanding the different values and attitudes of cultural groups (based on their perception of biogeography) could help to resolve cultural conflicts that may arise over management of natural resources and ownership of nature.

References

Carey, P. D. & Brown, N. J. (1994). The use of GIS to identify sites that will become suitable for a rare orchid. *Himantoglossum hircinum* L., in a future changed climate. *Biodiversity Letters*, **2**, 117–123.

De Groot, R. S., Kietner, P. & Ovaa, A. H. (1995). Selection and use of bio-indicators to assess the possible effects of climate change in Europe. *Journal of Biogeography*, **22**, 935–943.

Houghton, J. T., Meiro Filho, L. G., Callander, B. A., Harris, N., Kattenburg, A. & Maskell, K. (1996). *Climate Change 1995: The Science of Climate Change.* Cambridge, Cambridge University Press.

Hughes, L., Cawsey, E. M. & Westoby, M. (1996). Climatic range sizes of Eucalypt species in relation to future climate change. *Global Ecology and Biogeography*, **5**, 23–29.

IPCC (1990). *Climate Change: The IPCC Scientific Assessment*, ed. J. T. Houghton, G. J. Jenkins & J. J. Ephraims. Cambridge, Cambridge University Press.

Lindenmayer, D. B., Nix, H. A., McMahon, J. P., Hutchinson, M. F. & Tanton, M. T. (1991). The conservation of Leadbeater's possum, *Gymnobelideus leadbeateri* (McCoy): a case study of the use of bioclimatic modelling. *Journal of Biogeography*, **18**, 371–383.

MacArthur, R. H. & Wilson, E. O. (1967). *The Theory of Island Biogeography.* Princeton, NJ, Princeton University Press.

Neilson, R. P. & Mark, D. (1994). A global perspective of regional vegetation and hydrologic sensitivities from climate change. *Journal of Vegetation Science*, **5**, 715–730.

Peters, R. L. & Darling, J. D. S. (1985). The greenhouse effect and nature reserves: global warming would diminish biological diversity by causing extinctions among reserve species. *BioScience*, **35**, 707–717,

Scott, J. M., Davis, F., Csuti, B., Noss, R., Butterfield, B., Groves, C., Anderson, H., Caicco, S., D'Erchia, F., Edwards, T. C. Jr, Ulliman, J. & Wright, R. G. (1993). Gap analysis: a geographic approach to protection of biological diversity. *Wildlife Monography*, **123**, 1–41. Supplement to *Journal of Wildlife Management*, **57**(1).

Schulze, R. E. & Kunz, R. P. (1995). Potential shifts in optimum growth areas of selected commercial tree species and subtropical crops in southern Africa due to global warming. *Journal of Biogeography*, **22**, 679–688.

Wang Futang & Zhao Zong. (1995). Impact of climate change on natural vegetation in China and its implications for agriculture. *Journal of Biogeography*, **22**, 657–664.

Williams, D. W. & Liebhold, A. M. (1995). Herbivorous insects and global change: potential changes in the spatial distribution of forest defoliator outbreaks. *Journal of Biogeography*, **22**, 665–671.

Xiao, X., Ojima, D. S., Parton, W. J., Chen, Z. & Chen, D. (1995). Sensitivity of Inner Mongolia grasslands to climate change. *Journal of Biogeography*, **22**, 643–648.

Appendix I: Glossary

Abiotic. Not biotic, not of life. Part of the environment which is not biological; that is, water, soil, climate, geology.

Acclimatisation. Process by which an organism becomes adjusted to new conditions, a different climate or new environment.

Adaptation. The way in which an organism has evolved to become fitted for its way of life in terms of its behaviour, ecology, physiology, etc.

Adaptive radiation. An evolutionary process in which many species evolve and diversify from a common ancestor to occupy a wide range of modes of life.

Adventive. A species or taxonomic group that has arrived and become established in the wild outside its former geographical range either as a consequence of human activity or entirely independent of it.

Allelopath (allelopathy). An organism that releases compounds that are toxic to other species and thus inhibits other species.

Angiosperms (Angiospermae). A division of the plant kingdom commonly called flowering plants. Their reproductive organs are in flowers and the seeds are in a closed ovary or fruit.

Arbovirus. An arthropod-borne virus.

Benthic. On or near the bottom of water. Refers to organisms which are bottom living.

Binomial. Consisting of two names. Describes the system of 'double' names given to plants, animals and other organisms.

Bioclimatic (bioclimate). Microclimates in relation to fauna and flora.

Biocontrol. Biological control, particularly of pests.

Biodiversity. *See* Biological diversity.

Biofuel. Biological fuels.

Biogeochemical. Usually in reference to cycles of chemical elements though biotic and abiotic parts of ecosystems.

Biogeoclimatic. Used in association with classification of ecosystems and expressed as types of vegetation, climate and site characteristics. (The combination of biological, geological and climatic factors affecting distribution patterns.)

Biogeography. The study of the geographical distribution of organisms and their habitats.

Bio-indicator (biological indicator). Biological organisms which are used (according to presence, state or behaviour) to indicate a condition of the environment.

Biological community (biotic community). Populations of different species living in the same geographical area and within which there are interactions between the populations.

Biological conservation. An activity that aims to ensure the continued existence of all levels of biological diversity.

Biological diversity (biodiversity). The variety of life at different levels of biological organisation.

Biome. A geographical region which is classified on the basis of the dominant or major type of vegetation and the main climate. For example, the temperate biome is that geographical area with a temperate climate and forests composed of mixed deciduous tree species.

Biota. A general term for all living organisms.

Biotic. Pertaining to living organism or life.

Biotic community. Populations of different species living together.

Biotope. The smallest geographical unit of the biosphere, or of a habitat, that can be delineated by its own characteristic biota.

Budburst. The bursting of buds; the time at which buds open in the spring.

Buffer zone. An area or zone that helps to protect a habitat from damage, disturbance or pollution. It is an area (human-made or natural) that is managed to protect the 'integrity' of that area.

Climatic envelope. The area within which a species is found and which has specific climatic characteristics (the clime which is suitable for a certain species).

Climax community. The stable biological community at the end of successional changes.

Community. *See* Biotic community.

Conservation (in a biological sense). The continued existence of species, habitats and biological communities and the interactions between species and their environment.

Conservation biology. The integrated use of several social science and scientific disciplines to achieve conservation of biological diversity.

Contagion. This refers to the degree to which mapped attributes are clumped into patches of the same attribute class.

Coppice. Area of small trees. Coppicing is traditional management where trees are periodically cut at the base. This promotes new growth of shoots from the stool. Widely practised in Europe between AD 1500 and 1800. There has been renewed interest in coppicing as a method of sustainable management of woodlands.

Cosmopolitan (species). A species or other taxonomic group that is distributed widely throughout the world.

Cryptic species. A species which by virtue of its colour can blend into the background.

Cultivar. A plant variety maintained by cultivation.

Disjunct. A species or other taxon that has a widely separated and scattered distribution; discontinuous distribution.

Dispersal. The spreading of an organism's propagules (e.g. spores, seeds).

Dispersion. The spatial pattern of distribution of organisms.

Divaricating. Spreading at a very wide angle. Usually refers to a plant's structure where the stems diverge or are forked.

Ecological indicator. *See* Bio-indicator.

Ecological succession. A process where over time there is a sequence of changes in the biological communities leading eventually to a climax community.

Ecology. The science of the interrelationships between living organisms and their environment (other organisms and the physical environment including the soil, air, climate).

Ecoregion. An ecosystem of regional extent characterised by a particular climate and by indicator species unique to (or abundant in) that region.

Ecosystem. A term encompassing the living communities (biological communities) and their physical environment and the processes therein, including the flow of energy through the system.

Ectotherm. An organism that uses heat largely from the environment to help to regulate its body temperature.

Edaphic factors. Pertaining to the soil and influenced by soil characteristics or the substratum.

Edge effect. A greater variety of species or numbers of species occurs on an edge rather than within a biotic community.

Edge species. Species inhabiting edges or boundaries between biotic communities such as the edge of a woodland.

Elapid (snake). Refers to the Family of snakes (Elapidae) which includes cobras, mambas, coral snakes, etc.

Endemism, endemic. Native, and usually restricted, to a particular geographical region. Endemism may occur at different levels, subspecies, species, genus, etc.

Endotherm. An organism that uses heat largely from its own metabolism to regulate its body temperature.

Environment. All the surroundings but could be differentiated between the natural environment and the artificial environment.

Epiphyte. A plant that grows on another plant for physical support.

Ethnobotany (ethnobotanical). The study of people's classification, management and use of plants.

Eurytopic. Tolerant of a wide range of condition (habitat). Other terms such as eurythermal refer to temperature.

Evapotranspiration. The total loss of water from vegetation, soil and bodies of water.

Exotic species. A species introduced to one region from another geographical region. Alien species.

Fauna. A collective term for all kinds of animals.

Flora. A collective term for all kinds of plants.

Floristics. Structural attributes of the vegetation and the species which the biotic community comprises.

Fossil record. The remains or traces of past organisms. These remains are usually in the form of fossils.

Founder principle (effect). Amongst founder members of a new population or colony, there may be fewer genetic differences and less genetic variation.

Gap analysis. A technique to identify biota and communities that are not adequately represented in an existing series or networks of protected areas.

Genetic diversity (variation). The heritable variation in a population as a result of different variants (the alleles) of any gene.

Genetics. The science of variation and heredity in organisms.

Geographic information systems (GIS). Computer-based information systems that enable objects in the environment to be linked geographically to map features. Systems (usually computerised) that can capture and store data that describe places and conditions on the Earth's surface.

Grassland. A natural biological community composed mainly of species of grasses. The many kinds of grassland communities may be classified on the basis of the climate, the geology of the area and the dominant grass species.

Guild. A group of species with similar ecological requirements and similar feeding strategies.

Habitat. The typical locality or area in which a population of a species lives.

Habitat patch or fragment. A portion of the living space inhabited by populations of species. The habitat patch or fragment is part of a formerly larger area.

Heathland. A lowland biological community dominated by shrubs, mainly heathers.

Hedge (hedgerows). Boundary or fence consisting of shrubs, herbs and grasses, sometimes with trees.

Hemi-parasite. An organism that derives part of its nourishment from its host.

Index (environmental or ecological). A number or quantity compared to an arbitrary standard; often used as a simple way of expressing complex data sets.

Indicator (species). *See* Bio-indicator.

Indigenous (species). A species which is native to a particular region (cf. Endemic).

Insularisation. The process of habitat reduction, fragmentation and isolation.

Internet. A global information network; its services include electronic mail and the World Wide Web.

Iterative approach. Stated or checked repeatedly.

Keystone species (key species). A species in a community which interacts with other species and upon which many other species depend.

Landscape ecology (1). The study of the form, function and evolution of the visual aspects of landscapes, the attributes and spatial arrangements of attributes in landscapes and the landscape as an ecosystem. (2) Visual and spatial arrangements of landscape elements and of the ecological and cultural mechanisms that result in ecological change at a landscape scale.

Living fossil. A species or other taxonomic group that has persisted over long periods of geological time with little or no change.

Log–log relationship. Relationship shown in a graph where data on both axes are plotted as logarithms.

Macroclimate. The climate of a major geographical region.

Mark-recapture. In some population studies, individual organisms are captured, marked or identified then released. Some marked individuals may be recaptured – thus the marked, recaptured individuals.

Metapopulation. A population of populations or a set of populations which may, but not necessarily, interact as a result of individuals moving amongst those populations.

Microclimate. The climate of a habitat; a climate affected by the local topography, vegetation, soil, etc.

Monoculture. The cultivation of a crop of a single species.

Montane. Mountain regions below the tree line.

Nature (with reference to the environment). The whole natural physical and living world.

Nektonic. Swimming actively in water.

Niche. The 'space' or 'ecological role' occupied by a species and the resources used by a species. Conceptually the niche is multidimensional and each resource (food, time of feeding, etc.) and each abiotic factor (salinity, temperature, etc.) can be considered a dimension of the niche.

Non-target insects. Used in context of those insects which are not targeted for control by the use of insecticides.

Paramo. A plant community type found in tropical high mountain environments.

Parasite. An organism that derives all its nourishment from its host.

Particulates. Particles, as in particles in the air.

Perennating. Surviving for a number of years.

Phenology. The study of the temporal aspects of recurring events amongst organisms in relation to climate and weather.

Pheromone. Volatile chemical emitted in minute amounts by an organism, usually in connection with the behaviour of the organism and often as an attractant.

Phylogenetics. The study of organisms and their grouping for the purposes of classification based on evolutionary descent.

Phylogeny. Evolutionary relationships within and between taxonomic levels particularly the patterns of lines of descent, often branching from one species to another. Relationships between species as reflected by their evolutionary history.

Physiognomy. The appearance of features of a plant community which are characteristic to that community.

Physiography. The science and the surface of the Earth and the interactions of air, water and land.

Plankton. Aquatic organisms that drift with water movements and which generally have no locomotive organs.

Plantation forest. Stands of planted trees (usually of only one or two species) which are grown and then harvested as a crop.

Plate tectonics. The concept that the Earth's crust is divided into a number of rigid plates that move in relation to each other.

Poikilotherm (poikilothermic). An organism whose body temperature is variable and is largely determined by environmental conditions.

Polyphagous. Feeding on a wide variety of food or prey.

Population. A collection of individuals (plants or animals), all of the same species and in a defined geographical area.

Population viability (vulnerability) analysis. Used in attempts to estimate the probability that a population will survive for a given number of generations.

Quadrat (in ecological field work). A square device (sampling frame) of known size, used to set a limit to the area being studied. Typical field quadrats are a metre square and each line of the quadrat may have 10-centimetre divisions.

Radio-tracking. The use of miniature radio transmitters, attached to an animal, for the purposes of studying its movements and behaviour.

Rain forest. Tropical forest which has an annual rainfall of more than 254 centimetres (100 inches).

Realm. The largest of the biogeographical units.

Relict (species). Sole survivors of what were once more diverse in terms of species (taxonomic relict), or survivors of once geographically widespread groups (biogeographical relict).

Riparian. The edge of streams or rivers. Riparian biota is that frequenting or living on the banks of rivers and streams.

Sclerophyllous. Hard leaved; leaves resistant to drought.

Silviculture. The management of forests and of the trees of the forest.

Speciation. In biology, the evolution of new species.

Species. A group of organisms of the same kind which reproduce amongst themselves but are usually reproductively isolated from other groups of organisms.

Species–area curve. The relationship between the number of species (of a certain taxonomic group) and the area of an island or habitat fragment and presented in graphic form.

Species composition. The species or assemblage of species in an area or a sample.

Species diversity. A measure of the relative abundance of individuals of different species in an area or a sample (a measure of the evenness). High species diversity is when all species are represented by the same number of individuals. Low species diversity occurs when one species or a few species are represented by large numbers of individuals and the other species by few individuals.

Species richness. The number of species in an area or a sample.

Stenotopic. Tolerant of a narrow range of conditions (habitat). Other terms such as stenohaline refer to salinity.

Succession. *See* Ecological succession.

Sustainability. Used here in the sense of sustainable use; that is a use which can be continued through time without significantly changing the populations, species and habitats being used.

Sward (grass sward). Expanse of short grass.

Symbiont. An organism that has an association with organisms of another species whereby the metabolic dependence of the two associates is mutual (thus symbiosis).

Systematics. The classification of organisms into hierarchical groups and the study of their phylogenetic relationships.

Taxon (pl. taxa). *See* Taxonomic group.

Taxonomic group (taxon, taxa). Any defined unit or group of organisms used in classification of organisms, e.g. species, genus, tribe, family, order.

Taxonomy. The study of classification and the naming and classifying of organisms.

Tetrapod. Four-legged vertebrate.

Thermoneutral zone. The range of environmental temperatures over which an endothermic organism can maintain a near constant body temperature without additional physiological or metabolic activity.

Thermophilic (organisms). Organisms which thrive in warm environmental conditions.

Translocation. The removal and relocation of organisms from one location to another. Used in connection with conservation.

Tundra. Treeless polar region where subsoil is always frozen.

Turnover. Extinction of local populations and establishment of new populations in empty habitat patches by individuals moving from existing populations.

Tree crown. The leafy upper parts of a tree.

Vagrant. An organism that has expanded its geographical range independent of human activity but has not necessarily established itself in a new area.

Variance. A statistical measure of the dispersion of values around the mean value (square of the standard deviation).

Vascular plants. All the plants, excluding mosses, liverworts and fungi, etc., and having conducting tissue.

Vicariance, vicariated. The occurrence of closely related taxa in different geographical areas (separated by natural barriers).

Waka. A Polynesian canoe.

Wetland. A biological community in an area of wet ground; areas of marsh, peatlands or water whether permanent or temporary, with water which is static or flowing, fresh or brackish. The classification of wetlands is based partly on the types of plant species found there and on the physical characteristics.

Wildlife. A term commonly used to refer to non-domesticated mammals. In a biological sense wildlife means all kinds of living organisms that are not domesticated.

Woodland. A biological community dominated by trees. Each type of woodland is characterised by the species composition of the trees and other plants.

World Conservation Strategy. The first was published in 1980 by IUCN, UNEP and WWF and succeeded in 1991 by the sequel, *Caring for the Earth: A Strategy for Sustainable Living.*

World Wide Web (WWW). An information service developed at CERN (European Laboratory for Particle Physics at Geneva) attached to networks, usually the Internet, to allow access to 'documents'.

Appendix II: Addresses of relevant organisations

Australian Environmental Resources Information Network (ERIN)
World Wide Web species occurrence data http://kaos.erin.gov.au/erin.html

Australian Surveying and Land Information Group (AUSLIG)
World Wide Web http://www.auslig.gov.au/welcome.htm

BirdLife International (formerly International Council for Bird Preservation), Unit 3, Wellbrook Court, Girton Road, Cambridge CB3 0NA, UK.
email birdlife@gn.apc.org

The British Ecological Society, 26 Blades Court, Putney, London SW15 2NU, England, UK.
email general@ecology.demon.co.uk

British Trust for Ornithology, The Nunnery, Nunnery Place, Thetford, Norfolk IP24 2PU, England, UK.

Convention on International Trade in Endangered Species (CITES), Secretariat, 6 Rue Maupas, Case Postale 78, CH-1000, Lausanne 9, Switzerland.

Dorset Natural History and Archaeological Society, Dorset County Museum, Dorchester, Dorset DT1 1XA, England, UK.

The Ecological Society of America. 2010 Massachusetts Avenue, NW, Suite 400, Washington, DC 20036, USA.
World Wide Web http://www/esa.sdsc.edu/esa.htm

Intergovernmental Panel on Climate Change (IPCC). IPCC Secretariat, c/o WMO, Case Postale 2300, 41 Ave Guiseppe-Motta, C-1211 Genève 2, Switzerland.
World Wide Web http://www.unep.ch/ipcc

International Council for Birdlife International, *see* Birdlife International.

International Centre for Antarctic Information and Research (ICAIR), Antarctic Centre, PO Box 14–199, Christchurch, New Zealand.
World Wide Web http://www.icair.iac.org.n/

International Union for the Conservation of Nature (IUCN), World Conservation Union. World HQ Rue Mauverney 28, CH-1196, Gland, Switzerland.
email mail@hq.iucn.org

International Whaling Commission (IWC), The Red House, Station Road, Histon, Cambridge CB4 4NP, England, UK.

The Linnean Society of London. Burlington House, Piccadilly, London W1V 0LQ, England, UK.
email john@linnean.demon.co.uk

Montana Natural Heritage Program (MTNHP), Montana State Library, 1515 East Sixth Avenue, Helena, Montana 59620–1800, USA.
World Wide Web http://nris.msl.mt.gov
email mtnhp@nris.msl.mt.gov

National Rivers Authority (NRA), 30–34 Albert Embankment, London SE1 7TL, England, UK.

New Zealand Botanical Society, c/o Auckland Institute & Museum, Private Bag 92018, Auckland, New Zealand.

Royal Australian Ornithologists Union, 21 Gladstone Street, Moonee Ponds, Victoria 3039, Australia.

The Royal Society for the Protection of Birds (RSPB), The Lodge, Sandy, Bedfordshire SG19 2DL, England, UK.

Tasmanian Parks and Wildlife Service, Hobart 7000, Tasmania, Australia

UN Commission on Sustainable Development. Room DC2–2270, United Nations, New York, NY 10017, USA.
World Wide Web http://www.un.org/DPCSD

United Nations Educational, Scientific and Cultural Organization (UNESCO), 7 Place de Fontenoy, 75700 Paris, France.

United States Fish and Wildlife Service, Department of the Interior, Washington, DC 20240, USA.

Wellington Botanical Society, PO Box 10–412, Wellington 6036, New Zealand.

The Wildfowl and Wetlands Trust, Slimbridge, Gloucestershire GL2 7BT, England, UK.

Wildlife Society (United States), 5410 Grosvenor Lane, Bethesda, MD 20814, USA.

World Commission on Environment and Development (WCED), The Brundtland Commission. Palais Wilson, 52 rue des Pagnis, CH-1001, Geneva, Switzerland.

World Conservation Monitoring Centre. New Building, 219c Huntingdon Road, Cambridge CB3 0DL, England, UK.
email info@wcmc.org.uk
World Network of Biosphere Reserves, Division of Ecological Sciences, UNESCO, 1, rue Miollis, 75732 Paris Cedex 15, France.
email mab@unesco.org

WWW interactive species map of Tasmania.
World Wide Web http://life.anu.ed.au

Index